# Educating Eve

**A volume in the Open Linguistics Series**

*Series Editor*
Robin P. Fawcett, University of Wales, Cardiff

# Educating Eve

## The 'Language Instinct' Debate

Geoffrey Sampson

**CASSELL**
London and New York

Cassell
Wellington House
125 Strand
London WC2R 0BB

370 Lexington Avenue
New York, NY 10017-6550

First published 1997. Reprinted in paperback with minor changes 1999.

Reprinted 1999

**British Library Cataloguing-in-Publication Data**
A catalogue record for this book is available from the British Library.

ISBN 0-304-33908-3 (Hardback)
   0-304-70290-0 (Paperback)

**Library of Congress Cataloging-in-Publication Data**
Sampson, Geoffrey.
   Educating Eve : the 'language instinct' debate / Geoffrey Sampson.
      p.   cm.
   Includes bibliographical references and index.
   ISBN 0-304-33908-3
   1. Innateness hypothesis (Linguistics)   2. Language and languages—
Philosophy.   3. Creativity (Linguistics)   I. Title.
P37.5.I55S26 1997
401—dc21                                                      97-2322
                                                                 CIP

Designed and typeset by Ben Cracknell Studios
Printed and bound in Great Britain by Bookcraft (Bath) Ltd.

# Contents

To Victoria

# Preface

I should like to thank Gerald Gazdar, John Ohala, Geoffrey Pullum, Matthew Saxton, and Larry Trask for advice and help towards the completion of this book. They bear no responsibility for its shortcomings, and do not necessarily agree with its conclusions.

I am grateful to the editors and publisher of *Philosophical Papers* for permission to reprint material that first appeared in vol. 18 of that journal.

Readers interested in learning more about the intellectual background from which this book has emerged may care to visit the author's Web site at http://www.grs.u-net.com.

Waldron, Sussex
August 1996

# 1 Culture or Biology?

## A challenge to common sense

Many readers will know the story of Willy Russell's *Educating Rita*, first performed as a play in 1980, and turned three years later into an excellent film with Julie Walters as Rita and Michael Caine as Frank. Rita is a naïve and ignorant young Liverpool hairdresser, who finds her life unsatisfying and joins the Open University. The tutor assigned to her is Frank, a past-it don more interested in drinking than teaching, who tries to duck out of the job – but Rita insists. And so, slowly and uncertainly, Rita begins to climb away from her initial ignorance, taking the active intellectual initiatives and often taking them badly, but learning almost despite Frank from his fairly passive responses. As the relationship develops Frank becomes charmed and attracted; but after a while the tables are turned, because Rita goes on climbing intellectually, past Frank's level, until she has no real use for his teaching even if he wants to offer it. All she can eventually do to show she has a soft spot for the old wreck is to smarten him up with a haircut.

*Educating Rita* makes a vivid metaphor for the growth of human knowledge. We are born knowing nothing – we do not have, say, the beaver's instinctive knowledge of how to build a strong dam from branches and mud to raise the water level above his lodge entrance – but we have a natural curiosity, a propensity to come up with new ideas and put questions to Nature by practical experiment, so that Nature has to give us answers whether she will or no. And although many ideas are duds, experiment winnows away the mistaken ideas and leaves us the good ones, so knowledge grows unsteadily but cumulatively to such effect that, many generations ago, we largely left behind Nature as our first human ancestors knew it. If a twentieth-century Westerner is concerned with winning new knowledge, it is more likely to be knowledge about how to improve the efficiency of a car engine or about what sort of films will attract audiences next year – questions that have meaning only within a world created by the earlier growth of human knowledge – rather than, say, knowledge about what kinds of fruit are good to eat.

We are still fond of Nature. It is pleasant to prune the roses and mow the lawn on days off from the office; but, for many of us, that is as far as it goes.

Willy Russell did not write his play as an allegory, and I am sure the reader can find aspects of the developing human relationship between his Frank and Rita that fail to fit the metaphor. 'Any analogy will break down eventually', as Rita herself points out. Nevertheless, at a simple level the play does offer a memorable image for the way that mankind can learn anything, starting from nothing. Beavers are born knowing how to make beaver dams, and generation after generation they make them in the same way. If beavers found themselves living in grassland lacking the branches and tree trunks needed for a dam, or if new predators appeared which could swim underwater to get into beaver lodges (so that safety depended on raising habitations above ground level), then beavers would be out of luck, short of biological mutation. Because people develop knowledge from scratch rather than being born with built-in knowledge, we can adapt to different circumstances. Put humans in the Arctic, and they will invent the igloo. Put them in southern Africa, and they will invent the rondavel. Put them anywhere on Earth, and wait a while, and in time they will invent the Apollo rocket and the Lunar Excursion Module, or the Apple Macintosh, or other new things equally unexpected and marvellous.

The story of Rita and Frank makes a good metaphor, at least, for one view of the growth of human knowledge – a view that often passes for uncontroversial common sense. But my reason for writing this book is that, nowadays, quite a lot of people are saying that things are not like that at all. In the late twentieth century, there is a powerful current of intellectual opinion which holds that human knowledge consists of fixed biological instinct, like the beaver's knowledge of dam building. We do not really invent new knowledge, and we are not as intellectually adaptable as we like to think. Our instinctive knowledge base is richer, and lets us do a greater variety of things, than the beaver's; but it is just as biologically determined, so that if our environment changed in a way that called for new thinking, we would be as stuck as the beaver. Willy Russell got it wrong. Rita really knew all that university stuff before she met Frank; in fact she was born knowing it.

Stated briefly and baldly, this concept of human knowledge as biological instinct sounds almost mad. It seems so obvious that human culture changes, in a way that animals' lives hardly ever do. It seems self-evident that many of us in the twentieth-century West know about all kinds of ideas that were simply unknown to our forefathers just a few generations back, and often remain unknown to tribesmen living remote from our civilization today. Of course the people who argue that knowledge is instinct have answers to those points. They are as aware of the obvious facts of life as anyone else, but they have subtle reasons for urging that we have drawn the wrong conclusions from the facts.

Nevertheless, I believe the common-sense reaction is essentially correct. I am sure the idea of human knowledge as biologically built-in is quite wrong. The people who advocate the idea have arguments, and the arguments must be examined and countered – we cannot just dismiss out of hand a point of view which has succeeded in making converts out of a large proportion of the thinking public. But, if one does scrutinize the arguments carefully, they are easy to refute.

That is what this book is for. I have written it to reassert the common-sense view of human knowledge. Willy Russell got it right. Rita knew nothing to start with. And nor did our earliest human forefathers, the people who began the long process of cultural development of which we are the beneficiaries today. The name Eve in my title represents those first human ancestors. (If you wonder why I chose Eve rather than Adam, it was in order to focus on a biological rather than religious concept of human origins; for scientific reasons that will become apparent in a later chapter, the name Eve has special resonance in the context of human evolution.) What Eve and her present-day descendants such as Rita, you, and I inherit is not knowledge but the ability to gain knowledge, by taking initiatives in an environment which may be passive, but which cannot help showing whether our guesses are right or wrong when we try the experiment.

## Language and instinct

For the 'nativists' – the people who believe that knowledge is biologically built-in or native to the human mind – a specially important phenomenon is *language*. Indeed, language is crucial for both sides of the debate. To someone like myself who sees human knowledge as a cultural product, the outcome of many generations of trial-and-error experimentation, the languages that all human societies possess are cultural developments, just as their agricultural techniques or their beliefs about astronomy are; but the first languages were particularly significant cultural innovations, because they changed the process of getting knowledge from an individual to a communal activity. A newborn baby today is as devoid of inborn knowledge as were our first human ancestors; but, while any knowledge they gained was gained through their own testing of their own guesses, we can short-circuit this slow and uncertain process for the benefit of contemporary children. The baby has only the same resources which Eve possessed to try to make sense of his environment; but, once he succeeds in using those resources to master the complex system of behaviour patterns that we call a language, his elders can then simply *give* him the end results of many prior generations of painful knowledge-winning. We can use a language to teach the young, informally or in schools. Succeeding generations can continue the direct process of guessing and experimentation where their elders left off, instead of each individual having to go back to square one and start again.

The nativists see language quite differently. They tend to speak of 'language', rather than 'a language' or 'languages', because they think of the diversity of the world's tongues as a fairly superficial matter masking an underlying unity. Human language, for the nativists, is a sort of biologically inherited coding system for our biologically inherited knowledge base.

But, in addition, they say that language offers the clearest kinds of *evidence* in favour of this nativist picture of the human mind. Late twentieth-century nativism is a scientific theory, not a philosophical matter of pure conceptual analysis. The nativists claim that if we look at the observable facts with an unprejudiced eye, we are bound to concede that biologically inherited knowledge is the only reasonable explanation; and, overwhelmingly, the observable facts they point to are facts about language, about the structures of human language and about how children acquire their mother tongue. They argue that small children are too good at learning language to begin it from scratch – it must be that they know a lot about it before they start. They say that the various languages of the world are too similar to be freely developed cultural constructs: their structural framework must be fixed by our biologically inherited knowledge of language.

Nativism is not a belief just about language. The nativists make claims about the biological fixity of all sorts of human cognitive activity, including things like the graphic arts where language scarcely seems to play any role. But language is so overwhelmingly dominant among the categories of evidence cited in support of contemporary nativism that it makes sense to use the term 'linguistic nativism' for the movement that has revived nativist conceptions of Man in the closing years of our millennium.

I call this movement a revival, because nativism is a point of view with very deep roots in Western thought.* The first nativist was Plato; and in the field of intellectual name-dropping no name resounds with a louder clang than his. Most academics know Alfred North Whitehead's remark about the history of European thought being 'a series of footnotes to Plato'. More than two millennia before Darwin, Plato naturally did not think in terms of knowledge being implanted in human minds through biological evolution (he thought our immortal souls remembered things from a previous existence in a more perfect world than this one); but Plato was quite clear that knowledge is innate in children born into this imperfect world. Not some knowledge: all our knowledge. There is no true learning; 'what we call learning is really just recollection.'

In modern times, the seventeenth-century French thinker René Descartes advocated a very similar picture, though from a Christian perspective: our ideas were not remembered from a former life, they were present in the mind of a child within its mother's womb because God put them there. Descartes was somewhat less extreme than Plato about the extent of our innate intellectual endowment: 'all those [ideas] which involve no affirmation or negation are innate in us', in other words we do not actually begin with a knowledge of what is true and what is false, but we begin with a kind of menu of all possible propositions. The only way that experience after birth comes in is by filling in 'true' or 'false' against the various items on the menu. 'Innate proposition no. 2597923, *Oxford won the Boat Race in 1939*: postnatal experience shows that this one is FALSE, it was Cambridge; innate proposition no.

---

* Notes and references to quoted sources begin on p. 163.

10481387, *Initial array elements in C are indexed by zero*: postnatal experience confirms this as TRUE'; and so on, and on . . . Plato, on the other hand, would have had to claim that I knew from birth that Cambridge won in 1939 and C arrays start from zero. He must say that: I certainly know these things now, and what we call learning is really just recollection. (Incidentally, I decided to be kind to Plato by picking a Boat Race date earlier than my own birth: his picture of innate knowledge is problematic enough, without introducing the issue of innate precognition of the future.)

Of course, neither Plato nor Descartes supposed that tiny children were consciously aware of all these ideas they were supposed to be born with. If they had claimed *that*, then it really would have been impossible to take them seriously. But they agreed that the ideas were there even if a small child is not conscious of them. A baby before birth has the innate ideas in itself 'no less than adults have these ideas while they are not attending to them; the child does not acquire them later, on growing up', as Descartes put it; according to Plato: 'the truth about reality is always in our soul . . . and one must take courage and try to discover – that is, to recollect – what one doesn't happen to know, or (more correctly) remember, at the moment.' A newborn child, for Plato and Descartes, is like a very learned man who is asleep; the knowledge is in there all right, it just needs stirring up a bit before it is available for use.

Fans of these thinkers may feel I am being unfair to them by choosing such implausible illustrations as Boat Race results or the details of a programming language. But I am not being unfair at all: I am deliberately bringing home just how extraordinary a picture of human nature this is, if one takes these great names to mean what they certainly said. True, the specific examples of innate knowledge which Plato and Descartes themselves use as illustrations are very different in flavour from my examples. They discuss innate knowledge of the proposition that the diagonal of a square is $\sqrt{2}$ times the length of the side (Plato), or the proposition that God exists (Descartes), and of word concepts such as 'virtue' (Plato) or 'triangle' (Descartes). These are concepts from the realm of pure intellect, far removed from the messy incon-sequentialities of everyday life, so we do not react with the same immediate response of 'Come off it, Plato, pull the other one' which is likely to greet a suggestion of innate knowledge of Boat Race results. A lot of us are not too sure about the basis of geometrical theorems, and we would much rather leave it to the Vicar to sort out theological questions. We vaguely feel that there may possibly be something to be said for a claim that *these* ideas are based on innate understanding rather than observable evidence.

But that is no defence of Plato or Descartes. What it means is that they were using highly untypical, relatively digestible examples to smuggle into our thinking a far more general and much less plausible account of human nature. Plato's uneducated slave who turns out, allegedly, to possess unconscious knowledge of the ratio of diagonal to side 'will behave in the same way with all geometrical knowledge, *and every other subject*'; according to Descartes, as quoted above, '*all* [propositions] are innate in us' (my italics in both cases). We do not have to believe this stuff, just because it was said centuries or millennia ago by immensely famous men.

The contrary point of view was put by Descartes' English contemporary John Locke.

> How comes [the mind] to be furnished? Whence comes it by that vast store which the busy and boundless fancy of man has painted on it with an almost endless variety? Whence has it all the materials of reason and knowledge? To this I answer, in one word, from *experience*.

We are born with minds capable of executing various operations and of reflecting on their own operations, and our mental operations include a faculty of 'busy and boundless fancy' – human beings are obviously not sticks or stones, which will never come up with any thoughts or knowledge no matter what 'experiences' impinge on them. But we do not have any particular ideas or knowledge built in.

> He that attentively considers the state of a *child*, at his first coming into the world, will have little reason to think him stored with . . . *ideas*, that are to be the matter of his future knowledge. It is by degrees he comes to be furnished with them.

This view, that only experience generates knowledge, is called 'empiricism' (from Greek *empeiria*, experience – nothing to do with empires!).

Locke's wording is perhaps slightly florid for modern tastes, but the substance of what he is saying here seems to be such clear common sense that one feels slightly surprised it ever needed saying. And, indeed, at least in the English-speaking world Locke's empiricist point of view has been broadly taken for granted during almost all of the 300 years since he wrote the passages quoted.

Plato's and Locke's contrasting concepts of human nature have tended to correlate with contrasting political ideals. Plato, in *The Republic*, advocated a somewhat horrifically authoritarian state. Locke founded not only the empiricist philosophy of mind but also the liberal theory of politics which became the accepted political ideal wherever English was spoken. Empiricism and liberal politics are linked by the idea that freedom to experiment is needed in situations where authoritative knowledge is not given in advance.

On politics there is always room for argument, but on the issue of where the child gets ideas and knowledge from, I find it hard to see Locke's opinion, as expressed in the quotations above, as just one point of view among others. Surely most people would see it as the default viewpoint, to be accepted unless there are strong reasons to doubt it; it would take a very subtle philosopher to call such truisms into question. But we have seen that history has more than once produced such subtle philosophers. (Locke's *Essay* is believed to have been written as a direct response to Descartes, though the point is controversial.) In our own generation a new group of such thinkers has emerged and achieved influence.

## The return of the native

The first and still by far the most significant member of this group is Noam Chomsky, of the Massachusetts Institute of Technology. Chomsky, born in 1928, began his professional career within the academic discipline of linguistics – his first book on that subject, *Syntactic Structures*, was published in 1957 – but he quickly, in a stream of further books, transformed his style of analysing language into a subject of far broader intellectual interest than academic linguistics had ever possessed before.

Before Noam Chomsky, the scientific study of language was seen as a highly specialized affair, essentially a branch of social anthropology. (The first chair of linguistics in Britain was attached to an institute that had been founded to promote scholarly study of the peoples of the British Empire. In America, linguistic research was closely linked to ethnographic study of American Indian tribes.) Describing the languages of the world was like describing alien societies' marriage customs or religious beliefs, offering the lure of the exotic without much linkage with one's own life in twentieth-century Britain or America; but at the same time the intricate grammatical and phonetic detail found in any human language gave the study something of the same intellectually demanding character as legal training. Between them, these considerations ensured that the discipline remained a minority interest.

Those who pursued it did not doubt that they were studying an aspect of societies' cultural inheritance, so that where languages were not historically related to one another as descendants from a common ancestor language, they were liable to differ in any and every respect – there was no mechanism that could cause them to be similar. For linguistics scholars in the first two-thirds of the century, it was a public duty to emphasize the astonishing diversity of the world's languages. This was valuable, first, as a corrective to the Eurocentric assumption that our cultural norms were the only valid norms. Indigenous languages of other continents, which failed to reflect the intellectual categories of English or Latin, were not necessarily inferior as vehicles for thought – often, linguistic analysis showed them to express marvellously subtle intellectual distinctions unknown to the languages of Europe. Second, particularly following the horrors of Nazism, linguistics did society a service by making the point that culture and blood are independent spheres: the civilization and cognitive life which are the special glories of our species are uncoupled from the biological endowment which we mostly hold in common, but which creates limited differences with respect to skin colour or facial features.

Martin Joos in 1957 epitomized the received attitude to linguistic study in his own country as 'the American . . . tradition that languages could differ from each other without limit and in unpredictable ways'. British colleagues would have seen no reason to disagree.

Noam Chomsky completely changed this agenda. Rather than focusing on the differences between languages, he focused on what they have in common; and he argued that they have a lot in common – much more than can be explained as chance coincidence, or the result of similarities in the external circumstances facing societies which developed languages separately. The common features can only be explained, according to Chomsky, as reflecting innate linguistic knowledge which specifies in considerable detail what human language is like, and hence ensures that creatures endowed with this knowledge are capable of developing and using only languages that conform to the innate specifications. And if we consider the ability of small children to master their mother tongue, we see something quite different from the slow, plodding, sometimes unsuccessful learning that characterizes an older child's or adult's attempts to come to grips with a school subject or a body of knowledge needed for work. Any child born in (say) France seems to become a fluent French-speaker almost effortlessly at a young age, while a typical 13-year-old English schoolboy, try as he may, just does not get the knack of those genders and irregular verbs. Even if in due course he achieves an unusually good A-level result, it is quite unlikely that a Frenchman will ever mistake him for a compatriot.

It is as if a child no more has to 'learn' a first language, at a certain young age, than he has to 'learn' how to produce his first set of teeth, and then at a certain later age how to replace his milk teeth with adult teeth. Rather, Chomsky says, 'grammar grows in the mind'.

The obvious objection to this idea is that if a child's mother tongue grows in his mind as teeth grow in his mouth, we would expect everyone to grow up speaking the same language. Or, if there were differences, they ought to correlate with other genetic differences – perhaps white men would speak 'white languages', yellow and black men speak 'yellow' and 'black' languages, or the like. But people do not all speak the same language, and language differences certainly do not depend on biological ancestry. A newborn English child, brought up in a Chinese environment by Chinese-speaking foster-parents or in a Xhosa environment by Xhosa-speaking foster-parents, will become a fluent Chinese or Xhosa speaker, not a fluent English speaker (and vice versa).

Chomsky accepts this, but for him it is not very important. The differences between English, Chinese and Xhosa are superficial details: the bulk of what is known by someone who speaks any one of these languages consists of a rich set of structural principles that are common to all three languages, and to every other language on Earth. Our innate knowledge of language is not so perfectly complete that it fixes all details of language and hence permits only one human language. The innate knowledge leaves some matters open, and those matters do have to be learned by experience after a child is born. Consequently, separate societies have developed conventional patterns of speech which differ with respect to these 'open' issues, and we call these different 'languages'. But it is a mistake to pay so much attention to the superficial differences that we fail to notice the common underlying features. It is really rather provincial of us to think of English, Xhosa, Chinese, and so forth as 'different languages'; if an extraterrestrial alien visited Earth, Chomsky suggests, he might well think of all human beings as speaking one language, though with local differences in vocabulary. According to Chomsky's picture of the human mind, biology prescribes that we shall speak language; but it leaves some details open, so that there is a range – a strictly limited range – of alternative conventions for certain aspects of speaking.

And what is true of language is true, as Chomsky sees it, for other aspects (probably all other aspects) of cognition.

Scientists strive to understand the natural world, by developing theories that yield reliable predictions about various aspects of observable reality. Sometimes a theory that seemed well established turns out to be wrong, so that the relevant community of scientists have to cast about to construct some theory more adequate to the full range of evidence; and sometimes a class of phenomena obstinately fails to yield to scientific explanation over a long period. We usually assume that these are temporary problems of insufficient time and effort. Our current understanding of some field may be disconfirmed by new data, but give us time and we will surely find an account that explains the unexpected anomaly. Perhaps nobody has ever yet come up with a satisfactory theory in another field – it must be an unusually complex domain, but sooner or later someone will develop a structure of scientific laws that cover it.

To Chomsky, this is a wrong way of looking at things. Scientific theories, like languages, are mental products, governed by our biology. Our genes do not specify our scientific theorizing capacity so tightly as to allow just one theory in any domain: there is some free play for differences of scientific opinion, for one theory to displace another as we gather fresh data. But that flexibility is strictly limited. In particular, there is no reason to expect that the truth about every natural phenomenon is among the theories biologically available to us. In some sense there must be a true account, but it may not be a humanly thinkable account. In some domains there may be *no* biologically available theory we can formulate, true or false. If we have failed for a long time to come up with a satisfactory account of some topic, that may be because our genes give us no possibility of ever understanding it:

> an intelligible explanatory theory . . . can be developed by humans in case something close to the true theory in a certain domain happens to fall within human 'science-forming' capacities. . . . Thinking of humans as biological organisms . . . it is only a lucky accident if their cognitive capacity happens to be well matched to scientific truth in some area. . . . the class of humanly accessible sciences [is] possibly a small subset of those potential sciences that deal with matters concerning which we hope (vainly) to attain some insight and understanding.

Likewise in the arts. The history of painting and other graphic arts in Europe, and in some other traditions, shows a long series of developments as new generations have invented new techniques of celebrating or creating beauty, or expressing moods or ideas visually. We usually assume that nothing prevents this innovation process from continuing indefinitely into the future. True, some of what passes for art nowadays seems pretty rubbishy; but then, one hears that past artistic innovations often met the same response in their day, even if we recognize their value now – and in any case, what we retain

from earlier periods is the good stuff, whereas in our own time we are exposed
to the dross as well as the pearls.

Again Chomsky sees this as a misapprehension. Artistic innovation cannot
continue indefinitely: no human artist can ever do more than realize one or
another of the fixed range of artistic forms provided for us by our biology. As
with language and with scientific thought, biology leaves some limited
flexibility open, so more than one artistic genre is possible; and it has taken
humanity some centuries to work through the possibilities, because so few
people in previous ages had time and resources available to devote to artistic
endeavour. But, now that large numbers of people are in a position to pursue
artistic activity, we seem to have exhausted the possibilities; that is why
'modern art' often seems worthless. People would still like to be artists, but
our genes do not allow for any further genres of serious artistic innovation.
All that is left is for 'Mockery of conventions that are, ultimately, grounded in
human cognitive capacity . . . to become virtually an art form in itself'.

Another linguistic nativist, Ray Jackendoff, suggests that we inherit a
universal musical grammar, which biologically constrains the possibility of
developing new musical styles even more tightly than Chomsky's innate
knowledge of language constrains the diversity of human languages.

Incidentally, some people object to Chomsky and other nativists using the
term 'knowledge' for the innate biological organization which is claimed to
control our linguistic behaviour, though it might be acceptable with respect
to biological control of scientific theorizing. To have knowledge of a subject,
the objectors say, means being able to answer questions on it. Most people
have very limited knowledge about the structure of their mother tongue,
although they speak it perfectly well.

The nativists reject this as a dispute about semantics rather than reality, and
I think they are right to do so. Chomsky uses the phrase 'tacit knowledge' for
the mental arrangements that allow people to assemble words of their language
into meaningful sentences without being able to say explicitly what rules they
are following in doing so. If anyone dislikes the phrase 'tacit knowledge',
Chomsky is quite willing to use some different name, but the issue still remains:
is this, whatever we call it, something encoded in our genes, or is it something
we pick up purely through listening to our elders?

That is indeed the real question. And it means that the study of language
in Chomsky's style ceases to be a specialist branch of anthropology, focusing
on the exotic cultural developments of alien societies. It becomes a source of
evidence for a novel and startling picture of the biological nature of Man – of
all men and women, including you and me and the other inhabitants of our
own society.

It would be hard to exaggerate the impact that these ideas of Noam
Chomsky's achieved, beginning in the 1960s shortly after he began to propound
them. By many objective measures, Chomsky became the world's most
influential living thinker. For instance, there nowadays exist comprehensive
computerized registers of the references that scholars make to one another's
writings in the academic literature; within the sphere covered by the Arts and

Humanities Citation Index, Chomsky is the most-quoted living writer, and the eighth most quoted in history. (The only authors with higher scores are Marx, Lenin, Shakespeare, the Bible – treated as 'an author', Aristotle, Plato and Freud.) I happened to see a television sequence not long ago in which a London street trader was asked what he understood by the term 'intellectual': 'Noam Chomsky?' he offered uncertainly. Chomsky has been showered with virtually every honour that the international academic world has to bestow. In 1995 the University of Cambridge gave him an honorary doctorate in a ceremony at which the University Orator, speaking in Latin, likened him to Plato.

Initially, in the 1960s, Chomsky's message encountered a fair amount of scepticism, as well as (probably to a greater extent) a simple failure to understand what he was saying. Two of America's most eminent philosophers, Hilary Putnam and Nelson Goodman (both of Harvard University), when invited to debate Chomsky's linguistic nativism at a symposium in 1966, treated it as more a topic for sarcasm or hilarity than a serious contribution. But Chomsky drowned his intellectual adversaries in torrents of tireless argument. Very many of his critics, if they did not become converts, gave up the attempt to argue against him, and were consequently perceived by the audiences for intellectual debate as having lost the contest. By the 1970s, educated opinion had after 300 years sold pretty well all its stock in John Locke and empiricism, and reinvested the proceeds in Chomsky's nativism.

## The new wave

In the 1980s Chomsky's star waned. By 1990 it looked as though he was someone who had succeeded in making a sudden splash with an astonishing new idea, but that once the first wave of enthusiasm was past the temporary converts had re-examined the doctrine, recognized its inherent implausibility, and quietly dropped it. However, we shall see that this appearance proved to be mistaken.

There were several reasons for the 1980s' eclipse. One was that those were the Margaret Thatcher years, which meant that educated public opinion had other things to be interested in. Another significant factor was Chomsky's own politics.

Politics had given Chomsky much of his audience in the early days. He was the leading intellectual figure in the 1960s' movement against American involvement in the Vietnam War, which made him a person of great interest and attraction to a generation of American students who did not want to be conscripted to fight in South-East Asia. Many people came to listen to Chomsky on foreign policy and stayed to listen to him on linguistics. At that time, Chomsky spoke and wrote more about the concrete issues surrounding the war than about his general political ideals, which seemed to be an engaging if fairly dotty version of anarcho-syndicalism.

Later, though, Chomsky's political interventions became less congenial to many. He published statements about massacres in Cambodia and about a

French 'Holocaust revisionist' which some commentators found unconscionable. Martin Peretz, editor of *The New Republic*, took the charitable view that in this domain Chomsky was simply 'a fool'. In the 1980s the caravan moved on, and one heard less of Chomsky and less, in consequence, of linguistic nativism.

In the 1990s, though, nativism is back in the public eye again, benefiting from a current upsurge of interest in all kinds of popular science writing. The people making the running in the media and the bookshops now are not Noam Chomsky, but a new, younger generation of academics who are pursuing in their own style the nativist agenda which Chomsky set. The fundamental message is the same; but the manner of its expression is very different, and much more appealing to the general reader or television viewer.

Chomsky's books were never an easy read. Although his doctrines are scientific, in the sense that they are intended ultimately to stand or fall by their correspondence to observable facts, Chomsky is a very theoretical scientist. He freely admits it. 'Have you done any experiments with children to learn how they acquire language?' he was asked by the *New Yorker* essayist Ved Mehta; 'No', he replied. 'I hate experiments.' His books are characterized by relentlessly dense logical analysis, often in a semi-technical style interspersed with algebraic formulae, of the implications that he sees as following from a quite restricted range of observable facts – usually very everyday facts about the modern English language. No one would read Chomsky out of fascination with the data he quotes: the data are banal; the point of Chomsky's writing is the conclusions he purports to draw from them.

But in any case his prose is so forbidding that only a fraction of the people who chattered enthusiastically about linguistic nativism in Chomsky's 1970s' heyday are likely to have read attentively more than a token few paragraphs of his writings. They read secondary paperbacks and journalism by other writers, who simplified the master's message while sometimes glossing over the problems within it. It is hard to avoid the suspicion that some of them took a look at the original œuvre and decided 'If it's as hard as this it must be good' – Chomsky would not be the first intellectual guru to have profited from obscurity.

The nativists of the 1990s are quite different. Their books are full of fascinating information about languages and linguistic behaviour, facts that you will not encounter just by virtue of living an ordinary late-twentieth-century life in an English-speaking country but which are chock-full of 'human interest', so that people enjoy reading the books for the data alone. Although the arguments from linguistic data to nativist conclusions are there, some of the new writers lay the inferential framework on with a light brush. The reader is taken on a magical mystery tour of language and urged to agree that nativism makes a plausible account of it all – rather than herded through a bare corral in which every side exit is sealed off by barriers of logic and the only way out is the gate labelled 'innate knowledge'.

As a result, the new generation of linguistic nativists have succeeded very quickly in winning audiences and attracting praise from distinguished and sometimes influential onlookers. One of the first publications of the new wave was Derek Bickerton's 1990 book *Language and Species,* which draws strongly nativist conclusions from studies of prehistoric Man and of the pidgin and creole languages which have grown up in various areas of contact between widely different cultures. The dustjacket of my copy carries an endorsement by Michael LaBarbera, University of Chicago professor of anatomy and therefore, one imagines, well away from his usual beat, describing the book as a superb account of 'how we became human'. Ray Jackendoff's 1993 book *Patterns in the Mind* is among the offerings of a paperback book club, alongside erotic novels, histories of the more dramatic passages in our island story, and popular studies of the Holy Grail legend and the Turin Shroud; its dustjacket recommendation is by Francis Crick, discoverer of the double helix. And swamping all others is the splash made by Steven Pinker's 1994 book *The Language Instinct.*

Steven Pinker is a Canadian who is now a younger colleague of Noam Chomsky at MIT, and his book weaves a multicoloured web composed of strands from every fascinating byway of language study you can think of – the grammar of the Watergate tapes, the language of mothers talking to babies, linguistic clues to the way of life of our Indo-European ancestors, the speech of brain-damaged patients, all this and much, much more is there; and it is assembled into a pattern designed to convince a new generation of the truth of Chomsky's thesis: we speak because we inherit a 'language instinct'. Detailed knowledge of language is built into our genes; and what is true of language is likely to be true of other aspects of human knowledge and behaviour. What we take to be culture is mainly biology.

The level of acclaim which Pinker's book has received must be almost unprecedented for a popular book about science. Richard Dawkins of 'selfish gene' fame comments that 'Reading Steven Pinker's book is one of the biggest favours I've ever done my brain . . . exhilaratingly brilliant.' The *Independent* called it 'Dazzling. . . . Words can hardly do justice to [Pinker's] superlative range and liveliness.' Christopher Longuet-Higgins, writing in the august *Nature,* describes the book as 'marvellously readable'. BBC Television has shown a long documentary on Pinker's ideas.

And Pinker deserves the plaudits. His book is superbly well written (as well as very fully researched). I wish I were capable of using the English language half as well.

But of course a book can be very well written, and its conclusions quite wrong. Despite Pinker's verbal pyrotechnics, there is actually no such thing as a human language instinct.

There really isn't. Chomsky's arguments for it do not work; and Pinker's arguments do not work either. What they are telling us just ain't so. Believe me, it is not. The rest of this book is designed to convince you of that.

In fact the 'new wave' of linguistic nativists of the 1990s gain an unfair advantage in their struggle to win the hearts and minds of the educated public, stemming precisely from the fact that they are now several decades removed from the original development of the theory. Pinker's and the other recent

nativist writings make heavy use of references to the works of Chomsky and
his original followers, published twenty or thirty years before. When those
writings were new, readers who encountered them recognized that they were
being asked to believe a new idea, by one of its advocates, so it was up to each
reader to be on his mental guard and judge whether he was being given valid
arguments or hype and hand-waving. A sensible person who hears an
academic expounding his favourite new theory does not just surrender his
critical faculty and accept everything he is told, any more than we take
consumer advertising at face value. But in the 1990s Pinker and others discuss
the work of Chomsky and his early collaborators in terms that make this work
sound like established scientific findings from the past.

The new books do include plenty of footnotes which in theory allow the
reader to follow the audit trail back to the earlier passages in which some
relevant point was allegedly established. But it would be fantasy to imagine
that the average reader who takes the Penguin edition of Pinker's *The Language
Instinct* away for holiday reading is ever going to follow up the references and
check that facts said to be known since the 1960s were truly established then.
Most of us are not on our guard against too-ready acceptance of established
science, unless we are explicitly told that there were always reasons for
doubting it. And although some of the nativists of the 1990s write well, they
do not go out of their way to tell us that. They are barristers, not judges. They
are trying to win a case, and it is not their job to draw attention to its weak
points.

My task in this book, then, is to counter both waves of modern nativism,
and to show why we ought to prefer an empiricist view of human nature. If I
can deal adequately with Chomsky's version of nativism, this will give me a
good start towards demolishing the 'new wave' too – because their work
depends at many points on his. But the nativists of the 1990s have fresh
arguments of their own, and I must confront and defeat these also. All this I
shall do.

## Guessing and testing

Up until now I have been rather negative. I have given a clearer account of the
nativist picture of Man, which I disagree with, than of the picture I want to
put in its place.

Let me now be more explicit about what I am assuming human beings to
be like, so far as our intellectual life is concerned, so that when in later chapters
I object that a nativist explanation for some interesting fact sounds implausible,
the reader can check whether the picture I have in mind would fit any better.

The account of human nature which I aim to defend in this book is not
mainly due to John Locke. Locke was the first person in the modern world to
argue explicitly against innate knowledge, but – because he was first – the ins
and outs of the debate were not all as visible in his day as they later became.
Locke seems to have believed in broadly the same dialectic of guesswork and

testing which a twentieth-century empiricist would see as central to the process of human knowledge formation; but it is fair comment to say that Locke was much more concerned to discuss the relationship between knowledge and external objective realities than the relationship between knowledge and the guesswork from which it emerges.

The best individual guide to the general nature of human intellectual activity, I believe, is Sir Karl Popper, who was born in Vienna in 1902 but worked from 1946 onwards at the London School of Economics and died, not long before I undertook this book, in 1994.

Popper occupies an unusual role in twentieth-century thought. Among the coterie of professional academic philosophers busy doing the things that university staff have to do to struggle another rung up the promotion ladder, Popper's name does not impinge all that often. All academic philosophers know and respect his name, but they do not talk about him as much as they talk about many lesser men. Popper was never very interested in playing inward-looking professional games. On the other hand, the discipline of philosophy was originally intended to help Everyman understand what sort of universe he inhabited and how he should live his life. As a philosopher in this sense, Popper's achievements are unrivalled in our time. No other philosopher in the present century has had comparable influence on the thinking of statesmen and the conduct of public life, certainly in Britain and perhaps anywhere. And this influence seems to me to have been entirely for the good (even if, as a person, he had his difficult side).

Popper began his intellectual career as a philosopher of science. He was impressed, as any thinking person must be, at the great strides which physics had made since the Renaissance in understanding the laws governing the natural world. Living in early-twentieth-century Vienna, he was surrounded by the intellectual ferment created by two other self-styled sciences: Marxism, and Freud's and Adler's psychoanalysis. Popper felt there was a difference in kind between physics and these newer genres of discourse; there was a sense of responsibility about physics that seemed lacking in Marxism and psychoanalysis, which entitled the former to a degree of respect that Popper felt no obligation to extend to the latter.

Yet what did this responsibility amount to? It was not that the laws of physics were older and more solidly established than those of the Marxist science of history, or Freud's theory of the psyche. If anything, when Popper was a young man, the reverse was true. The ultimate, apparently unshakeable basis of physics was Isaac Newton's laws of motion, unchallenged for hundreds of years and confirmed through countless observations; yet within Popper's lifetime, Newton's laws *had* been challenged by Albert Einstein, who put forward an alternative and incompatible theory to account for the same facts – and in 1919, when Popper was 16 years old, observations of a solar eclipse demonstrated that Newton was wrong and Einstein right. It might appear that physics was the flaky discipline, while Marxism and psychoanalysis, though relatively new, had given little reason for anyone to disparage them. To Popper, though, that seemed to be the wrong way round.

The key difference, Popper realized, was that the laws of physics were
*refutable*. Newton's theory, and Einstein's theory, made predictions about what
can happen and, more important, what cannot happen in the natural world.
They each specified many 'potential falsifiers' – states of affairs which, if ever
observed, would force abandonment of the respective theory. One of Newton's
potential falsifiers *was* observed in 1919, so Newton's physics was abandoned
(other than as an approximation to the truth, adequate for many practical
purposes but not ultimately correct), and Einstein's alternative theory stepped
into the breach. But Einstein's theory had its own potential falsifiers, and it
would survive only so long as none of these was observed.

Marx's account of history might seem to have this quality too. It made
predictions about the future evolution of societies; it implied that nations
having capitalist economic systems would undergo Communist revolutions,
with the first nations to go Communist being the ones with the most fully
developed capitalist economies – Britain, the USA, perhaps Germany. The
trouble was, in 1917 one nation did have a Communist revolution, and it was
the wrong one: Russia. Yet Marxists did not treat this as a reason to abandon
Marxism, as physicists gave up Newton's laws; they just avoided talking about
the contradiction.

As for psychoanalysis, it seemed to Popper that nothing ever came close to
ranking as a potential falsifier there. He tried describing to Adler a case that
seemed not to agree with Adler's account of the psyche, but Adler promptly
fitted it into his system in a manner that suggested he envisaged no possibility
of any case not fitting.

True science, Popper concluded, was not characterized by certainty: it was
characterized by taking risks. Scientific advance was an interplay between
conjectures – guesses, in other words – and objective tests.

A scientist guesses that some observations might be governed by a general
law which he has somehow dreamed up, so he proposes it as a hypothesis. If
it is a scientifically worthwhile hypothesis it will make a strong claim, meaning
that there will be many potential future observations that would refute it; but
nothing can ever decisively confirm it (no amount of specific observations can
ever prove the truth of a general law). A hypothesis with no potential falsifiers
is safe from refutation, but it is empty – it tells us nothing.

Our scientific knowledge is the totality of guesses which we have put up
for potential refutation and which we have not yet succeeded in refuting. All
such knowledge is provisional. Even the best-established element of our
knowledge might unexpectedly be refuted tomorrow, as Newton was by the
eclipse observations.

Thus knowledge comes both from inside us and from objective external
reality. But what comes from inside is not true, authoritative knowledge, as
Plato and Descartes supposed: it is only a stream of highly fallible but original
guesswork – 'busy and boundless fancy', in Locke's words. It is experience
of external reality that converts a few of the guesses into provisional, tentative
'knowledge', by failing to knock those guesses out while it knocks out many
unluckier conjectures. Ultimate, authoritative knowledge about matters of

scientific fact is something that Man can never hope to achieve. The search for scientific truth must always be an *Unended Quest*, to borrow the title of Popper's autobiography. The real world is so complicated that very likely none of our theories will ever be perfectly true – in which case each of them will be refuted sooner or later. But, even if we did come up with a perfectly true theory in some domain, we could never know that we had achieved this. We would always be waiting to see whether a refutation was lurking round the next corner.

That is the picture which Popper painted of the special kind of knowledge-winning we call science. But what is true of the growth of science as a communal activity is equally plausible as a picture of how the individual child learns, at least in the years before he can talk (after that, his elders can speed things up by telling him the results of their and earlier generations' guess-testing). The newborn baby, for Popper, has no innate truths in its mind (Popper suggests that it might be described as having a few innate expectations, such as the expectation of being fed). What it has is a propensity to generate all sorts of hypotheses or guesses, many of them quite mistaken, and to winnow them out via practical trial and error. The guesses that seem to work are retained and built on as the foundation of further, higher-level guesses, and thus the child builds up an increasingly elaborate structure of knowledge.

Not that there is anything unique to Popper in this picture of infant learning, surely. Nelson Goodman described essentially the same view in these words: 'We . . . regard the mind as in motion from the start, striking out with spontaneous predictions in dozens of directions, and gradually rectifying and channeling its predictive processes.' The baby is a little research scientist, and one very energetic and rich in research ideas to try out.

The relevance of these ideas to public life is that we cannot expect errors not to be made, because progress comes only through making mistakes. We need to organize society in such a way that it can quickly learn from errors, recognize them for what they are and try alternatives. We need an 'open society' which encourages piecemeal social experiment and avoids grand schemes of Utopian social engineering, where mistakes lead to massive human penalties. One of Popper's most significant books, *The Open Society and Its Enemies*, written as Popper's 'war work' in the 1940s, argued that Plato was the first enemy of the open society, and that more recent continental philosophical traditions underpinned the totalitarian social systems which the Allies were fighting. This liberating attitude of mind, that errors were not things to be avoided at all costs but things to be used and profited from, became virtually Britain's 'house style' of thought about public affairs in the postwar decades.

Popper was fallible too, and I do not mean to hold him up as the sole and final arbiter on the nature of the good society and the basis of human knowledge. His LSE colleague Imre Lakatos quite correctly criticized Popper's account of scientific progress, for instance, by pointing out that in practice scientific theories are not considered in isolation and abandoned at the first appearance of a counterexample. Researchers use evidence in order to choose between alternative theories; if Einstein had not already challenged Newton, astronomers would never have thought of scrutinizing the 1919 eclipse in the way they did. What we should assess are not individual theories but theory sequences, programmes of scientific advance or 'problemshifts'. We should respect problemshifts that are 'progressive', responding to anomalies by modifications which yield ever-broader ranges of testable predictions, but not problemshifts that 'degenerate', avoiding refutation by reducing their sets of predictions, as Marxists gave up predicting the order in which nations would go Communist.

Popper was mistaken on some points, and where he was right others had often said similar things – as we would expect of a plausible account. But, if one wants a single name to associate with the concepts of mind and knowledge defended in this book, Popper's is probably the best name to choose.

For our present purposes, of course, I am not asking the reader to believe that a newborn child is a research scientist in miniature just because Karl Popper said so. Whether Popper's picture is the right one is what my book as a whole is intended to investigate. For the present, all I aim to do is to ask the reader to agree that this is a reasonable, coherent alternative to Plato's, Descartes' and Chomsky's and Pinker's picture of the newborn baby as sleeping savant. When I argue in later chapters that their account of speakers' internal mechanisms does not offer a good match to speakers' observed linguistic behaviour, I know the reader is sure to be thinking, 'What is your alternative account, then, and how well does that match the observations?' My discussion of Popper shows the alternative view of human nature that I shall be defending against the nativists. We shall see which matches the data better, as the book progresses.

It is important to spell out the view of human nature which I am defending, because the nativists sometimes try to win the debate by suggesting that anyone who disagrees with them must believe that human beings are some kind of mindless robot, and that 'learning' is an entirely passive and mechanical activity, something like the film in a camera registering impressions from the outside world. Noam Chomsky summarizes the debate as:

> The question whether 'the human mind [is] to be regarded simply as a responsive cog in the mechanism of nature,' as in empiricist doctrine, or as 'a creative, determinative force'

(internal quotations from Ellen Wood); he describes the view he opposes as:

> The doctrine that the human mind is initially unstructured and plastic and that human nature is entirely a social product . . . the concept of the 'empty organism,' plastic and unstructured . . .

If it were a forced choice between this picture and biologically inherited knowledge, probably we would all agree that the latter wins. But who seriously suggests that human beings begin life mentally as 'empty', 'plastic' organisms? Locke didn't. Popper didn't. Goodman doesn't. I don't.

As I said before, a stick or stone with *no* innate mental machinery will never learn anything, irrespective of the 'experiences' that impinge on it. But there is a world of difference between conceding that we have an innate propensity to create and test fallible, unpredictable guesses, and claiming that we do not need to do much guesswork because we know most things before we start.

Willy Russell's Rita began the play dead ignorant, as she would have put it. But she wasn't thick. If Rita had been stupid, even a more diligent instructor than Frank could have made nothing of her. The same, I suggest, was true for Eve. Our ancestors were given no knowledge prior to what they could learn from experience; but, having intelligence, they could use experience to gain knowledge.

The nativists claim that innate knowledge is a scientific theory, the best available explanation for the evidence. That means that it is not the only possible coherent theory – if it were that, they would not need to quote evidence. Since both sides in the debate evidently agree that different views of the nature of mind are logically admissible, surely the reader will allow that Popper's picture of the infant as a guessing-and-testing organism is at least a possible alternative to the nativists' sleeping savant? For the moment, that is all I need to ask.

## The book in outline

My strategy in the rest of this book will be as follows. First, I shall examine the detailed arguments used by the nativists to try to persuade us of their case, and I shall show that the arguments fail in every instance. Either the premises are factually untrue, or the conclusions do not follow from the premises (or, not infrequently, both). Chapter 2 deals with the 'first wave' of linguistic nativism, as put forward in the 1960s and 1970s. Chapter 3 deals with the 'new wave' of 1990s' nativism.

If, by the end of Chapter 3, the reader agrees that the nativists' case is in tatters, then we are back to where we were in thinking about human nature before the innate-knowledge merchants began their sales patter. The reader may feel that the Popperian view wins on inherent plausibility. But Chapter 4 will give positive reasons for believing in it, drawn from some of the same data about language structure that the nativists have mistakenly seen as buttressing their case.

In Chapter 5 we will consider some abstract, conceptual issues surrounding the concept of human minds as creatively original.

I should be precise about what I am undertaking to do, so that the reader can judge in due course whether or not I have achieved it. Linguistic nativism grew from one man's idea in the 1960s into a new branch of academic study that occupies literally hundreds of university staff internationally. Many of these people have been publishing books and articles which they would see as strengthening the case for nativism. If I were to deal individually with every one of these publications, I would be writing not a book but a small library. I have no time to do that; and, if I had, nobody would find time to read it all.

But there is no real reason to attempt this. Although there is now a vast literature that is at least tangentially relevant to linguistic nativism, the writings which have actually played a role in persuading the educated public at large are far fewer. It is those writings I need to address. If the leading works which actually have been instrumental in changing people's minds turn out, on critical re-examination, to have no force, there is no reason to expect the penumbra of lesser-known writings to make a better case.

Of course some of them may do. It is not logically excluded that a reader might respond to this book along the lines: 'Fair enough – you have demonstrated that Steven Pinker and Noam Chomsky, and the others you have discussed, give us no serious reason to believe in innate human knowledge. But have you seen Lynda Snell's argument in the latest *Borchester Language Skills Newsletter*? – it is really unanswerable.' Perhaps it genuinely is.

But then Lynda Snell will be in the position that Chomsky was in, back in 1960: she will have to convince the world that the implausible-seeming doctrine of nativism is right, using only her own powers of argument without any help from a climate of opinion created by others. Perhaps she can do it, and if she can, good luck to her. At the moment it is too easy for the Lynda Snells to seem to make a good case while taking a mass of crucial issues for granted.

The first group of nativist arguments I must address are obviously those produced by Noam Chomsky, during the period when he was changing people's minds. I would identify that period as broadly 1960 to 1980; I have taken pains to comb through Chomsky's œuvre from that period, and to identify each separate strand of argument that he deployed. I believe Chapter 2 is very complete in its analysis of the structure of Chomsky's nativist arguments in those decades.

Chomsky continued to write after 1980, but his subsequent writings have not been crucial in converting readers from empiricist to nativist beliefs. By 1980 he had already converted many readers, and I think there are very few people, if any, who have come to nativism chiefly because of some idea Chomsky put forward only after that date. Consequently I have not felt the same obligation to comb through Chomsky's post-1980 writings exhaustively. Here and there I mention them when some point seems specially relevant, but I do not claim to survey them thoroughly.

Other people were writing in the 1960s and 1970s in a way that harmonized with Chomsky's linguistic nativism but sometimes deployed rather separate kinds of data or argumentation. Chapter 2 examines these to the extent that, in my judgement, their output was both truly separate from Chomsky's (so that it could support the nativist case even if Chomsky's arguments are rejected) and also played a real part in making converts. Clearly, my selection of writers who meet these two criteria is fallible, and depends on personal impressions of what was widely read at the time. If readers feel I have overlooked writings which brought many people to nativism independently of Chomsky, that would be a valid criticism of my book. But I would defend my choices.

In Chapter 3, again, I am bound to exercise judgement about which contributors to the 'new wave' are being effective in making fresh converts to nativism. I believe few readers will disagree that the leading figure is Steven Pinker, and accordingly much of the chapter is devoted to his arguments and the findings of the researchers whom Pinker quotes. I deal also with two other contemporary linguistic nativists, Derek Bickerton and Ray Jackendoff; it is for the reader to decide whether my coverage responds adequately to various individuals' roles in the movement, but again I have made considered judgements.

Both Chapters 2 and 3 are longer than I should ideally like them to be. If I omitted to answer any argument that has played some part in winning people over to nativism, past experience suggests that critics might respond as if that argument were virtually the only one that mattered, however many other nativist arguments I had successfully refuted. So I have to be exhaustive in dealing with the influential writings. The reader might not thank me if I went on to cover the background publications equally exhaustively.

Then there is the issue of footnotes. There is a style of twentieth-century academic writing which, in the name of accountability, surrounds every direct statement with a plethora of references to earlier publications (or even to unpublished material). An inexpert reader may find himself persuaded less by the facts or arguments that are presented directly than by the apparent existence of a mass of further evidence lying behind the words on the page. This appearance can be misleading. Werner Cohn comments severely on Noam Chomsky's footnote style:

> Chomsky's writings are often praised by his admirers as packed with 'facts'. And indeed there are many footnotes and many references to apparently esoteric pieces of information. But I have found that these references, at least those that deal with crucial points, simply do not check out. Sometimes the source is impossible to track down, sometimes it is completely misquoted, very often it is . . . patently and completely biased . . .

Cohn is discussing Chomsky's political writings, but the same criticisms can equally be made of his writings on language and philosophy.

Clearly, readers must be on their guard against surrendering to a case that is not directly stated. In the exercise I have set myself in this book, I acknowledge responsibility for meeting nativist arguments where these are explicit; but if X says that we must believe in innate knowledge because Y has a good though unspecified argument for it, and hardly anyone in practice has read Y's argument, then I acknowledge no obligation to analyse Y's argument. Sometimes I do, but there is no reason why I should have to.

In taking issue with influential discourse produced by others, an author is bound to fight on the terrain his adversaries have chosen. Personally, I like prose dealing with abstract matters to be leavened with a high proportion of concrete examples to logical analysis. I think many readers share this preference. But the writings of the linguistic nativists vary greatly in this respect. As mentioned earlier, Steven Pinker's book has plenty of concrete, vivid illustrative data; but Noam Chomsky's writings are very abstract. When I address Chomsky's version of nativism, then, I shall necessarily focus on abstract issues of logical validity, as he does.

I shall bring in concrete examples where I can, though, to lighten the reader's burden. And, in taking on a case founded on many-layered pillars of abstract logical reasoning, there is one advantage: we only need to dislodge a single inferential brick to see the edifice collapse in ruins. We shall find no shortage of loose bricks.

If the reader will hear me out through the pages that follow, I am confident that he will agree with my conclusions. Nativism has been a thirty-year wrong turning in the progress of thinking about human nature. Eve was not a born know-all. She was ignorant. But she was a good learner.

# 2 The Original Arguments for a Language Instinct

## Drawing up the battle lines

In this chapter I deal with the various significant strands of argument for linguistic nativism put forward during the two decades, between about 1960 and 1980, when this idea first flourished and won converts. Overwhelmingly, those arguments were produced by Noam Chomsky, and most other linguistic nativists at the time were essentially interpreting and restating ideas of Chomsky's; so I begin by examining his writings. Later in the chapter, I shall take up a separate group of nativist arguments which were rather different in content and style from Chomsky's, but which in practice functioned to reinforce his case.

I begin by recapitulating the case Chomsky has advanced, in order to identify as precisely as possible the opinions which I aim to refute. Since Chomsky still holds and defends the views discussed, I shall use the present tense in expounding his doctrines, despite the fact that some illustrative quotations are now more than thirty years old. In outline, Chomsky's position is as follows.

No child speaks a language at birth. After some years of life in a speech community, all children (apart from a tiny minority who have physical disabilities which interfere with speech and/or hearing) become competent users of the language of their society.

Chomsky claims that this process of first-language acquisition must be determined in most respects by a genetic programme, so that the development of language in an individual's mind is akin to the growth of a bodily organ, rather than being a matter of responding to environmental stimulation by 'learning' a system to which the individual is not in detail predisposed. Human language, and the cognitive achievements (such as scientific theorizing) for which language is a prerequisite, are for Chomsky largely a product of biology, rather than being (as others have supposed) almost wholly a cultural product:

I would like to suggest that in certain fundamental respects we do not really learn language; rather, grammar grows in the mind. . . . In both [the development of physical organs and the development of language], it seems, the final structure attained and its integration into a complex system of organs is largely predetermined by our genetic program, which provides a highly restrictive schematism that is fleshed out and articulated through interaction with the environment (embryological or post-natal).

. . . our systems of belief are those that the mind, as a biological structure, is designed to construct. We interpret experience as we do because of our special mental design.

The writings in which Chomsky urges this point of view show great rhetorical skill. Chomsky really knows how to use words to win people over to his opinion. And he has always been blessed with a lively sense of the significance of his own work. Asked in 1971 to name any alternative leading thinkers in this field, Chomsky waved his hand dismissively: 'There aren't any.'

Considered as examples of logical argumentation, however, I shall suggest that Chomsky's nativist writings have very little merit at all. Chomsky has given us no serious reason to deny that human language, and the cognitive achievements which depend on language, are almost wholly cultural creations, constrained only in trivial ways by the nature of our genetic endowment.

Phrases such as 'largely a product of biology', 'almost wholly a cultural product', 'only in trivial ways' may suggest that my disagreement with Chomsky is merely quantitative. The issue between nativism and empiricism certainly is a more/less rather than a yes/no issue: everyone agrees that human beings bring some innate faculties to the task of learning, and everyone agrees that the mature human's cognitive world depends in some respects on his experience. Perhaps, as it were, Chomsky might be urging that the glass is half full while I am insisting it is half empty. That is a wrong view of the situation. To explain this, let me be more precise about the kinds of biological constraint on language and thought which I regard as 'trivial'.

It is common ground that human physiology is largely determined by biological inheritance. (Indeed, one of the ways in which Chomsky explains his thesis about human cognition is by saying that, logically, we ought to make our account of the as-yet mysterious mechanisms by which the cognitive aspects of human life are determined as similar as possible to our relatively well-established account of how human physiology is determined.)

Now, part of our physiology comprises the vocal organs by which we produce speech, and the sense organs by which we perceive both speech and all the various things in the external world to which speech refers. So it is not at all surprising if certain aspects of language which are quite closely connected with these 'input/output systems' are themselves invariant across the biological species, and independent of cultural variation. For instance, it seems to be true that, universally, the kind of vowels which phoneticians call 'front spread' vowels, such as [i] (roughly the English ee sound), and 'back rounded' vowels such as [u] (English oo), are more common than 'front rounded' vowels, such as [y], the French *u* or German *ü* sound. The great majority of the world's languages, including English, have none of the last sort of vowel at all, and in the minority of languages (such as French and German) which have all three kinds, the first two kinds of vowel are more frequent than the third. This fact has a straightforward explanation in terms of acoustic distinctiveness: languages prefer to use front spread and back rounded vowels for essentially the same reason that a system of signal flags is more likely to use bright red and green flags than drab-coloured flags. Similarly, there would be nothing very surprising if it turned out that every single language in the world had words which translated as 'sweet' and 'sour': the apparatus which creates our sense of taste responds distinctively to these properties.

What *is* surprising is to be told by Chomsky that aspects of linguistic structure which, on the face of things, seem entirely independent of our physical organs of speech and sense are equally predetermined biologically and independent of cultural variation. Such *prima facie* physiologically-independent aspects of language would include the grammatical organization of sentences, and the majority of vocabulary that remains after words for simple sense qualities such as 'sweet', 'hot' are subtracted. The former of these – grammar – is the aspect of language with which Chomsky's arguments are centrally concerned; and, though he says only a limited amount himself about biological determination of vocabulary, he gives his blessing to the work of colleagues who have argued at length for species invariance here too.

Thus the dispute between myself and Chomsky is qualitative, not merely quantitative. I believe that biological constraints on language are limited to matters which are 'trivial' because they follow from properties of our speech and sense organs which are known to be genetically fixed, while Chomsky believes that such biological constraints extend to areas of language which superficially seem to be independent of our physiological make-up, and which express the very structure of our thinking. In what follows, I shall show that Chomsky's arguments for this view give us no good reason to abandon the relatively commonsensical, Popperian account of language acquisition which I outlined in Chapter 1. (I shall not, in this chapter, give positive arguments in favour of that account – this will come in Chapter 4.)

There is a very weak nativist point of view according to which human beings do inherit a general propensity to learn and use a language – some language – although biology provides no detailed specifications of the language to be learned. This is far less controversial than the views of Chomsky and the other linguistic nativists I have mentioned, and I shall not consider whether it is correct. Karl Popper sometimes argued that it is; for instance, he wrote:

> The capacity to learn a language – and even a strong need to learn a language – is, it appears, part of the genetic make-up of man. By contrast, the actual learning of a particular language, though influenced by unconscious inborn needs and motives, is not a gene-regulated process and therefore not a natural process, but a cultural process . . .

Chomsky's theory of innate knowledge of language claims that 'the actual learning of a particular language' *is* a gene-regulated, natural process, although the genetic regulation leaves some leeway permitting the specific language learned to vary within narrow constraints. This is what I am concerned to refute. I personally doubt whether language learning is innate even in the very weak sense expressed in Popper's first sentence; I see no more reason to ascribe an innate language propensity to infants than to postulate an innate driving propensity in order to explain why modern British teenagers are keen to learn to drive – there are such obvious social factors which explain the keenness without needing a nativist postulate. But Popper may be right; 'linguistic nativism' in this weak sense has very little to do with the point of view advocated by writers like Chomsky and Pinker, and strikes me as a minor issue on which one could reasonably remain agnostic.

Notice (this will become important) that Chomsky does not normally claim that his own view of language as a biological 'organ' is the only view which is logically coherent. He cannot claim this, since he argues that a wide range of observable facts about language constitute evidence for his view. Contingent facts cannot be evidence for or against a logical truism. So, by putting forward empirical observations in support of his own view of the language acquisition process, Chomsky implicitly concedes us the right to construct an alternative account of that process and to check whether our account is more or less well supported than Chomsky's by the observable facts.

## Chomsky's premises

What are the empirical premises on which Chomsky bases his argument for innate knowledge of language? The many points he mentions in his various writings can be classified as follows. For ease of reference, I shall number the headings, and bold numbers in the subsequent text will refer back to these numbered subsections.

## 1  Speed of acquisition

Children learn their first language remarkably fast. Language acquisition contrasts in this respect with the acquisition of other bodies of knowledge, for example, knowledge of physics. Chomsky writes:

> Knowledge of language is normally attained through brief exposure . . .

> Mere exposure to the language, for a remarkably short period, seems to be all that the normal child requires to develop the competence of the native speaker.

. . . given an input of observed Chinese sentences, [the brain] produces (by an *induction* of apparently fantastic complexity and suddenness) the *rules* of Chinese grammar . . .

Grammar . . . [is] acquired by virtually everyone, effortlessly, rapidly, in a uniform manner . . . Knowledge of physics, on the other hand, is acquired selectively and often painfully, through generations of labor and careful experiment, with the intervention of individual genius and generally through careful instruction . . .

## 2  Age-dependence

Language acquisition in childhood works quite differently from language acquisition in later life. Adult language learning is relatively slow and halting, and its end result is less successful. Chomsky quotes as a 'commonplace but perfectly correct' observation the statement by Géraud de Cordemoy in 1666 that 'children learn their native language more easily than an adult can learn a new language'. Elsewhere, Chomsky remarks:

. . . there seems to be a critical age for learning a language, as is true quite generally for the development of the human body.

There is reason to believe that the language acquisition system may be fully functional only during a 'critical period' of mental development or, more specifically, that its various maturational stages . . . have critical periods.

Chomsky refers here to the work of Eric Lenneberg, who had discussed this notion of critical periods for language acquisition in greater detail.

The relevant factor is age, not whether the language being learned is a first or a subsequent one:

. . . a young child of immigrant parents may learn a second language in the streets, from other children, with amazing rapidity

– while on the other hand 'wild children' whose first exposure to language is seriously delayed are unsuccessful language learners: Chomsky discusses the well-known case of 'Genie'.

In reading Chomsky and other linguistic nativists, incidentally, it is worth bearing in mind that they use the term 'language *acquisition*' as a technical term contrasting with *learning*. Because they believe that much of our first language is not 'learned' in the ordinary sense, they use 'acquisition' as a neutral way of referring to the process by which someone becomes a competent user of his mother tongue. From the empiricist point of view, everything is learned; consequently the present book does not systematically distinguish the terms *learning* and *acquisition* as nativist writings often do.

## 3  Poverty of data

The child must induce the general rules underlying the linguistic behaviour of his elders from individual examples of that behaviour – children are usually given little or no explicit instruction about the structure of their first language. Furthermore, the sample of his elders' language to which a child is typically exposed during the acquisition period is both small relative to the totality of potential examples, and qualitatively poor (because adults make slips of the tongue, speak indistinctly, etc.).

> . . . it is clear that the language each person acquires is a rich and complex construction hopelessly underdetermined by the fragmentary evidence available.

> The native speaker has acquired a grammar on the basis of very restricted and degenerate evidence; the grammar has empirical consequences that extend far beyond the evidence.

> . . . we cannot avoid being struck by the enormous disparity between . . . the generative grammar that expresses the linguistic competence of the native speaker and the meager and degenerate data on the basis of which he has constructed this grammar . . .

> . . . many children acquire first or second languages quite successfully even though no special care is taken to teach them and no special attention is given to their progress. It also seems apparent that much of the actual speech observed [that is, observed by children during language acquisition] consists of fragments and deviant expressions of a variety of sorts.

## 4  Convergence among grammars

Although differing in level of intelligence and exposed to different finite samples of their elders' language, the various children in a language community all acquire essentially the same language as one another and the same language that their elders speak.

> . . . the grammars that are in fact constructed vary only slightly among speakers of the same language, despite wide variations not only in intelligence but also in the conditions under which language is acquired.

> To a very good first approximation, individuals are indistinguishable (apart from gross deficits and abnormalities) in their ability to acquire grammar . . . Individuals of a given community each acquire a cognitive structure that is rich and comprehensive and essentially the same as the systems acquired by others.

> . . . every child . . . acquires knowledge of his language, and the knowledge acquired is, to a very good approximation, identical to that acquired by

others on the basis of their equally limited and somewhat different experience.

With other skills, say, driving a car, we find a few people who keep on taking test after test but who never get a licence; we do not find people who never crack the task of first-language acquisition.


## 5  Language universals

All languages that are or have been actually used by human beings resemble one another with respect to a number of structural features that are by no means necessary properties of any conceivable 'language' – a system would not have to have these features in order to be called a language, but in practice all human languages have them:

> we discover a substantial system of principles that do not vary even among languages that are, as far as we know, entirely unrelated.

The language universals with which Chomsky is centrally concerned have to do with abstract properties of grammatical structure, such as the *structure-dependence* of grammatical rules – for instance, the rule which English uses to convert statements into yes/no questions (questions which ask whether the statement is true or false, as opposed to questions expressing a 'who', 'which', 'why' type of enquiry).

By calling the English question rule 'structure-dependent', Chomsky means that it 'appl[ies] to a string of words by virtue of the organization of these words into phrases'. Take the statement:

> The subjects who will act as controls will be paid.

To convert this into a question, we have to move a particular word to the front of the sentence – namely the second instance of the word *will*:

> Will the subjects who will act as controls be paid?

In order to pick out the second *will* from the statement as the word to work on to get the question, we need to know not just that *will* is a verb, but that the second instance of that word is not part of any clause smaller than the whole sentence. The first *will* is part of the relative clause 'who will act as controls', so we do not move that word to form the question – we do not say:

> *Will the subjects who act as controls will be paid?

(Linguists use asterisks to mark nonsentences – word sequences that do not 'work' in the language under discussion.)

Thus, if they are to frame questions correctly, English speakers must in some unconscious sense use knowledge of *phrase structure* – the implicit organization of words into increasingly inclusive groupings such as phrases and clauses. Yet, in order to function as a language, all English seems to need for yes/no questions is *some* way of modifying the wording of statements that gives a distinctive modified wording for each distinctive statement (so that the hearer is able to work out what question is being asked). There is no obvious reason why the system of modification has to depend on the invisible, inaudible phrase structure of the statements. As Chomsky says, 'It is easy to imagine *structure-independent* operations that apply to a string of elements quite independently of its abstract structure as a system of phrases.' For instance, one could postulate a rule 'Exchange the first and last words of the statement' – a rule that requires no understanding of grammar at all, and gives the question:

*Paid subjects who will act as controls will be the?

Or one could postulate a rule 'Move the first verb of the statement to the front', which requires a tacit knowledge of word classification but no knowledge of phrase structure (and yields the starred sequence of the previous paragraph). Either of these structure-independent rules, or many others that one could invent, would do the job. But English never uses structure-independent rules – for yes/no questions, or in other areas of grammar; and nor, apparently, does any other human language.

> ... all known formal operations in the grammar of English, or of any other language, are structure-dependent. This is a very simple example of an invariant principle of language, what might be called a formal linguistic universal ... Given such facts, it is natural to postulate that the idea of 'structure-dependent operations' is part of the innate schematism applied by the mind to the data of experience.

> There is no a priori reason why human language should make use exclusively of structure-dependent operations, such as English interrogation, instead of structure-independent operations, such as [a range of simple hypothetical operations like the rule 'Exchange the first and last words', just suggested above]. . . . Yet no human language contains structure-independent operations.

Apart from grammatical universals, Chomsky also suggests more tentatively that there are universal constraints on the diversity of concepts which human languages can express in single words; such a constraint might be:

> that proper names, in any language, must designate objects meeting a condition of spatiotemporal contiguity, and that the same is true of other terms designating objects ...

(Chomsky's former colleague Jerry Fodor has argued that innate limitations on the system of potential concepts are something close to a logical necessity. Fodor thus differs in his approach to the thesis of cognitive nativism from Chomsky, who normally treats the thesis as one founded on observable evidence. I have spelled out the fallacies in Jerry Fodor's argument elsewhere; his version of linguistic nativism is too unrepresentative of the movement as a whole to be worth examining again here.)

The precise identity of the language universals is a controversial matter; indeed the academic discipline of theoretical linguistics as a whole may be described as consisting in large part of a continuing attempt to refine the theory of linguistic universals. But Chomsky believes that the universals constrain the diversity of human languages very tightly indeed: in his later writings he suggests that there are probably only *finitely many* different biologically possible grammars.

Although the sample of his elders' language available to a typical child during language acquisition will be logically compatible with hypotheses according to which the language violates the universal constraints in various ways, children are never observed to make the kind of mistakes which would imply that they entertain such hypotheses; for instance:

> Children make many errors in language learning, but they do not assume, until corrected, that 'the candidates wanted me to vote for each other' [which violates the universal 'opacity conditions'] is a well-formed sentence meaning that each candidate wanted me to vote for the other [despite the fact that] relevant experience is never presented for most speakers of English . . .

> It surpasses belief that language-learners are regularly provided with specific instruction or evidence to bring them to recognize that [certain sentences violating the opacity conditions] are ungrammatical . . .

> It is certainly true that children never make mistakes about this sort of thing: no child ever tries [the structure-independent question rule 'Move the first verb to the front'] . . . then is told that is not the way it works and subsequently goes to the other hypothesis [ – despite the fact that] cases that distinguish the hypotheses rarely arise; you can easily live your whole life without ever producing a relevant example to show that you are using one hypothesis rather than the other one.

The universals correspond to built-in knowledge about language; these aspects do not need to be learned, so children never get them wrong.

## 6  *Non-linguistic analogies*

Occasionally Chomsky refers to other human cognitive achievements as resembling language in being uniform across the species and grossly underdetermined by experience:

> Think for example of the capacity to deal with the number system, common to humans apart from pathology and as far as we know, unique to humans. . . . One should not be misled by the fact that some birds, for example, can be taught to pick $n$ elements from an array for small $n$ – about up to seven. The very essence of the number system is the concept of adding one, indefinitely. The concept of infinity is not just 'more' than seven . . .

More frequently, Chomsky appeals to discoveries by other scholars about non-linguistic aspects of human cognition as providing precedents which render his nativist account of language more plausible; for example:

> Work of the past years has shown that much of the detailed structure of the visual system is 'wired in', though triggering experience is required to set the system in operation.

However, this particular allusion (and others like it) relates to genetic determination of human 'input/output systems', which as we have seen is relatively uncontroversial. Chomsky's own examples of alleged innate structuring of linguistic and other cognitive domains are far more radical than the suggestions he attributes to others, and Chomsky has been widely recognized by psychologists as the key figure in the modern resurgence of nativist psychology. The leading British psychologist Donald Broadbent, in his book *In Defence of Empirical Psychology*, identified a range of ways in which empirical psychology was under threat, but found Chomsky's linguistic approach 'much more interesting and relevant to human psychologists than the other divisions' of the anti-empiricist movement. I shall therefore assume that Chomsky's arguments stand or fall independently of other scholars' discussions of domains other than language.

## 7  Species-specificity

For completeness it should perhaps be added that Chomsky often makes the point that members of species other than Man do not master human-like languages even when given access to experience comparable to that available to human children. Since the 1950s there have been a number of experiments in teaching language or language-like systems to chimpanzees and other apes – the best-known experiment, by Allen and Beatrice Gardner, involved trying to teach the chimpanzee Washoe the sign language used by the deaf and dumb in America. This and later experiments achieved some success, but just how much success is a hotly debated issue. Chomsky is one of those who minimize what was achieved ('even the most elementary properties of human language . . . are beyond the capacities of apes'). However, it seems that Chomsky does not in fact regard species-specificity as evidence for innate cognitive structuring:

> Note that if it were discovered that some other organism had something like 'the number faculty,' [cf. 6 above] this would in any event not bear on the question of whether it is intrinsic to the human mind.

Whether or not Chomsky is right to describe the ape language-teaching experiments as unsuccessful, then, he does not see their results as relevant to his case. In assessing that case, we can leave these experiments aside.

For the moment, I shall also leave aside the argument from linguistic universals (subsection 5 above). This is in a rather different category from the other numbered subsections, and it deserves separate and extended treatment –

I shall provide that in Chapter 4. In this chapter, we shall look in turn at the evidence under the headings other than 5 and 7.

## Response to the argument from speed of acquisition (1)

The argument from speed of acquisition divides into two variants: (i) most commonly, Chomsky argues that language acquisition is *absolutely* fast, that is, it takes a shorter time than one would expect, given the complexity of the system to be acquired; (ii) less frequently, he argues that it is *relatively* fast, in comparison with acquisition of, for instance, knowledge of physics.

Clearly it is true that a theory which claims that much knowledge of language is innately available tends to suggest that language acquisition will be completed sooner than if the alternative theory, that everything has to be learned from scratch, were true. Nevertheless, the observed rate of language acquisition does nothing to support either theory against the other, unless the theories are made precise enough to yield concrete figures for predicted rate of acquisition; and Chomsky has never attempted to do this.

Children take years from birth, rather than months or weeks, to master the main grammatical structures of their mother tongue. (To give a precise figure, even for an individual child, would be arbitrary, because it depends on what degree of attainment is chosen as the threshold; but it is safe to say that no one would recognize an average child as displaying adult-like grammatical competence before the age of about 2 years.) Why is it appropriate to regard a learning period of two years or so as 'remarkably fast' rather than 'remarkably slow'? How long would human beings have to take to acquire language before Chomsky would no longer see the speed-of-acquisition argument as applicable? Ten years? Fifty years? Unless some particular figure for predicted acquisition-time without innate knowledge can be specified, variant (i) of the speed-of-acquisition argument is wholly vacuous. Chomsky not only has not specified such a figure, but could not consistently do so, because (as we shall see later) he argues that the data available to a language learner are so poor that accurate language learning would be impossible without innate knowledge – that is, *no* amount of time would suffice.

The truth is that the only reason we have for expecting language acquisition to take any particular length of time is our knowledge of how long it actually has taken in observed cases. So it is senseless to claim that acquisition is *in general* 'remarkably fast' (though one might describe some individual child as unusually fast by comparison with other children).

Adults tend to be favourably disposed towards small children. We find it natural to marvel at their perfectly formed little bodies and their delightful behaviour patterns – there is a mother in all of us. This emotional trait has perhaps caused many of Chomsky's readers to assent uncritically to the premiss of the speed-of-acquisition argument. It feels good to say 'Yes, isn't it marvellous how quickly they learn!'; one feels boorish if one denies that there is anything remarkable about children's rate of progress in this area. We should not underestimate the significance of emotional considerations of this sort when seeking an explanation of why a theory has succeeded in winning converts. But clearly they cannot be given any intellectual weight.

What of variant (ii), which compares learning-rates in the domains of language and of physics?

In the first place, Chomsky appears to be drawing a false analogy. The kind of language learning which each individual completes in a few years is acquisition of the 'tacit knowledge' that enables him to make his behaviour conform to the patterns appropriate to his linguistic environment. Conscious, explicit knowledge of the structure of a language is *not* acquired universally or rapidly. Descriptive grammars of English and other languages have been worked over by generations of linguists who often make the point that no natural language has yet been exhaustively described; studies of this sort are confined to a small circle of professional experts, and laymen commonly see them as impenetrably difficult. But the analogy, with respect to physics, of universal language acquisition is, surely, mastery of the 'tacit knowledge' which enables a person to conform his behaviour to the patterns appropriate to the physical world he inhabits: to pour a liquid without spilling it, to use a skipping rope, to succeed in throwing a ball roughly where he wants it to go, etc. I cannot see that these abilities are acquired strikingly less fast than the ability to speak.

Chomsky might reject this objection: at several places in his writings he argues that there is a much closer relationship between the tacit knowledge of language which every adult exploits in speaking and the expert linguist's conscious knowledge about the language than there is between the mental structures underlying our ability to perform ordinary physical activities and the physicist's conscious knowledge of the principles that make those activities possible. '[I]t seems easy enough to make the relevant distinction. . . . we take bicycle riding to be a skill, whereas [tacit] knowledge of language . . . is not a skill at all.'

I do not believe in Chomsky's distinction. It underestimates the logical problem of learning to perform physical activities, in very much the same way that (he complains) others have underestimated the logical problem of language acquisition. In order to pour a liquid successfully (to take a case much simpler than bicycle riding) it is necessary to have moved from observation of a number of particular instances of liquids in motion to some tacit grasp of general principles governing the movement of liquids within the gravitational field of the Earth, which must then be applied in dealing with fresh instances of pouring that will differ in detail (different shaped vessels, different distances apart, different quantities) from any of the previously observed instances. To dismiss this as merely a 'skill' is naïve. As I understand the word, both pouring water and speaking English are 'skills' among other things; but they both depend on internal mental attainments which cannot appropriately be described as skills.

However, even if Chomsky's distinction were accepted, it would remain true that nothing follows from the fact that physical knowledge has taken generations of scholarly activity to develop, while every child masters his mother tongue within a few years. In order to use this contrast to infer innate knowledge in the latter case, one would need to show that the degree of complexity of the two bodies of knowledge, and the accessibility of the respective bodies of relevant data, are equal or close to equal.

Chomsky has not done this; and he surely could not do so. The degree of complexity of domains as different as these is incommensurable – there are no units in terms of which they could be compared. Chomsky himself makes the point that 'There is no absolute sense of the notion "simplicity" in terms of which grammar is "simpler" than . . . atomic physics'; but he fails to spot the corollary, that there is equally no sense in which grammar can be called 'as complex as' atomic physics. Intuitively, to those who know about them, modern physics and the English language both seem very complicated; but to describe them as equally complex, or to claim that either one of them is 1.3 times – or 400 times – as complex as the other, would be as meaningless as a statement that the novel *War and Peace* is twice as long as the River Nile.

As for accessibility of the data, it is obvious that modern physics rests on an immense body of observations to which a young child has no access. Every university physics department uses many kinds of apparatus that are unfamiliar even to adult laymen. It is true that some theoretical physicists advance knowledge without themselves performing experiments, but they rely on the experimental findings of others. This guarantees that a child could not work out modern physics for himself. It is not similarly obvious and indisputable that the young child lacks access to data crucial for language learning. (There is an argument that children are indeed deprived in this sense; we shall look at that in our response to argument 3, below.)

A last point about Chomsky's comparison between rates of development of linguistic competence and physical knowledge is this. When Chomsky first drew that comparison, he was contrasting language, as a phenomenon for which we allegedly inherit specific cognitive organization, with physics, as a subject of which we have no special innate knowledge, and which accordingly is learned slowly and haltingly if it is learned at all. Later, though, Chomsky changed his tune about physics. He began to suggest that *anything* which can be learned by humans is learnable only because it happens to fall within the biologically determined range of humanly accessible subjects – remember the quotation on p. 9 above: 'an intelligible explanatory theory . . . can be developed by humans in case something close to the true theory in a certain domain happens to fall within human "science-forming" capacities.'

But this means that any differential in speed of learning, as between language and physics (or between language and anything else learnable), can no longer be an argument that knowledge of language is innate, because in Chomsky's later view that would not distinguish language from other intellectual domains.

Oddly, Chomsky continued to write in terms of there being a 'fundamental distinction' between grammar and knowledge of physics. The only passage I

have found in which he tries to resolve this blatant paradox in his thinking
runs as follows:

> Though [knowledge of physics], too, is derived on the basis of specific
> properties of mind, it does not reflect these properties in the same way as
> language. . . . Hence the vast qualitative difference in relative accessibility.

In the absence of some clarification of this notion of mental properties being
'reflected in different ways', with an explanation for why various 'ways of
reflection' should lead to different degrees of learnability, this passage can only
be described as pure hand-waving.

I conclude that variant (ii), as well as variant (i), of the argument from speed
of acquisition is empty.


### Response to the argument from age-dependence (2)

Chomsky claims that the human ability to acquire a (first or subsequent)
language diminishes sharply 'at a relatively fixed age, apparently by puberty
or somewhat earlier', which suggests biological determination.

With respect to *second* languages this claim is not obviously true, and
evidence for it is not given either by Chomsky himself or by Eric Lenneberg,
on whose research Chomsky depended in advancing this line of argument.
(Heidi Dulay and others have subsequently done empirical research on factors
affecting second-language learning success.) What appears to be true is that
people learn second languages (and, perhaps, many other things) relatively
easily and rapidly if they see the task as worthwhile. A young child of
immigrants will learn a second language rapidly 'in the streets' because he
aspires to full membership of the society whose language it is, although a child
of the same age may absorb very little from regular Latin lessons at school
because he sees them as pointless. An adult immigrant, who has already been
socialized into a different society, will often be much less than whole-hearted
in his identification with his adopted country; but there certainly are plenty
of cases on record of adults mastering a second language to native-speaker
standard apart from accent.

Lenneberg conceded this, and explained it by arguing that second-language
learning involves acquiring only those features of a language which are *not*
postulated by Chomsky to be innately known. The adult second-language
learner succeeds because he is able to exploit the mastery of the structures
common to all languages which he developed during the crucial pre-puberty
period in learning his first language. So second-language learning is neither
here nor there so far as the nativist issue is concerned.

What Lenneberg did convincingly demonstrate is that *first*-language
acquisition regularly occurs in a biologically determined period ending in the
early teens. Medical conditions which retard physical growth and maturation
equally retard language acquisition. Brain injuries which disturb language
ability, and thus force the first language to be wholly or partly relearned, are

overcome successfully only if they occur before puberty. 'Wild children' who are first exposed to a language after puberty, for instance because they have grossly inadequate parents who isolate them during childhood from normal social interactions, are unsuccessful at acquiring language when they do encounter it.

Do these findings support Chomsky's belief that the structure of language is genetically predetermined? No, because they fail to distinguish language learning from any other case of learning. Lenneberg's evidence seems to be perfectly compatible with the view that *learning as a general process* is for biological reasons far more rapid before puberty than later.

The idea that we are mentally more agile in childhood than adulthood is surely fairly commonplace. Philosophers such as Popper and Nelson Goodman, who describe the learning process in terms incompatible with Chomsky's idea that the structure of knowledge is foreordained, have not themselves suggested that our minds might 'strike out with spontaneous predictions' much faster in youth than in maturity; but I cannot see any reason why they should resist this idea. What is controversial in Chomsky's work, as I have put it elsewhere, is the claim that biology controls not merely quantitative aspects of learning but also qualitative: not just the rate at which hypotheses are produced, but also their content.

If 'wild children' are not merely very slow at language acquisition but actually fail to acquire normal mastery even after far longer exposure than normal children need, then that could surely be explained as a symptom of a general learning disability stemming from the great emotional damage caused by deprivation of normal social stimulation.

The best-known case is 'Genie', a girl born in 1957 whose father was insane: from the age of 20 months to 13 years 7 months she was kept in isolation from human company and from virtually all other mental stimulation, harnessed to an infant's potty seat by day, put to bed in a straitjacket-like sleeping bag at night if she was remembered at all, and beaten if she made any sound. Susan Curtiss has documented Genie's development during the first fifty-five months after society discovered her as an 'unsocialized, primitive, barely human' creature and began to try to help her towards normality. Within that period, Genie had not learned to speak English in anything like a normal sense; nor had she acquired the most basic non-linguistic skills. Even so, Genie did acquire non-trivial language abilities, and Susan Curtiss herself regarded Genie as refuting the strong version of Lenneberg's claim, that 'natural language acquisition cannot occur after puberty'.

The writings of the linguistic nativists have drawn heavily on the Genie case. Chomsky comments on it only briefly and what he says is reasonable, but, for instance, Derek Bickerton has recently argued that Genie's limited language ability cannot be blamed on emotional factors, because 'she suffered no lasting emotional damage'. I find no justification for that statement in Susan Curtiss's book, and in the circumstances it seems completely unbelievable.

Lenneberg was aware of the gap in his argument for his and Chomsky's shared view of language acquisition – namely, that what he presented as findings about language learning might alternatively be findings about learning in general; but he did little to fill it. I have found just one relevant remark, in his book of more than 400 pages:

> Do the time limitations postulated for language acquisition function across the board for all types of human learning? Probably not: there are many skills and tasks that are much better learned during the late teens than in early childhood and a great deal of general learning has no age limitation whatever.

Not one of these 'many skills and tasks' was identified. Of course, it is trivially true that a young child cannot acquire skill at, say, archery, before he has developed the physical strength to bend the bow. But, if Lenneberg meant that there are intellectual learning tasks which are tied to the post-puberty period for non-trivial reasons, he was simply making an unsupported assertion of personal opinion. Other eminent psychologists have asserted precisely the opposite. According to Jerome Bruner, 'any subject can be taught effectively in some intellectually honest form to any child at any stage of development'.

So much for the argument from age-dependence.

### Response to the argument from poverty of data (3)

The fact that a child has to derive general rules from particular examples in order to learn his mother tongue does nothing, in itself, to support the Chomskyan as against the Popperian view of language acquisition: for Popper, all learning has this logical form. Rather, the problem for a Popperian, guessing-and-testing account is allegedly posed by the fact that the examples of language available to the child are quantitatively meagre and qualitatively degenerate.

There are two objections to this argument of Chomsky's. In the first place, his claims about the linguistic data available to the child seem to be factually untrue. Second (and more importantly), it hardly matters whether or not Chomsky is right about the child's data, because his argument from poverty of data to innate knowledge of language is in any case logically self-refuting.

On the factual question about the nature of children's data, let me begin by considering the 'degenerateness' issue. Chomsky originally made statements about the child's data being qualitatively poor years before anyone had done serious research on the nature of the speech addressed to children ('Motherese', as it is often called). It subsequently emerged that the quality of such speech is far better than Chomsky supposed. Some writers have even suggested that adults provide children with something like an ideal graded series of language lessons.

These claims are controversial: Chomsky's associates Norbert Hornstein and David Lightfoot quote Elissa Newport, Henry Gleitman and Lila Gleitman as researchers who found evidence against extreme versions of the theory that mothers act as ideal language teachers. However, the point Hornstein and Lightfoot want to make is that a child lacking innate linguistic knowledge would find it difficult to work out the grammar of his elders' language if his data included 'defective sentences': 'If only 5 per cent of the sentences that the child hears are of this type, the problem will be significant because the sentences do not come labelled as ungrammatical.' But what Newport *et al.* give evidence against is the idea that mothers provide children with a graded series of language lessons of increasing complexity. Newport *et al.* do *not* support Chomsky's idea that the child's data are grammatically defective.

Quite the reverse: 'the speech of mothers to children is unswervingly well formed. Only one utterance out of 1500 spoken to the children was a disfluency.' (Newport *et al.* find that speech *between adults* contains 5 per cent of ungrammatical utterances, and Hornstein and Lightfoot suggest that since the child will overhear such speech these utterances will suffice to create the problem. But it will not, provided the child can tell the difference between speech addressed to him and speech addressed to other adults – which he surely can. An adult scientist faced with two sources of data, the more accessible of which proved much more amenable to analysis than the other, would surely concentrate his analytic efforts on the former: why should one not expect a child to act in the same way? Indeed, Steven Pinker quotes evidence that 'When given a choice, babies prefer to listen to Motherese than to speech intended for adults.') One ungrammatical utterance out of 1500 is surely a slender foundation to bear the weight of a conclusion as far-reaching as Chomsky's theory of innate knowledge.

I have encountered one recent source which continues to uphold the claim that Motherese is poor-quality language. Writing from deep within the nativist camp, Virginia Valian comments sternly that 'Any acquisition theory will have to come to terms with the fact that the child hears nongrammatical strings as well as grammatical sentences.'

But she supports this only by referring to an unpublished study of her own of conversations between twenty-one child/parent pairs, and the specific examples she quotes suggest a confusion about what is being claimed. 'Parents say to children things like "Want your lunch now?", and "Raining hard."' Valian counts such utterances as ungrammatical (though 'acceptable'), because they lack a subject. But this is using 'grammatical' to mean 'conforming to the artificial standards required for formal language in high-prestige contexts', and nobody would ever suppose that Motherese is unswervingly grammatical in *that* sense. For a small child learning to speak English, one of the things to be learned is that it is allowable and normal to begin an informal spoken sentence with its main verb; in the language he is learning, 'Want your lunch now?' *is grammatical*. The child is learning to speak English, not (at this stage) learning to write for *The Times*. Valian gives no real evidence that Motherese is 'ungrammatical' in other than this irrelevant sense.

If the premiss about degenerateness is shaky, the premiss about quantitative 'meagreness' is still less solid. Provided one agrees that a human language is a system comprising infinitely many potential well-formed utterances (a point which is common ground between the nativists and me), then it is trivially true that any finite sample of utterances is small relative to the totality of possibilities. But the set of utterances encountered by a child in the language-learning years can hardly be called 'small' in any absolute sense.

Indeed, it seems that Chomsky's point cannot be a numerical one. He cannot be saying that the number of utterances typically encountered during language acquisition is less than the number, $n$, which would be needed on the assumption of no innate knowledge, because he gives us no reason to believe that the latter assumption would yield any particular prediction about the numerical size of the sample required. Rather, we must interpret Chomsky as saying that a child's sample will typically lack *any* evidence bearing on some particular properties of the language being learned, and that the system ultimately acquired by the child nevertheless incorporates these properties.

This interpretation is supported by Norbert Hornstein and David Lightfoot, who describe the alleged fact that 'People attain knowledge of the structure of their language for which *no* evidence is available in the data to which they are exposed as children' as the 'central' problem to be explained by any theory of language acquisition. We have seen (in the last three quotations under 5 above) that Chomsky commits himself to specific examples of facts about English grammar for which (he believes) most English speakers are never exposed to relevant evidence.

But Chomsky's writings never suggest that he has empirical evidence to support his claims about non-occurrence of given constructions in a typical child's data. The quotations under 5 are characteristic in this respect: sometimes Chomsky simply asserts that given constructions do not occur in the experience of most children, while on other occasions he says that it 'surpasses belief' that they might occur.

Surely it is not very interesting what Chomsky finds easy or difficult to believe, in an area where the facts are readily available to observation. (One wonders how Chomsky would react to an intellectual opponent who argued in a similar style.) When Chomsky's claims are subjected to empirical testing, they fail.

The obvious example to consider is the one alluded to in 5, which deals with alternative hypotheses about the grammar of yes/no questions in English. Turning an English statement into the corresponding yes/no question involves operating on a finite verb in the statement: to spell the rule out more fully than I did before, either the verb itself is moved to the left (if the verb is a form of *be, do, have*, or a modal verb such as *will*) – thus 'The man is tall' becomes 'Is the man tall?'; or (in all other cases) the verb is put into the infinitive and an inflected form of *do* is placed to the left – thus 'The man swims well' becomes 'Does the man swim well?' Assuming that this much has been grasped by someone learning the rule, the problem then arises of knowing which verb must be used, in a case where the statement is a complex sentence containing more than one finite verb – say, 'The man who is tall is sad'.

Chomsky proposes two alternative hypotheses that a child learning English might conceivably try: (1) operate on the first finite verb; (2) operate on the finite verb of the main clause. (For ease of exposition, Chomsky assumes that the verb in question is always the verb *is* – but there is no reason to expect that a child would in practice formulate hypotheses of this sort about individual verbs separately: we should rather expect that a child, like a Popperian scientist, will adopt maximally general hypotheses, unless and until he is forced by counter-evidence to shift to less general hypotheses.) Hypothesis (1) is false (and it violates the 'structure-dependence' universal): applied to the complex statement of the last paragraph, it would give the ill-formed question *'Is the man who tall is sad?' Hypothesis (2) is correct, and gives the well-formed question 'Is the man who is tall sad?' But yes/no questions formed from simple statements, or from complex statements in which all subordinate clauses occur later than the main verb, fail to distinguish between the two hypotheses. The only sentences which reveal the falsity of (1) are yes/no questions formed from statements containing a subordinate clause which precedes the main verb.

According to Chomsky, 'the child could not generally determine by passive observation whether one or the other hypothesis is true'; because cases of this last kind 'rarely arise; you can easily live your whole life without ever producing a relevant example . . . you can go over a vast amount of data of experience without ever finding such a case'; the belief that each child encounters relevant evidence 'strains credulity'.

I described this example about the yes/no question rule as the obvious one to discuss in the context of Chomsky's poverty-of-data argument, because for many years it has been the standard example in Chomsky's own exposition of the argument. There is probably no other linguistic example having this degree of concrete specificity that is quoted so often in the body of Chomsky's writings. I have cited it from the proceedings of a 1975 symposium; but Geoffrey Pullum, in a recent review of Chomsky's poverty-of-data argument, shows the same example recurring down the years in one after another of Chomsky's leading works, from *Aspects of the Theory of Syntax* (1965) through *Language and Mind* (1968), *Problems of Knowledge and Freedom* (1972), *Reflections on Language* (1975), to *Language and Problems of Knowledge* (1988). Pullum mentions that Chomsky's claims about this example have been repeated by many other writers, including Gary Marcus in 1993, and Steven Pinker in *The Language Instinct* (1994).

Yet the claims Chomsky makes about this example are so extravagant that it is very easy to show that he is quite wrong.

Thus, it would be difficult for any English schoolchild to avoid an encounter sooner or later with Blake's *Tiger*, which contains the line 'Did he who made the Lamb make thee?' This sentence distinguishes between Chomsky's hypotheses; if hypothesis (1) were correct, the question would run *'Did he who make the Lamb made thee?' Of course, I am not suggesting that experience of this particular line of poetry is actually decisive for rejection of hypothesis (1) and adoption of hypothesis (2) in the biography of the typical English child; but the speed with which I was able to dredge up this example from my far from voluminous mental store of quotations suggests that relevant utterances are unlikely to be as rare as Chomsky suggests.

As a cross-check, I looked at a book which featured in the childhood of very many Britons (mine included) in the first half of the twentieth century,

Arthur Mee's *Children's Encyclopedia*, and ran my eye down the list of 'Wonder Questions' in its index. It would be difficult for Chomsky to dismiss this work as representing a level of intellectual sophistication too high to be relevant to the experience of the average English speaker. It describes itself on p. 1 as 'a Big Book for Little People, and it has come into the world to make your life happy and wise and good'; it was aimed, I would say, at the 6- to 10-year-old market of more innocent, pre-television days. The eleventh yes/no question (and the third yes/no question containing more than one finite verb) in the index is 'If a man flew above the air would he be able to hear?' Again this distinguishes between Chomsky's two hypotheses; if hypothesis (1) were correct, the question would run *'Did if a man fly above the air he would be able to hear?' Chomsky's claims about the rarity of evidence enabling a child to choose between hypotheses (1) and (2) for English seem to be grossly exaggerated.

Geoffrey Pullum felt that these examples of mine could be seen as anecdotal, so he conducted a systematic computer search for relevant examples in a corpus of English text. Pullum used the corpus available to him, which contained 40 million words of the *Wall Street Journal* over a period from 1987 to 1989: and he found that about 12 per cent of the many yes/no questions in this corpus were 'crucial examples' which refuted hypothesis (1). For instance, the question 'Is what I'm doing in the shareholders' best interest?' would, if hypothesis (1) were correct, run: *'Am what I doing is in the shareholders' best interest?'

My examples are anecdotal, and Pullum's are systematic but drawn from a source that is admittedly not representative of the language addressed to small children – neither he nor I currently has a suitable computer-readable corpus representing precisely the genre of English which children are hearing at the stage when they acquire the correct yes/no question rule. But, according to Chomsky, 'A person might go through *much or all of his life* [my emphasis] without ever having been exposed to relevant evidence'. Chomsky is not saying that there is something special about Motherese that makes it particularly devoid of relevant evidence. He is claiming that English usage in general is devoid of such evidence; and plainly he is wildly mistaken.

When we have a computer-readable corpus of English addressed to toddlers, who really believes that it will not contain any questions like:

Would anyone who is interested see me later?

Will those who are coming raise their hands?

Could a tyrannosaurus that was sick beat a triceratops in a fight?

– Pullum's examples, and all relevant for the choice between hypotheses (1) and (2).

'Hang on a minute,' I hear the reader say. 'You seem to be telling us that this man who is by common consent the world's leading living intellectual, according to Cambridge University a second Plato, is basing his radical reassessment of human nature largely on the claim that a certain thing never happens; he tells us that it strains his credulity to think that it might happen, but he has never looked, and people who have looked find that it happens a lot.'

Yes, that's about the size of it. Funny old world, isn't it!

Incidentally, we shall see in Chapter 4 that the Popperian account of language acquisition predicts that no child would try a structure-independent hypothesis about English question formation, *even if the child lacked evidence of its incorrectness*. My point here, though, is that children will *not* lack such evidence. And although I have discussed just the particular case of structure-dependent v. structure-independent rules for English questions, the point is a general one. Since Chomsky has never backed up his arguments from poverty of the child's data with detailed empirical studies, we are entitled to reject them on the ground that the data available to a child are far richer than Chomsky supposes.

But the detailed facts about the child's data scarcely matter, since the argument is in any case logically untenable. The obvious reply to anyone who asserts that a language has certain properties, no evidence of which is present in the data available to an individual learning the language, is 'How do you know?'

The adult's conscious knowledge of the properties of a language is based ultimately on observation of examples of the language – that is, on just the kind of experience which Chomsky alleges to be insufficient to determine the properties of the language. So, if data bearing on some particular point of grammar were too rare to be standardly encountered during language acquisition, there would appear to be no way that an adult could consciously ascertain that grammatical fact (unless by a great stroke of luck). The fact that Chomsky and his English-speaking readers all agree that questions formed according to hypothesis (1) are ungrammatical, in cases where they differ from the corresponding questions formed according to hypothesis (2), proves that evidence refuting hypothesis (1) *is* encountered in the life of any English speaker. Clearly, this point is independent of the specific nature of the deficiencies which Chomsky or other linguists believe to characterize the language learner's data.

Oddly, this self-defeating aspect of the argument from poverty of data has not been discussed by Chomsky, so far as I have read. The argument has been defended against this objection, however, by Steven Stich and by Hornstein and Lightfoot. They claim that an adult linguist's conscious knowledge of the properties of (his own or another) language rests on a wider range of data than those which are available to a child while he is acquiring the same language as his mother tongue.

This would be a good defence, if it were true. But what are these categories of data available to the linguistic researcher though not to the child?

Stich points out that:

Linguists . . . solicit from native speakers intuitions about grammaticality, about various syntactic properties and relations and about various semantic properties and relations. . . . But there is no reason to believe that the child has access to any significant cache of data about the intuitive judgements [of] his elders . . .

Hornstein and Lightfoot say that:

Crucial evidence . . . [includes] judgements concerning complex and rare sentences, paraphrase and ambiguity relations, and ungrammatical 'sentences', all of which are available to the linguist but lie outside the data . . . available to the child . . .

In other words: a child learning his first language is given only examples of the language; an adult linguist can also elicit speakers' beliefs about the language.

But – unless Stich, and Hornstein and Lightfoot, are happy to assume what they are claiming to prove, in other words to reason circularly – then, for the purpose of defending the poverty-of-data argument against the charge of self-refutation, they must concede that speakers' beliefs about their language derive purely from experience of examples of the language: in which case, interrogating a speaker does not give the linguist access to any category of data not available to the child. (It might seem that the adult linguist has a great advantage in that he can choose to interrogate a speaker about crucial constructions however rare they happen to be, while the child merely observes whatever language samples happen to come his way. But the linguist *cannot choose for his informant to have been exposed to relevant examples when acquiring the language*; so the fact that the linguist can select his questions does nothing to exempt him from problems allegedly posed for the child by the extreme rarity of crucial data.)

True, if Chomsky's view of language acquisition were correct, then an adult linguist who interrogated a speaker about his linguistic 'intuitions' would be gaining access to data that rested not just on the speaker's experience but also on the innate knowledge that the speaker had brought to the language-acquisition task – so the linguist really would have evidence which went beyond the experience available to the child language learner. But an argument for innate knowledge of language which works only if one grants the assumption of innate knowledge of language is less than impressive.

It seems possible that Stich, and Hornstein and Lightfoot, all stress the importance of speakers' intuitions as data for the adult linguist because they cannot see how a scientist could possibly succeed in formulating a satisfactory description of a language if he were limited to the type of data experienced by a child. Stich has described an earlier discussion by me of this issue as 'unpersuasive', though he does not say what is unpersuasive about it. Hornstein and Lightfoot list speakers' judgements about 'ungrammatical "sentences"' as one of the crucial categories of data for the linguist, which suggests that they might counter my viewpoint by asking, 'How could a linguist ever say that some sequence of words was ungrammatical if all he ever encountered were the utterances that do occur in the language?'

But although this latter question sounds as if the answer must be 'he couldn't', that is quite wrong. To see that, consider the analogy between this question and the question 'How could a physicist ever say that some hypothetical event would violate the laws of physics, if all he ever encounters are events which obey those laws?' That is indeed all a physicist ever encounters, and it is evidently all he needs in order to predict that many unobserved events are physically impossible. Popperian philosophy of science provides a straightforward answer to the question about physics (one seeks the strongest theory compatible with one's data); and the same answer will work equally well for the question about linguistics. I am perfectly willing to grant that children are innately predisposed to apply Popperian methodological maxims in their tacit learning behaviour; what I am concerned to deny is that the products of that behaviour are predetermined, to any greater extent than is implied by the nature of those maxims.

Stich also suggests that the adult linguist, but not the child, can draw on the products of instrumental techniques, for instance, 'the differences between sounds actually on a tape and what a subject reports hearing'. In principle, that would be possible. But in practice, linguists have made virtually no use of such data in describing the languages of individuals or of speech communities; when linguists have exploited data of this type, it has been in order to investigate how speakers process linguistic forms whose structural analysis is taken for granted by the researchers. The availability in principle of instrumental techniques is of little relevance to someone who argues, as Stich does, that we already know that children are better language learners than they could be if they lacked innate knowledge. It is logically possible that instrumental techniques could in future prove useful in discovering people's grammars, and that research using such techniques might show that children are even better at language learning than we now realize; but we have no reason to think that even the former of these possibilities is likely, let alone the latter.

Nothing remains, therefore, of the argument from poverty of data.

## Response to the argument from convergence (4)

Once the argument from poverty of data has been rebutted, the argument from convergence among different individuals' grammars can be disposed of quite quickly.

This argument is composed of two strands: (1) different individuals' level of mastery of the grammar of their native tongue (unlike their level of mastery of some other cognitive domains) does not correlate noticeably with their level of general intelligence (or education); (2) although the finite sample of his elders' language to which any one child is exposed is logically compatible with different hypotheses about the overall structure of the language, and different children are exposed to different finite samples, the members of a speech community nevertheless end up by acquiring near-identical grammars.

Point (1) was for some years treated as axiomatic by Chomsky, but he eventually retracted it. At the 1975 Royaumont Symposium, Chomsky admitted that it is both a priori plausible and empirically confirmed that individuals who are more intelligent and/or educated than others have a greater degree of mastery of their common mother tongue. That sounds like plain common sense, and it seems to leave nothing remaining of the first strand of the argument from convergence.

Individuals of very low intelligence do acquire quite a lot of language skill. The motive for learning to participate in a society's chief communicative activity is so strong that we would surely expect the least intelligent individuals to make this a high priority for whatever learning abilities they possess.

Strand (2) of the convergence argument can be answered by making a point analogous to my chief objection to the argument from poverty of data. How could anyone possibly find out that various individuals had formulated grammars which were more similar to one another than would be predicted from the fact that their data-sets were independent samples drawn from the speech of the same speech community?

Consider what one would need to do in order to establish that. One would have to construct descriptions of the speech of (at least) two members of the community, and one would have to show that the two grammars agree on various points for which there is good reason to believe that the speakers would not both have been exposed to relevant evidence. But, if the data available to a child fail to determine the exact nature of his elders' language, then it seems likely that the data about any two speakers which might be available to a linguist will fail to determine whether the rules of their idiolects are indeed identical with respect to any particular aspect of grammar.

The linguist is in one way better placed than the child, since he can ask the speakers to quote intuitions which they have distilled from observation of many utterances, rather than having merely to listen to individual examples uttered by the speakers. But in other ways the linguist is worse placed than the child. He has to construct two or more grammars, not just one; with an adult's various responsibilities, he is likely to have less time available for this task than the child; and, because intellectual inertia will tend to make his grammars of the second and subsequent speakers similar to his grammar for the first speaker by default, he must ensure that alternative analyses are considered and positively ruled out if they are inadequate, where the child can be content to adopt the first satisfactory analysis he hits on. If different speakers' grammars do seem to coincide on some particular issue, it is unclear how the linguist could ever disprove the possibility that both speakers' childhood data-sets had included relevant evidence. (And, if the linguist draws on speakers' intuitive judgements about their language, rather than just recording their utterances, it may also be difficult to disprove the possibility that shared 'intuitions' reflect exposure to a common cultural tradition of discourse about language, rather than common tacit grammatical rules.)

When Chomsky discusses the convergence argument, he does not refer to detailed comparative studies of different individuals' idiolects. The argument might feel more persuasive if we found that in practice different members of a single speech community almost invariably agreed as to the fine details of their judgements about hypothetical examples.

But of course they do not. It is notorious among linguists that (as discussed, for instance, by William Labov) investigations of individuals' grammars via elicitation of their judgements keeps throwing up unexpected, apparently unsystematic differences between members of a single speech community (however narrowly the boundaries of the 'community' are defined – this seems to be nothing to do with regional or class dialects). To quote just one example: can we say in English *Every one of the boys didn't go there*? When twenty-four subjects were asked to judge this word sequence by ticking one of four descriptions of its status, three ticked 'Only a foreigner would say a thing like that', nine ticked 'Maybe some speakers of English would say it, but I've never heard it', nine ticked 'Some people would say it, others wouldn't', and three ticked 'Anyone raised speaking English would say it naturally'. Findings like this show up over and over again, and the harder one scrutinizes them the less patterning there seems to be in the ranking of related word sequences.

Chomsky is in a cleft stick here. If (as Labov argues) these numerous individual differences relate to speakers' beliefs about their respective idiolects, rather than to the idiolects themselves, then speakers' judgements are an inadequate guide to their grammars – in which case, convergence between the grammars of individual language learners could only be demonstrated by constructing grammars for two or more speakers on the basis of the kind of evidence (raw observation of usage) which Chomsky insists is insufficient to determine one grammar. Alternatively, if the individual differences do reflect genuine differences in the speakers' 'tacit knowledge', then the speakers have *not* completely converged.

Perhaps the argument from convergence could be rescued if there were reason to believe that without innateness one would expect the limited and non-identical data-sets available to different children to lead to much *larger* differences than the ones observed – but what reason have we got to believe that?

Chomsky gives none – I have seen no passage in which he thinks through the implications of his argument from convergence as far as this. Steven Stich has tried to persuade us to believe it, by means of an argument which introduces and makes heavy use of a concept of *rough equivalence*, which is a relationship that some pairs of individual grammars are said to have to one another. Stich offers 'no precise definition' of the 'rough equivalence' concept, but sketches what he means by saying that 'roughly equivalent' grammars are not so wholly identical that the observable differences between the idiolects of members of a speech community establish that their grammars lack rough equivalence, but 'roughly equivalent' grammars are too similar to one another to be arrived at (unless by chance) by linguists separately working out the structure of a language on the basis purely of the sort of data-sets available to children. Stich goes on to argue that we can discover whether two speakers' tacitly known grammars are 'roughly equivalent', without needing to know anything about the rules of those grammars.

There is a logical fallacy in that argument, which I had already pointed out in the article to which Stich's piece was intended as a response. But we do not need to go into those details here, because for present purposes the significant point is what Stich has done by introducing his concept of 'rough equivalence'. One cannot begin to engage with Stich's discussion, unless one grants him that it is reasonable to use this concept. But the question whether there *is* any relationship between grammars that combines both the properties Stich attributes to 'rough equivalence' – grammars in this relationship are too similar to have been constructed from data of experience without innate knowledge, and yet are not so similar that they fail to throw up the kinds of difference discussed by Labov and others – is exactly what is at issue. A version of the argument from convergence which begins, as Stich's does, by requiring the reader to grant the legitimacy of the term 'rough equivalence' amounts to reasoning in a circle.

Thus the argument from convergence fails. As said above, I shall defer until Chapter 4 discussing **5**, the argument from linguistic universals.

### Response to the argument from non-linguistic analogies (6)

The non-linguistic analogies quoted by Chomsky merit only brief discussion, because it is a mystery to me why Chomsky believes that the cognitive systems he mentions are common property among our species (as they would need to be, in order to support his case).

Take Chomsky's discussion of 'the' number system, quoted in **6**. If this passage means anything, it must surely mean that all human communities have counting systems with no highest integer, together with the concept of infinity. But these claims are quite false. In South America, Australia and elsewhere there are indigenous languages whose speakers cannot count even as high as the seven managed by the birds Chomsky mentions. As for 'infinity', I seriously wonder whether most twentieth-century English speakers understand this word in its mathematical sense, as distinct from the concept of a very large finite quantity. And the earliest uses of 'infinite' or 'infinity' in anything close to that sense which are reported in the *Oxford English Dictionary* date only to the seventeenth century. James Thomson states that the modern numerical concept of infinity was developed as recently as the mid-nineteenth century.

Are we to conclude from these facts that speakers of languages which lack expressions for large numbers, and our own ancestors until a few centuries ago, are or were less than fully human with respect to their cognitive equipment? This borders on absurdity. Surely it is obvious that the proper way of thinking of the situation is that our modern number system, incorporating an endless series of integers and a separate concept of infinity, is a case of cultural development – a rather clear case, I should have thought. The reason why Chomsky, I and no doubt the reader all share these concepts, while certain contemporary inhabitants of South America and Australia, together with all our ancestors up to the sixteenth century, do or did not share them, has nothing to do with biological equipment built into Chomsky, me and the reader, and missing from the others mentioned – it has everything to do with the fact that Chomsky, I and the reader, but not those others, have been exposed via the mechanisms of cultural transmission (schoolteaching, for instance) to ideas that were developed at particular places and times.

It is true that the modern European number system, like many other comparable intellectual developments, does not simply follow from the nature of our experience – as Chomsky puts it, these developments 'far transcend . . . the limited environmental factors that trigger and partially shape their growth'. But so what? Popper does not suggest that the ideas which people throw up in their attempts to make sense of their experience are in some way mechanical copies of the contents of experience; he insists that our ideas are free creations, not determined by the nature of what we observe. Inappropriate ideas are eliminated when their consequences turn out to be contradicted by experience; but it is only in this sense that our environment 'shapes' our ideas. (In the case of a mathematical system, presumably the environment will not play even this role; it is hard to see how experience of the physical world could 'refute' a system of numbers. I suppose only discovering internal contradictions could provide a reason for discarding a mathematical system.)

Chomsky writes:

> Were it not for [the rich innate cognitive endowment which he attributes to our species], individuals would grow into mental amoeboids . . . each merely reflecting the limited and impoverished environment in which he or she develops . . .

Who says they would? Why should they? This is just a way of making Chomsky's own theory seem more plausible or attractive, by contrasting it to a straw man, the grossly implausible picture of the mind as a passive camera film which I mentioned in Chapter 1. This was not the view of Locke or the other classic philosophers of empiricism; as H.H. Price pointed out more than forty years ago: 'It is, of course, historically false that the Empiricists thought the human mind passive.' It was not Popper's view. It is certainly not my view.

It is worth pausing for a moment to think about what nativists like Chomsky are doing when they use this sort of argument, as they quite often do. It is rather as if someone were to announce 'We have established that human beings are descendants of a race of gods from the planet Venus', and then, to someone saying 'Actually I don't believe that's true', to respond 'What, you mean you think that people are just clods of earth that lifted themselves off the ground and formed into human shape spontaneously? – hey, fellows, get this, there's a guy here that thinks human beings are just clods of earth!' But of course the objector never believed either alternative. I do not believe that human beings are born with knowledge built in, and I do not believe that we are just empty organisms with passive, 'plastic' minds either. I boringly continue to believe what most people believed before the linguistic nativists came along. It made good sense then, and nothing the nativists say stops it making good sense still.

The clue to the way Chomsky saddles his opponents with an obviously wrong point of view may lie in one of his earliest writings, which was a slashing review of a book about language by the American psychologist B.F. Skinner. Chomsky's criticisms of Skinner were quite fair: Skinner confused the method of psychological research with its object, and suggested that because all the researcher can observe are the stimuli that impinge on a person and his behavioural responses, that is essentially all there is. Skinner scarcely seemed to believe in the reality of a complex mind that often leads a person to behave in ways that are linked only indirectly, if at all, with the stimuli that recently impinged on him. Chomsky's later writings often refer back to Skinner. But to treat Skinner's unreasonable theories as representative of the centuries-old tradition of empiricist thought is a travesty. So far as I know, Skinner was never much read outside the USA. To expect the world at large to believe in innate knowledge, because some half-forgotten American psychology professor did not believe in minds at all, is surely a bit rich.


## Question-begging idealizations

The preceding sections have dealt with all the actual arguments Chomsky used to support his claim that we have innate knowledge of language. However, quite an important part of the support Chomsky's writings lend to that claim comes from Chomsky's use of certain strategies of discussion which cannot, properly speaking, be called 'arguments'.

Chomsky repeatedly points out that he quite deliberately makes various counterfactual 'simplifying assumptions' when discussing language and language acquisition, in order to render the topic amenable to analysis. He argues that any successful empirical science must abstract away from many of the complexities which actually exist in its subject matter. He sometimes sounds exasperated by commentators who object to his own simplifying assumptions:

> Opposition to idealization is simply objection to rationality; it amounts to nothing more than an insistence that we shall not have meaningful intellectual work. . . . you *must* abstract some object of study, you must eliminate those factors which are not pertinent . . . if you want to conduct an investigation which is not trivial. In the natural sciences this isn't even discussed, it is self-evident. In the human sciences, people continue to question it.

One problem with this passage is that it ignores an important difference between two kinds of simplifying assumption. It is one thing to ignore aspects of one's subject matter that are beside the point. The branch of physics called kinetics, which deals with the motions of material bodies, says nothing about the colours of the moving bodies, and nobody supposes that it should; moving bodies are all coloured one way or another, but colour has nothing to do with their movements. It is quite another matter, and not so obviously a good idea, to pretend for argument's sake that some aspect of the subject matter which *is* relevant is different from and simpler than the way it really is. In the context where the passage just quoted appears, Chomsky seems to be justifying idealizations of this second, counterfactual type. But what he actually argues for in the quoted passage is only the former sort of simplification, and it is only that sort which everyone can see is self-evidently necessary.

Still, we may well concede that 'model' sciences do also use the second, counterfactual kind of simplifying assumption, and are often justified in doing so. For many purposes, kinetics treats sizeable material objects as if their whole mass were all concentrated at their centre of gravity. In fact it is not; but the calculations are far simpler if one makes that assumption, and in most cases, as it happens, the results of the calculations are not affected by it.

However, when one resorts to using the counterfactual kind of simplifying assumptions, it is obviously vital (as Chomsky mentions) to be on one's guard against the possibility that they may distort the substantial point at issue. Not every attractive assumption that simplifies calculations will leave the results unaffected.

Unfortunately, the counterfactual simplifying assumptions about human language which Chomsky makes in his theorizing keep falling into this trap. Each of the assumptions is incompatible with the Popperian account of language acquisition; and in consequence, they artificially protect Chomsky's theory from refutation, because they eliminate a plausible alternative from consideration through what is presented as a harmless, uncontroversial assumption.

One of Chomsky's counterfactual simplifying assumptions is that language acquisition 'can be conceptualized as an instantaneous process'. The language learner is envisaged as moving from his full set of data to his final grammar in one fell swoop. (Indeed, although Chomsky usually acknowledges the status of this postulate as a counterfactual simplification, the third quotation in subsection 1 above suggests that on at least one occasion Chomsky confused his simplifying assumption with reality. A first language takes several years to acquire, and to describe a process lasting over years as fantastically sudden is an odd use of words.) But it is a crucial prediction of the Popperian account that language learning cannot be instantaneous. Popperian learning is a matter of many small, fallible steps, and we shall see in Chapter 4 that it is precisely by way of this gradual property of the learning process that the Popperian approach succeeds in predicting the Chomskyan linguistic universals.

Chomsky urges that his assumption of instantaneous learning must be harmless; if it mattered,

> then we would expect to find substantial differences in the result of language learning depending on such factors as order of presentation of data, time of presentation, and so on. But we do not find this . . .

But that is wrong. We shall see in Chapter 4 that the Popperian explanation for Chomsky's linguistic universals depends *only* on learning taking place in a stepwise, Popperian fashion; it does *not* depend on the order or time of presentation of individual items of data. To claim that it is harmless to pretend that language acquisition is instantaneous is, in effect, to assume that language acquisition does not work in a Popperian fashion, without going to the trouble of arguing the point.

Although Chomsky does usually concede that the instantaneity postulate is counterfactual, his description of the true state of affairs still embodies a questionable assumption:

> We might, more realistically, say that children proceed through a series of cognitive states . . . [terminating in] a 'steady state' attained fairly early in life and not changing in significant respects from that point on. . . . Attainment of a steady state at some not-too-delayed stage of intellectual development is presumably characteristic of 'learning' within the range of cognitive capacity.

Here, Chomsky is acknowledging that an individual does not really move from initial ignorance to adult mastery of his mother tongue instantaneously, but he is still assuming that the learning process is one that comes to a stop, even if it lasts a while before terminating.

I cannot make out from Chomsky's word 'presumably' whether, in his own mind, his 'steady state' postulate is an uncontroversial assumption that he sees as making discussion easier and as being harmless whether or not it is true, or whether he believes there is hard evidence to support the idea that after a certain fairly early point in a person's life his idiolect ceases to change in 'significant respects'. If the latter, Chomsky quotes no evidence; and the 'steady state' idea is sharply at odds with the views of eminent linguists of the past. For instance, Leonard Bloomfield wrote:

> there is no hour or day when we can say that a person has finished learning to speak, but, rather, to the end of his life, the speaker keeps on doing the very things which make up infantile language-learning.

W.D. Whitney put the same point in this way:

> We realize better in the case of a second or 'foreign', than in that of a first or 'native' language, that the process of acquisition is a never-ending one; but it is not more true of the one than of the other.

What is clear is that the steady-state assumption is incompatible with the Popperian approach to learning. It is central to Popper's account of knowledge acquisition that it is a process which never reaches a well-defined termination. Even if a scientist succeeded in producing a theory which was in fact wholly true, there is no way he could ever know that he had done so: theories which in everyday life we rely on as 'true' are just ones which have escaped disconfirmation over a long period, and a theory which has survived test after test ought to be held only provisionally – nothing can guarantee that it will not turn out to be refuted tomorrow. Well-entrenched scientific theories have often been refuted in the past. What is more, in view of the 'open-ended' character of the range of possible hypotheses that might potentially be formulated and tested, it would seem a remarkable chance if a wholly true theory were put forward in any domain having the degree of complexity that most natural phenomena display. It seems more plausible to imagine that our theories about the natural world will go on developing indefinitely, as Popper often suggests – with luck forming 'progressive' rather than 'degenerating' problemshifts', but never managing to be more than partly false approximations to the truth.

Accordingly, if language learning is just a particular aspect of human learning as a general Popperian process, then it will not terminate in any well-defined 'steady state'. It may be that learning of all kinds slows down sharply at puberty (cf. p. 37 above); but, since we know that learning in some domains continues after puberty, we must predict that learning continues, even if more slowly, in the domain of language too. It seems a reasonable prediction; I do not believe that I ceased to deepen my knowledge of English after the 1950s. But the relevant point here is that by asserting his steady state postulate without quoting evidence for it, Chomsky is choosing to make an assumption that is incompatible with the Popperian account of language acquisition: hence he is ruling out the rival view by fiat.

Finally, an explicitly counterfactual simplifying assumption that Chomsky makes is that:

> Linguistic theory is concerned primarily with an ideal speaker-listener, in a completely homogeneous speech community, who knows its language perfectly . . .

Chomsky describes this assumption as being 'of critical importance' for his approach to linguistics. It is obviously false, of course, and Chomsky knows that it is false; but he regards it as 'innocent', and expresses surprise that it has 'aroused quite a storm of protest'.

One reason for protest is that, yet again, this assumption excludes the Popperian approach without argument. I have just pointed out that learning in Popper's eyes is a non-terminating process. If this view is appropriate for the domain of natural science, it should be even more appropriate for the domain of language acquisition, because in this domain the concept of a 'wholly true theory' seems to have no application even in principle. Nature (scientists normally assume) works in accordance with fixed laws, so that a theory which described some of those laws with perfect accuracy could not be surpassed in its domain – even though the inventor of the theory would not know that it was destined never to be refuted, and even though it may seem unlikely that such a perfectly true theory will ever be created in practice. In the linguistic domain, on the other hand, a 'language' has no independent existence over and above the representations of the language in the minds of the various individuals belonging to the speech community that uses it.

What the language learner is trying to bring his tacit linguistic theory into correspondence with is not some single, consistent grammar inhering in a collective national psyche, the sort of mystic entity that a sociologist such as Emile Durkheim would call a 'social fact'. Rather, he is trying to reconstruct a system underlying the usage of the various speakers to whom he is exposed; and these speakers will almost certainly be working at any given time with non-identical tacit theories of their own – so that there will not be any wholly coherent and unrefutable grammar available to be formulated, quite apart from the fact that the language learner would be extraordinarily fortunate to hit on the 'correct' grammar even if there were one correct grammar to be discovered. The notion of a speaker-listener knowing the language of his community 'perfectly' is doubly inapplicable – both because there is no particular grammar, achievement of which would count as 'perfect' mastery of the language, and because even if there were such a grammar, there is no procedure by which a learner could discover it.

From a Popperian perspective, these points remain true even if we think about 'ideal' rather than real speaker-listeners. An ideal language learner would be one who never holds on to grammatical hypotheses after he has encountered evidence sufficient to refute them, and perhaps one who always selects new hypotheses for testing in such a way that his theory series is 'progressive' rather than 'degenerating'. No doubt, real language learners are not ideal in these respects; but *even if they were*, they would not attain 'perfect' mastery of the language of their community. Popperian learning is not an algorithm which, if followed without deviation, leads to a successful conclusion.

Therefore, to assume that it makes sense to describe even an 'ideal' speaker-listener as inhabiting a perfectly homogeneous speech community and as knowing its language perfectly amounts, once again, to surreptitiously ruling the Popperian view of language acquisition out of consideration.

Chomsky argues that anyone who regards this idealization as illegitimate is committed to the view that 'People are so constituted that they would be incapable of learning language in a homogeneous speech community' (or alternatively to a weaker variant of that thesis which it is not necessary to quote here). Chomsky describes this position as 'hopelessly implausible', and later in the same book he strengthens these words (without further discussion) to 'quite absurd'. It is true that a supporter of the Popperian account of language acquisition is committed to the quoted view, because it is just a special consequence of the Popperian principle that – in Chomsky's sense of 'learn', where this implies 'attain a steady state of perfectly accurate knowledge' – people are so constituted that they are incapable of learning language in *any* circumstances. (A Popperian would not want to use the word 'learn' in that sense, though.) Likewise, a Popperian is committed to the view that people are so constituted that a speech community composed of people cannot be homogeneous. But these views are not in the least unreasonable or quixotic; they have seemed quite natural to many commentators.

Chomsky's characterization of the former view as 'hopelessly implausible' and 'quite absurd' merely functions to frighten people away from the

Popperian approach, without the need to provide arguments against it. Throughout this section, we have seen how Chomsky persuades his readers to agree with his picture of human cognition by insisting that he has the right to make idealizing assumptions that seem harmless, but in reality smuggle in the conclusions he is claiming to prove. However much Chomsky tries to make us believe that 'Opposition to idealization is simply objection to rationality', we are obviously rationally entitled to reject counterfactual simplifying assumptions if they lead to circular reasoning. Indeed, this aspect of Chomsky's argumentation is appropriately answered in words of his own:

> Specific arguments with regard to native endowment should be assessed on their merits, without intrusion of a priori doctrine as to the nature of legitimate idealization . . .

This concludes my survey of Noam Chomsky's arguments for nativism. I have striven in the foregoing sections to represent his arguments fully and fairly, avoiding distortion through quoting out of context, and not suppressing relevant qualifications. I believe I have succeeded in that endeavour.

If so, I submit that, insofar as the case for linguistic nativism is based on Chomsky's arguments, it collapses.


## Input/output systems

The original case for linguistic nativism was in fact even weaker than we have seen so far. On p. 24 I was quite willing to concede that biological determinism may operate to fix aspects of language that are closely related to human 'input/output systems'. There seemed no reason to deny that concepts such as 'sweet' or 'hot' might be independent of culture and universal across the species, since they are connected directly to our physiological sense apparatus, which certainly is genetically determined; likewise our production and perception of speech sounds is mediated by biologically fixed anatomical arrangements. It is with respect to more knowledge-dependent concepts such as 'carbon' or 'conservative', and to abstract properties of language such as grammatical structure, that it seems important to challenge claims for biological determinism. However, the evidence suggests that much less is innate, even in areas of language where an empiricist could happily live with innateness, than the nativists claimed at the period we are discussing.

In the following sections, it is no longer Noam Chomsky whose writings are in my sights. Chomsky wrote little about 'input/output-related' aspects of language. (I apologize, incidentally, for the phrase 'input/output-related': it is an ugly one, but I cannot find any other concise way of summarizing what I mean.) During the high tide of linguistic nativism in the 1960s and 1970s, though, others did argue that in these areas, too, biology controlled language to a greater extent than people had previously imagined. Chomsky sometimes gave such theories his blessing, even if he did not himself develop them; and there is no doubt that some of the work on 'input/output-related' linguistic nativism significantly reinforced Chomsky's message in many readers' minds.

This work is rather different in style from Chomsky's work. Chomsky's argumentation is strongly logical and formal in flavour; and this has the advantage, from an opponent's point of view, that if one can uncover a fallacy, the structure of argument immediately topples, so that refutations can be fairly concise. The writings on 'input/output-related' linguistic nativism draw more heavily on detailed studies of concrete evidence of various sorts. This means that someone such as myself, who aims to show that the conclusions do not follow from the evidence, unavoidably has to take longer to deal with each strand of argument, to allow the reader to grasp the nature of the concrete realities under discussion. But these realities are often quite interesting in themselves, so the following pages may make a congenial counterpoint to the abstractions we dealt with earlier in the chapter.

## Speech perception and production

One issue has to do with categorical perception of speech sound.

The physical variables which distinguish one speech sound from another are in most cases continuous variables: a pair of related sounds will represent different points on a scale along which any number of slightly different sounds are physically possible. For instance, the variable distinguishing the English [d] as in *da* from [t] as in *ta* is *voice-onset time*: the interval, measured in milliseconds, between the release of contact between tongue-tip and palate (which is common to [d] and [t]) and the moment when the vocal chords or folds within the Adam's apple begin to vibrate, as they do in [a] or any other English vowel. Time is obviously a continuous variable; but the English language treats it as if it were discrete in this case. The language uses just two distinctive values of the variable, so that *da* is typically pronounced with a voice-onset time close to zero (that is, vocal chords begin to vibrate more or less simultaneously with release of tongue/palate contact), while *ta* typically has a voice-onset time of about 60 milliseconds.

Timings in successive utterances of either consonant will not be perfectly identical; but timings for utterances of the two consonants will vary around two well-defined means. Other than as an occasional slip, one will not find English speakers producing consonants halfway between [d] and [t] – even though, physically, such a sound is quite possible and unproblematic.

In itself, all this says is that a language constructs a finite set of symbols by attributing distinctive symbolic value to a limited number of positions in an inherently continuous medium – rather as the traffic-light system attributes special value to three positions in the colour spectrum. Not every green traffic-light is an identical green to every other, but you will not see a traffic-light whose colour is halfway between green and amber, or halfway between amber and red, even though there are such colours. This is natural and unsurprising, whether we are discussing traffic-lights or the sounds of a language.

The novel twist introduced by nativists such as Alvin Liberman was that this discrete categorization of physically continuous variables might be biologically built into our perceptual mechanisms. Artificial auditory stimuli were created, in which voice-onset timing differed by a series of small equal steps between the [d] and [t] values, and people were tested on their ability to hear pairs of the artificial stimuli as the same or different. They were not asked 'Is this a D or a T?', they were asked to make identity or difference judgements among sets of the artificial stimuli. Instead of responding in line with the physical properties of the sounds, subjects perceived the stimuli as falling into two classes – any two stimuli with voice-onset times below about 25 milliseconds were heard as identical, even if the specific times were different in the two cases, and likewise for the stimuli where both times were greater than 25 milliseconds. Pairs of stimuli which spanned the 25-millisecond threshold were usually heard as different, even if the physical difference was smaller than in the case of many pairs which were judged identical.

Outside the context of language, physically continuous sound variables are perceived as continuous. Tones on different pitches, or silent pauses of different lengths interrupting a tone, are not lumped into large classes of 'perceptually equivalent' pitches or lengths. But the implication of these experimental data seemed to be that the discrete use, for linguistic signalling purposes, of the voice-onset variable (and other continuous phonetic variables tested in parallel experiments) had been sufficiently important in the history of our species that it led to evolution of special perceptual mechanisms attuned to speech sound. Other sounds are heard in ways that mirror their physical properties fairly faithfully; but when incoming sounds are identified as representing speech, they trigger a separate perceptual processing system, which analyses their properties in a manner that reflects their function as linguistic signals rather than their physical form.

The linguistic nativists could not claim that all aspects of speech perception had this categorical quality. Notably, the differences between the various vowel sounds are physically continuous and are perceived as continuous – small differences are heard as small differences, irrespective of how the differences relate to the boundaries between distinct vowels in one's language. (The acoustic differences between vowels relate to the frequencies of complex features of speech signals called *formants*.)

But even in this area the linguistic nativists had a trump card to play. According to scholars such as Philip Lieberman and Jeffrey Laitman, the reason why adult humans are capable of producing a diverse range of vowel sounds is that we have a vocal tract that is notably different in shape from the vocal tracts of other primates such as the chimpanzee (our closest evolutionary relative), from the shape reconstructed for Neanderthal Man (a still closer, though extinct relative), and even from ourselves when newborn. All these latter creatures have or had vocal tracts that resemble one another in shape, and cannot produce a large variety of vowel sounds; adult *Homo sapiens* is claimed to be the odd man out with respect to vocal tract shape.

The implication, Lieberman claimed, is that our vocal tract must be a relatively recent evolutionary development (the newborn child would in this respect resemble the adult stage of our evolutionary forebears, as is true in many other respects). This must be an instance of biological evolution geared specifically to the needs of language, according to Lieberman, because in another respect our distinctive vocal tract is a *dis*advantage. It allows us to choke to death on food lodged in the windpipe, as people sometimes do (other primates and Neanderthalers are or were safe from this).

Because he originally believed that this evolutionary innovation must have been quite recent, Philip Lieberman allowed himself to speculate about a connection between this finding and the anthropologist R.A. Dart's claim that there was a great acceleration in the growth of human culture about 30,000 years ago. Perhaps this cultural explosion was the consequence of evolution suddenly giving us the wherewithal to speak to one another? More recently, Philip Lieberman has changed his mind about the timescale (in 1991 he described the modern *Homo sapiens* vocal tract shape as at least 125,000 years old); but he still believes that the anatomy of modern man gives us a superior ability to pronounce distinctive vowel sounds, and that 'these phonetic differences are sufficient in themselves to account for the late stages of hominid evolution. The small selective advantage for more perceptible speech of anatomically modern *Homo sapiens* could account for the extinction of late hominid forms like the classic Neanderthals.' We triumphed and the Neanderthalers went extinct, Lieberman believes, because we spoke more clearly: a lesson for every sloppy-tongued teenager.

But these various nativist arguments about the medium of language have worn even less well than Chomsky's arguments about the abstract structure of language and its acquisition.

Take, first, the point about continuous phonetic variables being perceived categorically. Considering that the variables in question are ones which function categorically in speech, the idea that our perceptual mechanism has become biologically geared to language has some apparent force: why else would we hear these sounds in a fashion at odds with their physical reality, if not because linguistic considerations are built into our perception?

This argument was knocked very effectively on the head by P.K. Kuhl and J.D. Miller, who looked at how voice-onset timing is perceived by another species. They used the chinchilla, a rabbit-like rodent. In brief, Kuhl and Miller found that artificial stimuli spaced along the *da–ta* dimension are perceived just as categorically by chinchillas as they are by human beings. Indeed, the chinchilla discrimination function, plotted as a graph, is near-identical to that of an English speaker.

Now, I do not know (and nor does anyone else) why chinchillas perceive voice-onset timing categorically; but it is certainly not because they need to distinguish words beginning with D from words beginning with T. So evidently Alvin Liberman was letting two and two make twenty-five when he inferred linguistic nativism from categorical perception. The chinchilla experiments show that biological evolution is quite able to yield categorical perception of a continuous phonetic variable in animals that do not use phonetic variables for language. There is no reason not to suppose that Man acquired categorical perception in the same way as the chinchilla; then, when eventually we developed language, naturally we exploited this pre-existing perceptual mechanism to choose distinctive speech sounds. In one sense, this could still be called a case of linguistic mechanisms being biologically innate; but one might as well say that, because a driver changes gear using a genetically inherited grasping ability in order to manipulate the gearstick, gear-changing is innate in humans.

As for the clear vowels of adult *Homo sapiens* versus the indistinct utterances of the Neanderthaler, the first relevant point to make is that when Philip Lieberman writes about modern Man having a distinctively shaped vocal tract, he does mean Man. John Ohala points out that 'the larynx is *not* remarkably low in adult [human] females', who in this respect remain closer to the ape. So, although we can probably never do more than speculate about exactly what sounds a Neanderthaler could make, the evidence surely cannot justify a conclusion that Neanderthalers were unable to talk: modern women manage it. That is not to say that women's vowels are physically identical to men's vowels: the differently shaped vocal tracts make a difference to the airwave patterns produced, but we unconsciously allow for the different vocal tracts and hear a woman's utterance of, say, *peep* as sounding like a man's *peep* even if, physically, it is more like a man's utterance of *pip*. What we do not seem to find is that people regularly understand men's speech but fail to make out what words are said by women. If women can speak English comprehensibly with their high larynx, why suppose that Neanderthalers could not have done the same?

John Ohala agrees that adult male *Homo sapiens* shows a distinctive vocal tract anatomy by comparison with our close evolutionary relatives, but this is better explained by considerations not related to language. Ohala marshals a number of lines of evidence to argue that this development in Man, together with similar evolutionary developments in various distant species such as the elephant seal, are most plausibly explained as adaptations which functioned to deter potential attackers or competitors. The distinctive vocal tract, and the distinctively long vocal chords also found in adult male *Homo sapiens*, make the calls of this creature low in frequency: many animals can recognize that deep notes tend to come from big things. It is easier to understand why men but not women developed an improved ability to frighten off the opposition in the dawn of human history, a hundred thousand years and more before political correctness, than it would be to understand why men but not women should have developed clear speech. And although the modified vocal tract shape affects vowel sounds as well as pitch, the distinctively long vocal chords of adult men function *only* to make the voice deep – they have no effect on vowel acoustics.

On top of that, Ohala points out that the distinctive adult male vocal tract develops only at puberty; until then the sexes are virtually identical in this area of their anatomy. Again, it is understandable that boy children, as well as women, might have had no use for deep voices because they functioned socially as non-combatants; it would be harder to explain why efficient speech became adaptive only after puberty.

To sum up: even if the evidence for language-specific evolutionary developments in our vocalizing or hearing mechanisms had been good, it is not obvious that defenders of an empiricist account of the human mind should have felt threatened. These mechanisms are not closely related to our intellectual functions. But in any case the evidence is not good. So far as we can tell, human language simply exploits vocalizing and hearing capabilities that evolved in our ancestors to serve other biological functions. These pre-existing capabilities just happened to come in handy when we began to invent the sophisticated techniques of making thought concrete which we call 'language'.


## Basic colour terms

Phonetic matters are technical, and of correspondingly narrow interest. An aspect of 'input/output-related' linguistic nativism which is more accessible to the average reader is the claim that vocabulary relating to the data of the senses reveals subtle underlying structures, common to all the world's languages but not contained in the external physical realities that give rise to the sense data, and which may therefore reflect a genetically determined structuring of concepts in the human mind.

In particular, Brent Berlin and Paul Kay's 1969 book on colour terminologies did a great deal in its day to reinforce the appeal of the case for linguistic nativism; and it is still widely quoted as the standard account of its topic.

Berlin and Kay's book made an impact for one thing because colour is something that engages almost everybody's interest and emotional response; and also because it seemed to refute the absolutely classic example of languages as independent systems which encode the diverse intellectual structures of separate cultures. Before the rise of linguistic nativism, introductory textbooks on linguistics very often used differences between languages' colour terminologies as an easily grasped illustration of this idea.

H.A. Gleason's *Introduction to Descriptive Linguistics*, first published in 1955, is typical. After a few pages of generalities, on p. 4 Gleason illustrates the way in which one language will structure reality into units that speakers of another language will find arbitrary or illogical by showing how the vocabularies of various languages segment the colour spectrum. The English language divides the continuous spectrum up into chunks called *purple, blue, green, yellow, orange, red*. By contrast, the Zimbabwean language Shona, for instance, has three words: *cips$^w$uka* covers orange, red, purple, and some orangey yellows and purplish blues; *citema* includes most blues and some bluish greens; *cicena* includes the bulk of the English 'green' and 'yellow' areas of the spectrum. To an English speaker, Shona illogically lumps together different colours, and treats as if they were separate a range of hues which are 'really' shades of the same colour. But, for a Shona speaker, the same objections would apply to the English terminology.

Again, according to Harold Conklin writing in the same year, in the Philippine language Hanunóo the reference of 'colour' terms is not even wholly determined by chromatic properties; it is partly determined by the variable of wetness or dryness. The association of greenness with fresh growth and yellow/brown hues with dead, desiccated vegetation means that perception of wetness or dryness can override the hue variable in determining the suitable Hanunóo colour word to apply in a particular case.

Colour words make a convincing and appealing illustration of cultural relativism. It was easy to believe that this is an area in which 'languages could differ from each other without limit and in unpredictable ways'.

People got excited, then, when Berlin and Kay argued, on the basis of a survey of basic colour terms in ninety-eight languages from many parts of the world, that there is much more predictable patterning in this aspect of language structure than was previously realized. (Berlin and Kay use the word 'basic' to indicate simple words such as English *red*, *white*, *grey*. They excluded, as non-basic: words for subdivisions, such as *scarlet* as a subdivision of *red*; words with internal structure, such as *bluish*, or having restricted application, such as *blonde*; words referring to objects having a distinctive colour, such as *peach* for an orange/pink shade; words borrowed from other languages, such as *cerise*, which an English speaker will not necessarily connect with 'cherry' but may well perceive as a French word; and so on.)

According to Berlin and Kay, languages do differ from one another in the *number* of basic colour terms they possess; but that is essentially the only way they differ in this area. If you know how many basic colour terms a language has, you broadly know what they will be: in the sense that there is a universal linear sequence of 'focal colours' – points on the colour chart which attract names – and a language with *n* basic colour terms will use them for the first *n* focal colours in the sequence. The range of shades covered by a single colour term will depend on how many focal colours have names: hues not at a focal point will be grouped under an adjacent named focal colour, so that if there are few names, each name will cover a wider range of hues.

Using the English names for focal colours, the universal sequence is:

$$\left\{ \begin{array}{l} \text{white} \\ \text{black} \end{array} \right\} \text{---} \text{ red } \text{---} \left\{ \begin{array}{l} \text{green} \\ \text{yellow} \end{array} \right\} \text{---} \text{ blue } \text{---} \text{ brown } \text{---} \left\{ \begin{array}{l} \text{purple} \\ \text{pink} \\ \text{orange} \\ \text{grey} \end{array} \right\}$$

Colour terms are not useful unless there is more than one of them, so the first two focal colours cannot be ordered with respect to one another; and the universal linear sequence breaks down after seven terms. Apart from that, the only complication is that a four-term system may include either *green* or *yellow* (a system of five or more terms will include both).

Berlin and Kay do report a handful of exceptions to their neat schema, in the sense of cases where a language lacks a word for some 'early' colour while including various words for 'later' colours, or includes a single 'late' colour while lacking various 'earlier' colours. But these exceptions are so few, in the context of almost a hundred languages examined, that their findings seem quite impressive if taken at face value.

However, if one penetrates beyond Berlin and Kay's conclusions about a universal colour sequence to scrutinize the details of the data on which the conclusions are founded, it becomes hard to take them at face value.

One reason has to do with the way the data were gathered. A large proportion of the data were not assembled by Berlin and Kay themselves, or by other professional scholars, but by students on one of their courses at the University of California. Individual students each picked a language, found out about its colour terminology as best they could, and handed their findings in to the authors as their coursework for the term. For the students it was probably a good course – they had fun and learned something; but some of us in the university teaching profession would gasp and rub our eyes at the thought of turning a collection of student essays into a contribution to the world of international scholarship. It is hardly surprising if the data often seem rocky.

A particularly egregious example is the treatment of Homeric Greek. Berlin and Kay list four basic colour terms for Homeric Greek, including the word *glaukos*. Standard reference works, such as Liddell and Scott's Greek dictionary, say that *glaukos* at the Homeric period meant something like 'gleaming', with no colour reference, and in later Ancient Greek meant something like what its English derivate 'glaucous' means now: roughly bluish-greenish-grey. But Berlin and Kay's theory requires a term for 'black' in a four-term system, so they translate *glaukos* as 'black'. Ancient Greek had a standard word for 'black': *melas*, the root of 'melancholy' (black bile) and 'Melanesia' (black islands) – but *melas* does not appear in Berlin and Kay's list of four Homeric basic colour terms.

Is this, perhaps, because this particular word is missing from the Homeric texts? That would be interesting in itself if it were so, but it is not: *melas* is actually (by far) the commonest colour word in Homer. (If you wonder how I know that, the answer is that W.E. Gladstone counted and tabulated the figures in the monumental work on Homeric Greece which he wrote in his spare time from statesmanship.) The data available to Berlin and Kay somehow omit the standard, common word for black, but they need one, so they declare that a word meaning something different was the basic colour term for black – and Homeric Greek becomes yet another confirmation of the theory.

There is a lot of this sort of thing. Korean and Vietnamese are similar languages in that, while belonging to language families separate from Chinese (and from each other), both have for historical cultural reasons borrowed Chinese vocabulary wholesale, rather as English incorporates numerous words derived from Greek and Latin roots. Berlin and Kay are ambivalent in general about whether foreign loan words can count as basic colour terms, but the arguments for including or excluding Chinese loans seem to be the same for Korean and Vietnamese: either Chinese colour terms should be included in both cases or excluded in both cases. However, Berlin and Kay exclude the Chinese loans from Korean (to produce a five-term system agreeing with their theory), but include them in Vietnamese. I do not know whether this is because the student who took Korean knew how to detect Chinese loans and the one who took Vietnamese did not, or whether it was done to make Vietnamese fit the theory better. (Even with the Chinese loans included, Vietnamese presents a slight exception to Berlin and Kay's law, but without them it would be grossly exceptional, having a six-term system of black, white, red, brown, purple and grey.) Either way, the procedure is not impressive.

Berlin and Kay dither about whether they should treat a Chinese word for 'grey', pronounced *hui* in Mandarin and *fui* in Cantonese, as non-basic because it refers primarily to a thing, like English *peach*: 'there is some evidence that it refers to "ashes" ', 'we ... plan to obtain more data for this language in future research'. The question does not need research, it needs a moment with a Chinese dictionary or someone who speaks Chinese: *hui/fui* is the standard, common Chinese word for 'ashes'. (Its written form is based on the symbol for 'fire'.)

When students are let loose on the great languages of civilization, such as Greek or Chinese, it is not too hard to detect their errors (at least, one would have thought not). When Berlin and Kay list analyses for languages such as Nez Perce or Masai, most readers have little possibility of assessing their reliability; but there is no reason to assume these analyses are more reliable.

All this is not to deny that Berlin and Kay were on to something, though not as much as they supposed. Linguists such as Gleason who discussed colour vocabulary in the 1950s thought of the two-dimensional colour chart defined by the variables of hue and brightness as inherently featureless – which, in terms of the physics of light, it is: so that languages were free to chop it into whatever segments they chose, and one would expect no language-universal patterning. But human perception of colour is mediated by sensory apparatus which is not equally sensitive to all areas of the colour space. Our eyes can detect great intensity of colour in the 'focal red' region, for instance; conversely, in the pale blue-green region we are much less sensitive, so that the most intense colour we can experience in that area is not too different from a pale grey. One would naturally suppose that if a language has few words for colours, the words it does have will refer to the strongest sensations; and a comparison of Berlin and Kay's focal points with the regions of greatest human colour sensitivity indeed shows a near-perfect match.

In this respect, then, it is true that human biology does influence the conceptual structure of human language. (Incidentally, the influence is not totally consistent across the species: one reason why blue occupies a relatively late position on Berlin and Kay's sequence is that dark-skinned people have pigment in their eyes making them less sensitive than Europeans to blue light, and their languages correspondingly often lack a word for 'blue'.) But this degree of biological influence really would be easy for an empiricist to accept, even if the influence exerted complete control over those aspects of language to which it related. As I said earlier, it is not the concepts directly connected to immediate data of sense, but all the many concepts which involve a component of knowledge or imagination, that an empiricist insists on seeing as developed individually by separate cultures.

And in any case, even with colour terminology the biological influence does not amount to complete control. We saw that Hanunóo makes non-colour considerations relevant for the use of its 'colour' vocabulary. Noriko McNeill offers an interesting point about the traditional Japanese colour vocabulary, as it existed before Japan's nineteenth-century opening to Western technology. Before that time, she claims, Japanese used a five-term system whose focal colours would translate as black, white, orange, turquoise and yellow. This would be a serious counterexample for Berlin and Kay (they discuss only the modern Japanese colour vocabulary, which is much larger); but it is explained by the fact that the main natural dyestuffs available to the Japanese yielded orange, turquoise and yellow colours respectively.

In other words, as a language community evolves ways of talking about colours, it is influenced by diverse kinds of experience. Often, the direct experience of which perceptions are most intense proves decisive; sometimes, as in the Japanese case, the external question of what intense colours exist in the outside world (or which colours are open to manipulation by human action) is more important. Nothing in the least surprising for an empiricist there, surely?

And I do not believe there were other significant types of argument put forward by linguistic nativists in the 1960 to 1980 period, independent of the various strands of argument that we have scrutinized in this chapter. Linguistic nativism achieved a remarkable intellectual hegemony during those two decades. Looking back, it is hard to see how.

# 3 The Debate Renewed

## Out of Africa

When nativism revived after the 1980s' lull, one feature distinguishing the new wave from those who initiated the debate was a far livelier interest in Darwinian biological evolution. If knowledge of language were built into our biological endowment as the nativists claim, then it seems to follow that our ancestors must have got it through the gradual process of evolution. But Noam Chomsky never showed much interest in discussing this apparent implication of his ideas. On the odd occasion when he did refer to biological evolution, Chomsky was quite negative about its ability to account for innate language knowledge: 'It is perfectly safe to attribute this development to "natural selection," so long as we realize that there is no substance to this assertion.' He suggested that human language might have emerged as an evolutionary saltation, a sudden discontinuous leap rather than a gradual development from simpler precursors.

Many commentators have been puzzled by the brief remarks along these lines scattered in Chomsky's writings. They seemed unmotivated in the context of Chomsky's main focus of interest, namely the basis of language ability in the individual modern human; and they were not developed sufficiently to reveal their rationale. But recently Derek Bickerton, a linguistics professor at the University of Hawaii, has developed these hints into an elaborate theory of the evolutionary origin of human language. Bickerton's book *Language and Species* tries to construct a new and independent pillar to shore up the nativist case.

At the heart of Bickerton's picture of language origins is a claim that there is a sharp discontinuity between adult human language and various language-like systems which people commonly take to be way-stations along the road towards adult language. In itself this is a statement about present-day phenomena, and we need to understand what Bickerton means by 'discontinuity' in the context of present-day linguistic behaviour before moving on to what he says about prehistory.

The obvious 'way-station' is the speech of small children. To illustrate his discontinuity claim, Bickerton contrasts the language of a child, Seth, as recorded by one of his Ph.D. students at the ages of 21 months and 27 months respectively.

At the younger age, some typical utterances by Seth were:

Get up.

Get.

Please?

Please.

Thank you.

Apple.

Fan.

Six months later, Seth was producing sentences such as:

I want to put the squeaky shoes some more, Daddy.

Let's get a piece of rock and make it go ding.

Where'd the ball go? Where's the ball?

There's Geoffrey. There's ya cookie monster. There's the nother cookie monster.

I saw Robert, and saw Kevin, and saw Luanna.

The 27-month-old's English is far from perfect, but that is not the point. It has the characteristic adult language feature of fitting words together into grammatical patterns which allow sentences of considerable length and complexity to be built up. At 21 months, Seth's utterances were either single words or, at most, stereotyped two-word phrases.

So far, so what? would be most readers' reaction. If one assumes that a child has to learn everything from scratch, then surely it would be quite natural and to be expected that he would first learn to use individual significant words and set phrases, and would only later begin to grasp the rules that allow words to be built up into meaningful sequences. You cannot do anything with grammar rules before you have learned at least a small vocabulary; and the rules of grammar are more abstract than the individual nouns and verbs. Quite inevitably grammar will come later than the use of separate words.

Furthermore, once grammar does start to be learned, we would expect the child's sentences to become complicated very fast, because the grammar rules of human languages are 'recursive'. That is, by their nature they apply to their own output, so that a few simple rules yield endlessly complex structures. One simple rule of English says that a preposition such as *in* can form a unit (technically known as a 'prepositional phrase') when followed by a 'noun phrase' such as *the kitchen*: the sequence *in the kitchen* makes sense. Another simple rule says that one way to build up a noun phrase is to modify a noun with a following prepositional phrase: *the crayon in the drawer* makes sense. But just those two short rules give you structured word sequences as long as you care to make them, because a noun phrase can contain a prepositional phrase which contains a noun phrase which contains a prepositional phrase . . . and a child who has mastered the two rules can say things, if he wants to, like *the crayon in the drawer by the door to the kitchen in Granddad's house*. Long utterances by small children are not always long in this repetitive way; but lots of English grammar rules are recursive, not just the pair I have mentioned, so it only needs a few rules to be learned for a wide variety of sentence structures to become available. There is nothing controversial about this way of looking at grammar. As a matter of fact, it is the linguistic nativists who have taken pains to stress the recursive nature of grammar rules, and in this respect at least they are entirely correct.

Bickerton, though, does not agree that there is a natural progression from the 'Get up. Apple.' stage to the 'Let's get a piece of rock and make it go ding' stage. If you look closely at the passage from one to the other, he argues, you do not see anything gradual; you see more of a sudden flip, as when a light is switched on. For child language Bickerton does not really offer concrete evidence to support this, but he goes into more detail in connection with something which he regards as a different instance of essentially the same discontinuity: the difference between *pidgin* and *creole* languages.

Pidgin languages are communication systems that came into being in various parts of the world where adult speakers of different languages needed to talk to one another for work or trade purposes but, for one reason or another, neither group had the time or opportunity to learn the other's language properly. Speakers of pidgins can get quite a lot of information across, but their utterances are said to be grammatically chaotic in ways that no ordinary human language ever is.

A pidgin was used on Hawaii, based on elements of English and of the indigenous Polynesian language, and spoken by immigrants from many parts of East Asia. Bickerton quotes, for instance, a comment by a Japanese immigrant talking about the advisability of building a temple as an act of piety: 'Ifu laik meiki, mo beta *make* time, mani no kaen *hapai*.' (The words in italics are Hawaiian: *make* is pronounced 'mah-keh' and means 'die', whereas 'meiki' is the pidgin pronunciation of English 'make'.) A word-by-word rendering is 'If like make, more better die time, money no can carry.' Bickerton translates it into ordinary English as 'If you want to build (a temple), you should do it just before you die – you can't take it with you!'

By definition, a pidgin is spoken only by people who have other mother tongues, and acquired the use of the pidgin later than early childhood. In some communities, a pidgin is the language which children are exposed to during the years when they are acquiring a mother tongue, so they will grow up speaking a version of that pidgin language as their first language; but a pidgin-spoken-as-a-first-language is not called a pidgin, it is a 'creole'. This sounds like an arcane matter of terminology, but Bickerton says it is much more than that. As soon as a pidgin becomes a creole, it loses its grammatically chaotic nature. A creole language may be unusual in not having a single 'parent' language – it will be a *mélange* of the two or more mother tongues of the people who developed the pidgin; but in other respects creoles are 'ordinary' languages. From the moment they are spoken as anyone's mother tongue, they display all the same kinds of grammatical resources possessed by languages of more respectable ancestry. The transition from pidgin to creole is, in terms of language structure, abrupt rather than gradual – resembling in this respect, according to Bickerton, the transition between the speech of a child up to about 2 years old and the speech of the same child after that age.

Bickerton quotes, as an example of first-generation Hawaiian creole, *They wen go up there early in the morning go plant* – glossed as 'They went up there early in the morning in order to plant (crops)'. One respect in which this is a typically 'creole' rather than 'pidgin' utterance is that it involves a systematic method for marking verb tense. The word *wen* derives from 'went' but has been converted into a past-tense marker that can be prefixed to any verb, including 'go': *wen go* is the creole translation for English 'went'.

The point of stressing discontinuity is that Bickerton wants to persuade us that the kind of speech which precedes the discontinuity – pidgins, and the speech of children before age 2 – is a system in its own right: what he calls *protolanguage*. Protolanguage is not a stage on the way to fully fledged language, any more than a bicycle is something that is going to turn into a car but has not yet been completed. Protolanguage is a separate phenomenon. We inherit an ability to acquire and use protolanguage from our remote ancestors – very remote, because even non-human primates such as Allen and Beatrice Gardner's chimpanzee Washoe can be trained to use a protolanguage-type communication system. From rather less remote ancestors we inherit an ability to acquire and use (ordinary, full) language; but unlike the protolanguage ability, this second ability has the biological characteristic that acquisition is constrained to occur during a critical period of early childhood. Seth at 21 months was thrown back on protolanguage, because his language ability had not yet switched on. The people who create pidgins produce protolanguage systems, because they are past the age when their ability to develop new full languages switched off; but as soon as their children encounter the pidgin at their own critical age they use it as the raw material to create a creole.

After arguing for the separate identity of protolanguage and language systems, Bickerton tells us that it corresponds to a discontinuity in the evolution of mankind. 'The evidence . . . indicates that language could not have developed gradually out of protolanguage, and it suggests that no intermediate form exists. If this is so, then syntax must have emerged in one piece, at one time.' This is likely to have happened as a result of 'an event, presumably a mutation of some kind, that affected a single female living in Africa', probably between 140,000 and 290,000 years ago. That mutation, Bickerton believes, is what created the species *Homo sapiens*, as a new kind of animal utterly different in its abilities and potential from the existing populations of *Homo erectus* and *neanderthalensis*.

For millions of years, hominids had grunted at one another in staccato utterances which would have translated into the equivalent of 21-month-old Seth's 'Get up. Please. Apple'. Then, one particular day, at one particular spot on the savannah, in one particular 2-year-old's head, a light came on. She opened her mouth; and adverbial phrases, relative clauses, sequence of tenses, concord of number and gender, flowed out in an articulate stream of eloquence. Unlike 27-month-old Seth, she made no errors: there were no standards against which her usage could have been judged erroneous. And we are all her many-times-great-grandchildren.

It is a charming story. But, as an account of human prehistory, it embodies some fairly basic misunderstandings of recent genetic research.

In explaining my book title in Chapter 1, I mentioned that 'Adam' would have suggested an inappropriate biblical connotation but that 'Eve' is more closely associated with human origins in a biological sense. The reason for that has to do with genetic material in the bodies of humans and other animals called 'mitochondrial DNA'. The DNA in the nuclei of an individual's body cells is inherited partly from the mother and partly from the father, hence the mixing of genes that occurs generation by generation. But cells also contain structures called mitochondria, which contain DNA of their own; and an animal's mitochondrial DNA, whether the animal is male or female, comes exclusively from its mother, without mixing.

Because of this, mitochondrial DNA permits some kinds of research that are not possible using nuclear DNA. The genetic code sequence in mitochondrial DNA changes only occasionally as generation succeeds generation, through mutations but not through mixing of father's with mother's sequences; so one can use comparisons between the mitochondrial DNA in different individuals to reconstruct remote evolutionary relationships. Where comparison of mitochondrial DNA points to individuals having a common ancestor at some past time, the common ancestor directly indicated must necessarily have been female (even though individuals with a common female ancestor probably also had a common male ancestor at about the same time).

Now it is a mathematical inevitability that some particular individual was the most recent common female ancestor of all living humans, and this individual was probably human herself (if she was a pre-human ape, various of her descendants must independently have evolved into human beings, which is unlikely). She was not necessarily the *first* human being, even if it is meaningful to identify a specific first human; there could have been many previous human generations, if the individual in question happened to be the only female in her generation to have left lines of descendants who survived until now. But, inevitably, this hypothetical common great-grandmother is called 'mitochondrial Eve'.

Just to say that there once was a mitochondrial Eve is not really to say anything – there must have been. But researchers using mitochondrial DNA to reconstruct prehistory think they have found out interesting things about mitochondrial Eve. She may have lived, in Africa, far more recently than the age usually assigned to Man; which implies that modern Man may descend from a biological variety which spread and entirely replaced large, long-established populations of close relatives. (All this is irrelevant to my book title, of course, where I use 'Eve' merely as shorthand for early mankind.)

Even if these latter findings are right (which they may well not be – this is highly controversial stuff), and even if the thing that gave our ancestors the edge of adaptive fitness which led them to eliminate all other hominids was language (which is utterly speculative), and even if language started in one individual rather than in several at about the same time (which would be a reasonable assumption, *if* language is the specific consequence of a biological mutation), none of this gives us any reason to assume that that first language user was female rather than male (or vice versa). Mitochondrial Eve was female, because her identity is defined in a way that requires her to be female; but she was not necessarily the individual in which some significant mutation occurred. The first language user could have been her mother or her great-grandmother; but it could have been her father, or one of her boyfriends, or indeed some man she never met.

So Bickerton's assumption that the first possessor of a 'language gene' must have been female suggests that he may be rather out of his depth when he writes about palaeontology. But, giving him the benefit, let us go back to the question of discontinuity between protolanguage and (true) language. Everything else depends on our accepting that.

## Big true, me no lie

Bickerton argues for this discontinuity by analysing a sample of a conversation in the pidgin language Russenorsk, used between Russian and Norwegian seamen. (Bickerton spells it 'Russo-', but others spell it with an E.) The speakers in the sample are trying to barter Norwegian fish for Russian flour. In word-for-word translation the sample runs:

R: What say? Me no understand.

N: Expensive, Russian – goodbye.

R: Nothing. Four half.

N: Give four, nothing good.

R: No brother. How me sell cheap? Big expensive flour on Russia this year.

N: You no true say.

R: Yes. Big true, me no lie, expensive flour.

N: If you buy – please four pood. If you no buy – then goodbye.

R: No, nothing brother, please throw on deck.

(A pood is a Russian measure of weight; four pood is about ten stone.)

According to Bickerton, the grammar of this dialogue is 'hardly more complex' than that of Seth at 21 months. This sounds surprising: the Russenorsk utterances are far *longer* than 21-month-old Seth's. But Bickerton argues that this is misleading: when sentences are long in a true language, their words group into phrase and clause structures, but in the Russenorsk example 'both words and utterances are simply strung together like beads, rather than assembled according to syntactic principles'.

That seems manifestly false. Judging by the sample, Russenorsk has grammatical rules. Both prepositions and demonstratives precede the nouns they modify (*on Russia, on deck, this year*) – the same rule as in English, and the opposite of the order in Basque or the African language Songhai, for instance. Negation precedes the verb and any modifying adverb (*no understand, no true say*): the same rule as in Chinese, and the opposite of the traditional English rule (*I know not* – modern English uses a more complicated negation rule, giving *I do not know*). The Russenorsk intensifier which Bickerton translates 'big' (on the basis of his own discussion, 'very' might be a more appropriate choice of gloss) precedes what it modifies. The longest sentence in the extract seems to have a reasonably intricate constituent structure:

[ [ big expensive ] [ flour [ on Russia ] [ this year ] ] ]

If Russenorsk words are really just 'strung together like beads', then any permutation would have done as well; for instance, the Russian might have said, 'Expensive on this Russia big year flour.' My guess is that this would have had the Norwegian scratching his head.

Bickerton comments that the 'Big expensive . . . ' sentence, the longest in the sample, contains no verb. From what I know of Russian, I believe I am correct in saying that a direct translation of the Russenorsk sentence into educated, polished, adult-native-speaker's Russian would have no verb. (Russian sentences often lack a verb when English uses 'to be'.) Where verbs do occur, Bickerton mentions that they often omit logically necessary arguments which have to be understood from context; for instance, 'please throw on deck' does not specify what is to be thrown. Has he never encountered sentences such as 'Insert in slot B' or 'Destroy after reading', written by adult English speakers for adult English speakers?

I am not saying that the Russenorsk sample is grammatically as complex and conventionalized as a translation into ordinary English, Russian or Norwegian would be. It seems to have less grammar than an ordinary language; it has a lot more than Seth at 21 months. It is intermediate between these extremes. Where is the discontinuity?

Bickerton apparently supposes that, if Russenorsk has less grammar than an ordinary language, this must be because something in the speakers' brains prevents them from developing more: they cannot deploy their innate language faculty, only their innate protolanguage faculty, in the context of adult development of a pidgin.

But why suppose this, when there is a more obvious explanation? It takes two to tango, and at least two to use a communicative convention. Nothing is achieved by one pidgin speaker incorporating new conventions into his speech, even though they might make his meaning more precise, if his various hearers do not know what the conventions are.

Take a concrete instance. From Bickerton's sample it looks a good guess that Russenorsk lacks definite articles, corresponding to English 'the'. English surely gains in expressive power from the availability of the word 'the', so one could imagine the Norwegian mariner trying to improve Russenorsk by introducing a word for 'the' into it. He would have to choose some particular word and try to get Russians to grasp that it is intended for 'the' rather than, say, 'few' or 'my'; and he would have to guess what grammar for 'the' is most likely to be understood – should it go before the noun, as in English, or after, as in his own language? (Norwegian says e.g. *bord* 'table', *bordet* 'table-the'.) And after all this effort, as it happens he would get nowhere, because Russian has no word for 'the', and Russians find it a difficult word to deal with. On the other hand, if the innovation had worked, what would really have been gained? – these pidgin languages are by definition only a minor part of their speakers' mental lives, the speakers all have 'real' languages of their own, and the word 'the' is not as valuable as all that. (I can find no place in Bickerton's Russenorsk sample where 'the' would add anything.) It takes only a very rudimentary cost-benefit analysis to suggest that trying an innovation like this is not worth the bother.

For creole speakers, on the other hand, the creole is their sole medium of modelling and thinking about the world, so introducing fine logical distinctions into it is as valuable to them as the presence of similar distinctions in English is to us. The creole represented on p. 68 marks past tense with *wen*, for instance, whereas Russenorsk seems to get along without tenses. The balance of advantage is quite different.

This point may be obscured for some readers because it seems to depend on pidgins being spoken less regularly than they sometimes are. Russenorsk may be untypical in being restricted to occasional encounters between ships in Arctic waters; Bickerton does not discuss the point, but I believe there may have been immigrants in pidgin-using communities such as Hawaii who rarely or never spoke to other people except in pidgin, having no social contacts who shared their native language. But that would affect the point only if communication with other people were the sole purpose of language. It is not. This is one issue on which Bickerton does seem to me to be very sound. I agree with his assessment that language 'is not even primarily a means of communication. Rather it is a system of representation, a means for sorting and manipulating the plethora of information that deluges us throughout our waking life.' Knowing English or another 'real language' is all-important even to a Robinson Crusoe. If, when a Man Friday shows up, conversation is limited to the level of 'you catchee fishee, me cookee', then too bad.

## In the beginning was the main clause

Our examination of the Russenorsk example suggested that the alleged discontinuity between protolanguage and language – this 'immense gulf', as Bickerton describes it – shrinks rapidly when contemplated from the protolanguage side: pidgins have an intermediate amount of grammar. Contemplating the gulf from the other side shrinks it further still.

Take another of Bickerton's comments on the Russenorsk sample. He says that the utterance 'Big true, me no lie, expensive flour' translates as three disconnected statements – 'It's absolutely true, I'm not lying, flour is expensive' – while an ordinary language enables the message to be incorporated into a single complex structure in which the later statements are nominal clauses subordinate to what precedes them:

[ I tell you [ (that) it's absolutely true [ that flour is expensive ] ] ]

Bickerton is not quite explicit about whether he thinks two adult native English speakers bargaining with each other by word of mouth would be more likely to say 'I tell you it's absolutely true that flour is expensive' than to say 'It's absolutely true, I'm not lying, flour is expensive'. My own studies of the grammar of real-life spoken English suggest to me that they would not. Natural, unrehearsed spoken language does not make much use of heavily embedded clause structures: they tend to be reserved for writing, which not even the nativists see as a biologically innate form of behaviour.

Perhaps Bickerton just means that an English speaker *could* choose to express the thought via subordinate clauses even if in practice he probably would not: pidgin speakers have no such possibility available even in principle. This is not altogether obvious from the data in Bickerton's book (as one can see above, both his Hawaiian pidgin and Russenorsk examples include 'if' clauses, which are one kind of subordinate clause). But Bickerton knows far more about pidgin languages than he spells out in his book, and it may be that he could make good the claim. Even if he could, though, that does not mean that all languages used natively by adults have always had the full panoply of grammatical resources that are in principle available to a literate speaker of modern English.

This is an area that is very little talked about by linguists nowadays, for a reason which is not far to seek: it risks violating the great social taboo of our day. In the seventeenth century, many old women living alone with a cat for company must have been terrified that someone would take it into his head to accuse them of witchcraft. Professionals in the 1990s are running scared of being accused of racism. They guard their tongues, and indeed their minds, from anything that could be construed as linking inferior and superior capacities with ethnic groupings.

In the area of language there is some virtue in this attitude: earlier in the twentieth century, people often made very ill-informed statements about the languages of technologically backward people having simple, primitive structures. But of course the fact that some views of this sort were mistaken does not mean that others are not well-founded. I think few knowledgeable people would deny that richness of vocabulary is a rough index of a language community's degree of cultural advancement – this is clear in the case of the differently sized colour vocabularies discussed on pp. 61–4, for instance. And the issue of clause subordination to which Bickerton alludes is also highly relevant in this context.

It was a cliché of late nineteenth-century linguistics that the early stages of languages with a long recorded history showed a development from what was called *parataxis* to *hypotaxis*: from a state in which simple expressions followed one another like beads on a string, to a state in which logical relationships were made explicit via subordination of simple expressions into grammatically complex structures. Karl Brugmann, for instance, took it as indisputable that 'Originally people spoke only in sentences having the form of main clauses'. This was not a matter of a priori speculation; the claim was that Homeric Greek and Biblical Hebrew are tangible examples of nearly pure paratactic languages, regularly stringing together elements whose logical relationships would be reflected by subordination in any modern European language. Eduard Hermann wrote an article entitled 'Did Proto-Indo-European have subordinate clauses?'; he concluded that it probably did not. Not everyone agreed; for instance, Hermann Paul argued that hypotaxis had existed from the earliest stages. I am not qualified to adjudicate, but in context Paul's statement reads like an aprioristic refusal to consider concrete evidence cited by others, rather than vice versa.

Present-day linguistic nativists often make remarks such as 'the earliest written documents already display the full expressive variety and grammatical complexity of modern languages' (to quote Ray Jackendoff), but they say little to suggest that they have looked at the facts. Writers such as Walter Ong, who discuss the difference between oral and literate cultures from a different scholarly standpoint, continue to urge that hypotaxis is a product of long-established literacy, and is consequently absent from works which stem from an oral tradition.

Consider the opening words of the Book of Genesis. Ong compared the Douai translation, which remained faithful to the paratactic constructions of the original, with a modern translation which adjusts the language 'to sensibilities shaped more by writing and print'. His point comes out even more clearly if we compare a word-by-word gloss of the original Hebrew with the 1970 New English Bible.

Original:

*B'reshit bara Elohim et hasshamayim w'et haaretz:*
In beginning created God the heavens and the earth:

*w'haaretz hay'ta tohu wabohu w'choshek al-p'ne t'hom*
and the earth was waste and desert and darkness on the face of abyss

*w'ruach Elohim m'rachepet al-p'ne hammayim:*
and wind of God moved on the face of the waters:

New English Bible:

In the beginning of creation, when God made heaven and earth, the earth was without form and void, with darkness over the face of the abyss, and a mighty wind that swept over the surface of the waters.

An adverbial clause (*when God made . . .* ); a verbless *with* clause; a relative clause (*that swept . . .* ) modifying *wind*, which itself becomes subordinate to the *with* construction – all this is grammatically foreign to the original, which consists of a simple, majestic sequence of main clauses. It would be interesting to know whether present-day languages with little tradition of literacy show similar patterns; for the reason already given, this is not a popular topic of research in linguistics departments.

If modern Englishmen make as little use of subordinate clauses in speech as do pidgin speakers, it is open to Bickerton to say that there is nevertheless a difference: an English speaker *can* use richer structures of subordination, and in writing he often does, even if in speaking he typically refrains from exploiting the possibility. Surely, though, no nativist is going to say that the language of Greeks or Jews three thousand years ago included a rich system of hypotaxis, which was not manifest in speech, because nobody uses much hypotaxis in speech, and was not manifest in writing either, because writing had not been invented yet? If there was little or no hypotaxis in these languages, that is a real difference between them and more recent languages.

But note that this difference can have nothing to do with biology. The Greeks and the Jews, not many generations later, produced some of the greatest flowerings of the human spirit that the world has ever seen (including as much hypotaxis as anyone could ask for). If there was a development, in the languages of mature adult speakers, from parataxis to hypotaxis, this must have been a purely cultural development. So, wherever we look, we seem to find smooth transitions bridging over the 'immense gulf' between Bickerton's protolanguage and true language.

And if discontinuity disappears, Bickerton is left without a leg to stand on.

Even if one were willing to accept the idea of discontinuity, there are strange *non sequiturs* in the way Bickerton uses it to reconstruct the early history of our species. He argues at one point that there could well have been a delay of 100,000 to 250,000 years between the time when early Man suddenly acquired the language capacity and the time when this began to have a significant effect on his technology, but at another point he urges that it would not be reasonable to postulate a delay of a million-and-a-half years between the same events. (Both of these claims are needed in order to underpin his arguments about the intellectual relationship between *Homo sapiens* and *Homo erectus*.) If a quarter-of-a-million years is not too long for language to fail to transform technology, why is a million-and-a-half years too long? Bickerton offers no reason at all for regarding one of these figures as more plausible than the other. If the language capacity really did emerge through an overnight genetic saltation, some might think it surprising if there was a delay of one thousand years before technology was radically changed.

But if there is no discontinuity anyway, we need not worry about trying to make sense of this sort of thing. Bickerton gives us no reason to believe that a special one-off change occurred in Seth's mind at some time between 21 and 27 months. Seth just went on learning more English, including some of its recursive grammar rules. And in doing so he recapitulated the process by which our ancestors moved from one-word utterances to the kind of thing I am doing now.

There are other aspects to Bickerton's book. For reasons that are not altogether clear, Bickerton feels it necessary to found his discussion of protolanguage/ language discontinuity on an analysis of logical semantics. Bickerton patronizes Bertrand Russell for Russell's naïve failure to grasp that a personal name such as 'Bill Bailey' must refer to a concept, not to a real person, since otherwise it would be impossible for people to contradict one another by saying, for example, 'Bill Bailey is honest' and 'Bill Bailey is a rascal'. But this does not follow, unless Bickerton assumes that there can be no such thing as a false statement; and, unless Bickerton is using the term 'refer' in some private sense, his statement about what names refer to is just not true – someone who calls Bill Bailey a rascal is not saying that a concept is a rascal, whatever that would mean. I shall be sticking to Bertrand Russell as a guide to philosophical logic.

In his final chapter, Bickerton identifies a problem about Man's intellectual uniqueness. Earth is not likely to be the only planet in the universe on which a language-using species has evolved, he argues, so how come no extra-terrestrials have got in touch to date? Bickerton has an answer. He believes that language may be 'terminally dysfunctional': any species which acquires it thereby acquires, and will inevitably exercise, the ability to destroy its environment, through rash applications of technology.

Gee, could be . . . On the other hand, perhaps there is no life elsewhere; or perhaps there is but it has better things to do than send off messages to the stars; or perhaps they have been sending messages for millennia and we have mistaken them for cowpats; or . . . This stuff must be a real hit with Green students on Hawaii, but I think we shall allow ourselves to leave Bickerton there.

### Hands, tongues and brains

I shall devote fewer pages to Ray Jackendoff's *Patterns in the Mind*, but not because it is poorly written. Jackendoff is one of the best writers among the linguistic nativists, and he is refreshingly lacking in the lawyerly, win-the-argument-at-all-costs attitude found with some of them. But the same evidence and arguments recur in many of these authors (which is no criticism – it would be highly suspicious if they derived their joint conclusions from non-overlapping premisses); quite a lot of the arguments Jackendoff deploys either have already been analysed in Chapter 2, or will be most conveniently taken up in connection with Steven Pinker's *Language Instinct* below.

One topic on which Jackendoff is more informative than other nativist writers is the sign languages of the deaf. This is certainly a fascinating subject, and one where real advances in understanding have been achieved during recent years. Not so long ago, otherwise well-informed people commonly believed that sign language was a matter of *ad hoc* pantomiming, of the kind that two hearing people who are suddenly thrown together while lacking a common tongue might cook up spontaneously for basic communication; or else sign language was taken to be parasitic on spoken languages, with signers using some system of manual equivalents to give a word-by-word representation of sentences in English (or whatever spoken language was used locally).

Since the 1960s it has become clear that these pictures are both completely false. Sign languages are independent systems, as spoken languages are. They are as conventionalized as spoken languages – signers do not just make the system up as they go along – and they have no particular relationship with individual spoken languages. American sign language and British sign language, for instance, are different languages; users of one cannot understand users of the other.

Jackendoff is keen to persuade his readers that American sign language, as a fully fledged linguistic system, is as much under the control of the innate linguistic mechanisms as spoken languages are. For instance, he quotes evidence that proficiency in signing depends on encountering the system by a critical age, as Eric Lenneberg argued for spoken language.

But here Jackendoff is trapped in a dilemma. He is anxious to assure us that sign languages have characteristic features of their own, relating to their special manual medium and not paralleled in spoken languages. The fact that sign languages in different parts of the world share these features, and individual deaf children all grasp them easily – despite the fact that they get no support towards grasping them from the spoken languages of the hearing majority which surround them – creates a case for believing that the features might be elements of innate knowledge. On the other hand, the more 'special' these features are to sign language, the less likely it is that they could be innate: as Jackendoff realizes, it is grossly implausible, biologically, that mankind as a whole would inherit sophisticated intellectual mechanisms which serve a useful purpose only for the tiny minority of people who happen to be born deaf or go deaf at an early age.

So, for instance, Jackendoff discusses how differences in hand movements which represent a verb, with respect to features like location, direction and rate of repetition, express a range of precise distinctions that far exceed what English verbal inflexion can express. (For instance, they indicate whether the action 'takes place at a point in time, over a long period of time, incessantly, repeatedly, or habitually'.) But then, if such distinctions could not be expressed in *any* spoken language, it would be very unlikely that they were an aspect of 'innate knowledge of language'; so Jackendoff hastens to point out that there are some spoken languages which can incorporate far more information into the inflexions of a single verb than English does. In the Onondaga language of the Great Lakes region one word means 'he handed a basket to her', in

Hungarian the word *beadogattathattuk* translates as 'we could make someone hand them in piece by piece'.

Perhaps so; but the stranger the sign-language properties which nevertheless have parallels in some spoken language, the harder it is to argue that we have innate knowledge of language which forces all human languages to be cut to a common pattern. Jackendoff does not seem fully to appreciate the bind he is in here. In one paragraph he stresses that, relative to spoken languages, American sign language makes 'much greater use of simultaneity rather than sequencing' – sounds have to occur along the time dimension, while hand and face gestures can co-occur; but then he turns round and says that 'ASL only takes the possibilities for simultaneity in . . . spoken languages and extends them to a greater degree . . . the abstract principles that organize these degrees of freedom are drawn from the same menu'. It is not at all clear that a specific 'menu' of possibilities covering both sign and spoken languages could have any real substance.

Indeed, Jackendoff has shortly beforehand pointed out that one aspect of American sign language grammar is not paralleled in any spoken language. The sign-language equivalent of third-person pronouns (*she, they, his*) consists of gesturing (with hand shapes and movements that depend on whether the reference is singular, plural or possessive) to locations in 'signing space' which have been assigned to successive topics of conversation. 'The effect is that there are as many different third-person pronouns available as there are discernible locations in signing space.' No spoken language has a pronoun system remotely like this, so how can it be part of our innate knowledge?

Jackendoff is oddly ambivalent, also, about Eric Lenneberg's concept of a biologically determined 'critical period' lasting from about age 2 to age 12 for language acquisition. Jackendoff says that this is often taken to mean 'that language learning ability is switched on before age twelve and then switches off'. Much of the material in Lenneberg's book (notably, the diagrams illustrating 'Factors which limit the acquisition of primary language skills') suggests that that is exactly what Lenneberg did mean. But Jackendoff disagrees: 'What Lenneberg actually proposed – and what subsequent evidence also suggests – is that there is a steady decline in language learning ability.' A light switch turns on at about age 2, but from then on the light gradually dims throughout life, with no special transition at age 12. Jackendoff realizes that many of the data he discusses are not really compatible with the idea of a sudden extinction of our language-learning ability at age 12.

Yet, if the nativists do not claim that the innate mechanisms switch off while people are still young, many of the arguments we have been looking at would never begin to get off the ground. Nativists or not, we all know – alas – that mental functioning gets slower as life goes by. A few pages later, Jackendoff reverts (because he needs it for what he is discussing at that point) to the idea that the light does go off abruptly: 'children hav[e] a specialized piece of their brains that is devoted to constructing a mental grammar. This piece is not only genetically programmed, but even genetically programmed to *turn off*' [Jackendoff's italics].

Which is it to be? Does it turn off, or doesn't it? If the nativists cannot settle that crucial part of their story, they have little basis for persuading the rest of us of anything at all.

Jackendoff believes that our innate knowledge of language extends not just to grammar but to the properties of sounds. Understanding speech, he believes, involves mentally reconstructing successive configurations of a speaker's vocal tract from the inadequate clues provided by the airwaves that reach our ears; this requires that a language-learning child 'already "instinctively" or "intuitively" . . . knows . . . which [sounds] are made with the tip of the tongue and which with the back, and so forth'.

We could debate whether the former genuinely requires the latter, though it may not be necessary: the phonetician John Ohala denies the premiss, arguing in a recent article that 'Speech perception is hearing sounds, not tongues', and even Jackendoff's fellow nativist Steven Pinker believes that babies have to learn how to make speech sounds by experiment. But anyway Jackendoff undercuts his own case as soon as he makes it. He claims that evolution has adapted human beings' perceptions of one another so delicately that we instinctively 'hear' a single blurry sequence of sound-waves as, on the one hand, a series of vocal tract configurations and, separately, as an index of the speaker's emotional state. There is some initial plausibility in the idea that this could have happened; but Jackendoff argues that not only do we do these things, 'We even "instinctively" . . . attribute emotional tone to acoustic events like a rumble of thunder or bird song.' How could that be? There is no old man in the sky who is angry when it thunders. Bird song does not genuinely express carefree pleasure on the bird's part, and whether or not birds are happy has no consequences for human survival. This is not how evolutionary biology works. If Jackendoff reaches for the word 'instinct' so hastily in these cases, how can we trust him to use the word judiciously when there are real questions to be resolved?

That is one of the problems about the nativism of the 'new wave': it is preaching to an audience which in the 1990s is half converted already, so it cuts corners. Hints that nativism might be semi-plausible are offered as if they were cogent demonstrations. Jackendoff has an interesting section on what is currently known about brain functioning – it is now clear that separate areas of the brain serve distinct functions, the brain is not an undifferentiated general purpose device – but in summarizing this he slides within a single paragraph from saying that this modular picture of the brain is 'altogether compatible with' the concept of innate knowledge of language to a claim that the facts 'strongly indicate' that grammar is an organ that grows in the mind, as Chomsky put it. My work commitments over the summer are altogether compatible with my visiting the Olympics and winning the 1500 metres; they do not strongly indicate that I shall do it.

If human beings are born with a rich body of detailed knowledge of language, it is surely true that we would expect to find some identifiable brain module housing or embodying that knowledge. But the fact that the brain has modules does not in itself imply that innate knowledge of language occupies one of them. There are plenty of other cognitive functions for brain modules to serve. Jackendoff has a good discussion of vision, for instance, and there is little doubt that many visual capacities – for instance, our ability to see an elliptical two-dimensional pattern of retinal stimulation as a circular disc at a certain angle to our line of sight – depend heavily on innately built-in neural machinery. Such things are genuinely independent of culture (we do not find Frenchmen seeing the same sight as a different three-dimensional shape); and they are not closely related to conscious reasoning, as language and its structure are.

It is known that (in most people) language functioning is localized in the left brain hemisphere; according to Steven Pinker, it is probable that 'a variety of mental processes requiring sequential co-ordination and arrangement of parts co-reside in the left hemisphere'. Speaking requires a lot of sequencing and arranging of parts, so if mechanisms for doing those things are found in one part of the brain, that is the part which language would need to use. (Susan Curtiss argued that Genie's eventual pattern of intellectual successes and failures could be explained on the assumption that only her right hemisphere functioned.) To call language innate because it uses an innate ability to arrange parts in order would be like calling driving innate because it exploits an inherited ability to grip objects like gearsticks. Jackendoff tries to pin more specifically linguistic functions on particular areas of the left hemisphere, Broca's and Wernicke's areas. Steven Pinker's comment on attempts to make such precise links is 'to be honest, no one really knows what either Broca's area or Wernicke's area is for'.

Sometimes Jackendoff seems so rooted in a nativist mind-set that he overlooks the possibility of learning from experience even when this seems utterly compelling. Discussing the 'paradox' that children grasp the structure of their mother tongue rapidly while scientific descriptions of languages take much effort and time to produce, he asks 'Why can we think more clearly than children about simple things like income taxes and going to the dentist, but not about the organization of language?' We saw in Chapter 2 that comparisons like this are misguided; conscious and 'tacit' knowledge are very different things. Focusing on the first half of Jackendoff's question, though, is it not self-evident that we cannot expect children to think clearly about tax or dentistry because they lack relevant experience? A child is bathed in language. Even an accountant's son will only catch glimpses of the intricacies of income tax.

Jackendoff urges that if we look at young children's language behaviour, we must agree that they are formulating general grammatical rules, not just imitating what they hear – for instance, because they get some of the rules systematically wrong. Three children observed by E.S. Klima and Ursula Bellugi at about 3½ years old were asking questions in the form:

What he can ride in?

Which way they should go?

Why kitty can't stand up?

They had the English rule partly correct, but they had not formulated the part about inverting subject with auxiliary verb. The children did not hear questions like this from their parents, Jackendoff points out, so they must be using a general rule – an incorrect one.

Who doubts it? The child is a little scientist, formulating hypotheses about regularities in his data; like an adult scientist's, his initial hypotheses will often be wrong. (Perhaps it might suggest innate grammar if separate children often converged on the same wrong rule *and this was not an obvious simplification of the correct rule* – but we are offered no evidence of that sort.) Jackendoff points out (I remove italics in quoting his words) that deaf children whose hearing parents develop *ad hoc*, unsystematic habits of signing to them 'construct rules . . . despite the fact that the environmental input is not systematically rule-governed' – they behave like the children Bickerton describes as developing creoles out of pidgins. Why wouldn't they construct rules? An adult scientist will assume there is patterning in his data and try to construct hypotheses to predict it, even if the attempt is ultimately vain. (Gamblers try to find regularities in the behaviour of the roulette wheel even though, at one level, they *know* the wheel is designed with great care to produce no regularities.)

These kinds of evidence do nothing to show that children have knowledge built-in rather than seek it by research. Jackendoff writes well, but it is plain that he has already excluded the empiricist case as a serious contender from page one.

## Sugaring the pill

As I have already said, the star among the new wave of nativists is Steven Pinker. *The Language Instinct* ranks far above other recent or Chomsky-era nativist writings in terms of readability, and it is being more widely read than the other books. In the rest of this chapter we will examine Pinker's case for linguistic nativism, which is many-sided and cleverly constructed.

I should say to start with that I am far from wanting to contradict every point that Pinker makes in his book. Quite a lot of Pinker's material has little or nothing to do with the nativism issue and is not at all controversial, at least not among people versed in the findings of scientific linguistics. It is possible to read *The Language Instinct* as a general survey of the state of contemporary knowledge about human language, and quite a few people seem to be reading it in just that spirit. One chapter, for instance, includes a very readable account of the development of modern English from Middle and Old English and, earlier, from the Germanic branch of the Proto-Indo-European mother tongue – all perfectly correct, and not really related to the innate knowledge issue. And Pinker moves on from this well-worn passage of linguistic history to examine fascinating recent theories according to which Proto-Indo-European and other language families previously thought to be quite separate, including the Hamito-Semitic and Eskimo-Aleut families and the near-isolated language Japanese, might all descend from a single very remote common ancestor,

'Nostratic' – and Nostratic and other superfamilies of languages may in turn be groupable into a tiny number of linguistic super-superfamilies which cover the whole world and which, according to the geneticist Luca Cavalli-Sforza, seem to correlate with the major racial divisions of mankind. These last ideas are highly controversial, but Pinker presents them as such. He describes the theories to the reader for the sake of their intrinsic interest, but he warns the reader that many scholars believe the evidence for them is inadequate.

Pinker makes some excellent points about the irrational nature of many popular attitudes to language. People who bewail the modern corruption of English object to the loss of semantic distinctions when speakers use *disinterested* to mean *uninterested* or *infer* to mean *imply*; and at the same time they object to the influx of novel slang words unsanctified by appearance in the dictionary. But these attitudes are contradictory, as Pinker rightly points out. Slang neologisms, such as e-mail *flaming* or sixth-form *vegging out*, often fill new semantic niches which before had no fully satisfactory expression – if fine semantic distinctions are worth having, then *flame* versus *lose one's temper* is not obviously less valuable than *disinterested* versus *uninterested*. (The corollary, which Pinker does not state, is presumably that both popular attitudes cannot be wrong any more than both can be right. The judicious conclusion, I take it, is that fine distinctions are indeed useful, so we should embrace skilful use of slang, in suitable contexts, and reject *infer* for *imply* even though Milton used *infer* that way in *Paradise Lost*. Since Milton's day, we have developed a worthwhile new distinction that merits being kept up.)

As Pinker says, people who complain that youngsters are carelessly mishandling the wonderful and delicate resources of their mother tongue consistently land their blows on the wrong targets. Slang is not the point. The real problems with bad writing lie elsewhere:

> For example, a banal but universally acknowledged key to good writing is to revise extensively. Good writers go through anywhere from two to twenty drafts before releasing a paper. . . . Imagine a Jeremiah exclaiming, 'Our language today is threatened by an insidious enemy: the youth are not revising their drafts enough times.' Kind of takes the fun out, doesn't it? It's not something that can be blamed on television, rock music, shopping mall culture, overpaid athletes, or any of the other signs of the decay of civilization.

As a university teacher myself I am often staggered at the propensity of the 1990s' undergraduate to hand in written work in the form of a jumble of phrases and clauses which he expects me to assemble into a finished piece of prose before marking it. To this point of Pinker's I can only respond 'Right on!' (I hope I have the slang correct.)

When a book explores as rich a diversity of material as Pinker's, it is inevitable that the author cannot equally master every branch of his subject and will rely in some areas on 'things everyone knows' that are not always true. Pinker is somewhat prone to retail the received unwisdom of academic linguistics. He tells us, for instance, as do the authors of most introductory linguistics textbooks, that languages have rigid rules governing how sounds may and may not be assembled into words: 'any native speaker recognizes that *thale, plaft*, and *flutch* are not English words but could be, whereas [a long list of non-words such as *sram*] are not English words and could not be.' It just is not true that English has fixed rules of this kind, though there are clear statistical propensities to prefer some sound patterns to others. The allegedly 'illegal' consonant cluster of *sram* occurred in the name of the distinguished Anglican liturgist James Herbert Srawley. When I studied linguistics, the dentist father of a fellow student had a patient named Sringer; knowing his son's interest in these matters, the dentist quizzed Mr Sringer about his name – did he think of it as an unusual one? The patient could not understand the point; his name seemed a perfectly ordinary English name to him. Taking other allegedly 'illegal' combinations, in an English shop window I once saw an electric blanket with the trade name *Fnug*, evidently a version of 'snug' with added friendly fuzziness. There is quite a common houseplant called a *vriesia*. And so on.

Even when Pinker seems to misrepresent the realities of language, though, this sometimes helps make his message more palatable. If language is controlled by the genes then, Pinker suggests, we will expect to find that some individuals inherit special propensities for sweet-talking, for wit, for wordiness, and some people will find themselves 'not playing with a full linguistic deck' – he suggests that ex-President George Bush may be one of these unfortunates deprived of their proper complement of language genes, instancing a remark of Bush's that ran as follows:

> I am less interested in what the definition is. You might argue technically, are we in a recession or not. But when there's this kind of sluggishness and concern – definitions, heck with it.

To me this recorded comment seems linguistically impeccable. It makes a reasonable point in a manner which is both clear and in conformity with all the norms of fluent spoken English. (Some of the wording would need to be modified for a written text, but a man who talked 'like a book' in informal conversation really would be linguistically incompetent.) In the academic world of the 1990s, though, it is an understood thing that any weapon will suffice to attack our rulers. The days when university teachers saw themselves as natural partners of the governing class are long gone; nowadays any politician who makes hard choices, and particularly any politician who seeks to control public spending on higher education, is automatically a philistine buffoon. George Bush's comment was fine, but fairness – heck with it; getting in his licks on Bush helps to establish Pinker as a regular guy.

And the fact that Pinker writes about many interesting byways of language that have little to do with the nature/nurture debate, as well as making explicit his *bien pensant* status with regard to politics, lends a lot of extra power to his central message. Pinker's main purpose (as his title suggests) is to persuade the reader that:

Language is not a cultural artifact that we learn the way we learn to tell time or how the federal government works. Instead, it is a distinct piece of the biological makeup of our brains.

It is an admirably clear statement of the nativist manifesto, and all the more persuasive for being argued intermittently in the course of a book which, as a whole, can be read as a general survey of the state of knowledge about all aspects of language.

What is more, as a theorist of nativism Pinker ranks in one important respect well ahead of Noam Chomsky and the other writers we have looked at. He is much more sophisticated than they are about the nature of biological evolution. Pinker has no patience with Chomsky's and Bickerton's arguments that language must have emerged abruptly through a large genetic saltation. Chomsky and other linguists suggest that it must have happened that way, because there would be no survival value for our ancestors in having only bits and pieces of the total panoply of language structure – most of the elements would be useless in isolation. Pinker recognizes this as just one more example of a kind of objection that has been repeatedly levelled against evolutionary explanations ever since Darwin's *Origin of Species*, and which biologists have repeatedly answered without difficulty. Analysing some of the unique and quite remarkable features possessed by the elephant's trunk, Pinker argues that if biologists were elephants they might find it very hard to believe that trunks could possibly have been produced through gradual evolution. No related species has an organ that is at all comparable. Yet in the elephant's trunk case there is no real doubt that Darwinian evolution did the job.

On this issue my sympathies are with Pinker. *If* detailed linguistic knowledge is part of human beings' biological endowment (and if, with virtually every serious observer nowadays, we accept Darwinian evolution as a general explanation of how species have come to be what they are), then there is no good reason to claim that language is a special exceptional instance of biological evolution.

But obviously the prior question is whether linguistic knowledge is part of our biological endowment at all. Here, we shall see that Pinker's arguments are no better founded (though they are often better expressed) than those of other linguistic nativists.

In many cases, naturally enough, Pinker makes his case by quoting arguments we have already considered when they were made by others. It would be redundant to go through those again here. But Pinker has some new variations on old themes; and there are nativist arguments I have deliberately saved to examine now, because Pinker develops them in more persuasive ways than his predecessors.

## Infant prodigies

The central issue for Pinker, as for all the linguistic nativists, is that young children seem just too good at language learning. They learn fast, and without being given the kind of formal training which is quite necessary when the subject to be learned is (say) algebra. We dealt with this type of argument in Chapter 2.

If the speed of children's language learning is caused by knowledge being innate, this ought to lead to testable predictions about which aspects of a language are learned faster than others. We know that not everything is innate, otherwise all human beings would speak exactly the same language. Grammatical structure is claimed to be in large part innate; on the other hand, even Chomsky recognizes that vocabulary differs massively from language to language. Presumably, then, children should acquire the grammar of their mother tongue quickly, but learn new words ploddingly. Yet Pinker stresses that they are fast at learning vocabulary as well as grammar: 'A bit of arithmetic shows that preliterate children . . . must be lexical vacuum cleaners, inhaling a new word every two waking hours, day in, day out', achieving an average vocabulary of about 13,000 words by age 6.

Not all aspects of grammar are claimed to be innate, of course: the innate principles leave some free play, allowing adjectives to follow nouns in French, for instance, while in English they precede. But we succeed in acquiring the grammar of our mother tongue, according to Pinker, only because we know before we start what we ought to be looking out for, in order to fix the local details applying to Universal Grammar.

> The child, constrained by Universal Grammar, knows what to focus on in decoding case and agreement inflections: a noun's inflection might depend on whether it is in subject or object position; a verb's might depend on tense, aspect, and the number, person, and gender of its subject and object. If the hypotheses were not confined to this small set, the task of learning inflections would be intractable – logically speaking, an inflection *could* depend on whether the third word in the sentence referred to a reddish or a bluish object . . . whether the sentence was being uttered indoors or outdoors, and billions of other fruitless possibilities that a grammatically unfettered child would have to test for.

I sort of see what he means. If children were not born knowing that choosing the right verb inflexion can only depend on Pinker's short list of possible relevant variables, they would never finish mastering their mother tongue. It would take too long to check and eliminate endless ridiculous possibilities, such as the variable of whether the person you are talking to has a higher social status than you have, or the variable of whether the previous word happened to be 'and'.

The trouble is, if you innately know that these last two variables cannot be relevant, you will be innately incapable of growing up as a speaker of Japanese or Hebrew, respectively. Implausible as it perhaps sounds to English speakers, these variables are or were central to choice of verb forms in those languages. (By 'Hebrew' I mean Biblical Hebrew; I understand that the rule of *vav consecutiva* by which 'and' converts the interpretation of a following past tense to future tense and vice versa is no longer used in the language of Israel today – but Biblical Hebrew was spoken by 3-year-olds once.) Pinker's list of variables potentially relevant to verb inflexion is too short; and if he tried to enlarge it in response to counterexamples he would just end up with a rag-bag list of variables which happen to matter in one or another of the several thousand languages of the world – if there were more languages, the list would be even longer. I do not know a language which inflects verbs differently indoors and out; but I do not know that there is not one, somewhere. There are aboriginal languages in Australia in which a man has to switch to an entirely separate vocabulary, making more use of derivational rules in order to construct terminology from fewer roots, when in the presence of his mother-in-law.

Children never make mistakes that Pinker says we would expect them to make if they had to learn from scratch. He quotes an unpublished investigation by Karin Stromswold of the speech of thirteen pre-school children, which focused on how far the children were seduced by tempting but false analogies in the use of auxiliary verbs such as *can*, *do*. For instance, one might expect a child to say things like *He cans go*, on the analogy *I like going* : *He likes going* : : *I can go* : *???* Yet for 'virtually all' the patterns tested (the pattern quoted was one of several dozen), Karin Stromswold 'found *no* errors among the 66,000 sentences in which they could have occurred'.

On the other hand, that does not mean that children never make mistakes in learning grammar. Just a few pages later, Pinker tells the story, famous within the profession, of the dogged resistance by the daughter of the psycholinguist Martin Braine to her father's attempts to correct her phrase 'other one spoon' to 'the other spoon'. So what exactly is Pinker saying that Karin Stromswold's data demonstrate? Is he claiming that the young Miss Braine was able to adopt the hypothesis that the placeholder *one* (as in 'I need the other one') may be followed by the noun it stands for, because our innate linguistic knowledge does allow a language to be like that (even though English is not); but that no child could try a hypothesis that a verb such as *can* inflects to agree with its subject, because innate knowledge forbids any language to be like that? No, that can't be it; innate knowledge would have forbidden sixteenth-century English children to speak sixteenth-century English:

I like : thou likest : : I can : thou canst

All we really seem to be able to conclude is that children find some aspects of grammar easier to learn than others, and that it is not always obvious what distinguishes the easy bits from the harder bits.

If one does not begin by ruling out the nature of the child's experience as a legitimate answer to this question, then a good guess is that what makes one aspect of grammar easier to learn than another has something to do with the detailed nature of the speech typically heard by children at different ages – for instance, the frequency with which evidence for various features crops up.

Nativists often resist the idea that this could adequately explain the patterns observed in young children's speech. Derek Bickerton suggested in an early book, *Roots of Language*, that the sort of structural developments which occur when pidgins become creoles (for instance, the creation of a tense system) are observably innate in children who acquire an 'ordinary' first language: these children converge on principles for using adult forms which Bickerton thought it implausible they could infer from the Motherese they hear. But Yasuhiro Shirai and Roger Andersen have shown, via a careful study of relevant mother/child conversations, that Motherese does contain evidence for the principles that Bickerton took to be innate. I do not claim to know exactly what features of English Motherese lead to children getting *he can* right sooner than they get *the other spoon* right; but then, the nativists do not claim to identify the detailed brain structures that embody innate linguistic knowledge. They just say, 'children get this right because it is innate', which is a very easy thing to say.

My references to Motherese might seem to imply that children could not learn to talk unless their mother (or whoever looks after them) gave them careful language lessons. Of course, mothers do not give formal lessons, such as older children get at school for Latin or French (what language would mothers use for teaching?) – though, in the culture I inhabit, it is noticeable that mothers and other adults do speak in special ways to small children; for instance, they enunciate clearly and use a limited vocabulary. But Pinker says that there are many societies in which parents speak very little to their small children, so that the children learn to talk through 'overhearing adults and other children'. Actually, although Pinker repeatedly says that this is a common pattern, his only reference is to Shirley Brice Heath's description of one black community in rural South Carolina, and the picture conjured up by Pinker of children reconstructing a language from overheard scraps is not really what Shirley Heath describes. The main point she makes is that adult members of this community differ from whites in not using special 'baby talk' when speaking to small children, and speak directly to them less overall than is typical of white parents – but the black children do hear plenty of speech, including speech addressed to them by older children, and speech between adults within social groupings in which the children are included. (There is no reason to suppose that the speech the children hear is poor in quality – as Pinker himself points out, casual working-class speech tends to be highly grammatical in its own terms; ungrammatical utterances occur most commonly when middle-class speakers discuss difficult topics.) If there are societies which expose small children only to ordinary adult speech, then an empiricist should presumably predict that the pattern of grammar acquisition by their children will reflect the evidence available in the adult speech they hear, while the pattern in our society will reflect the evidence available in Motherese. Pinker gives us no reason to disbelieve this.

Why do children learn language at an early age, Pinker asks, while 'the rest of the child's mental development seems to proceed at a more leisurely pace'? A 3-year-old who is already a competent English speaker, he says, may still 'be flummoxed by no-brainer tasks like sorting beads in order of size, reasoning whether a person could be aware of an event that took place while the person was out of the room, and knowing that the volume of a liquid does not change when it is poured from a short, wide glass into a tall, narrow one'. Intellectual achievements such as these might also be innately programmed to occur at fixed ages (as the Swiss psychologist Jean Piaget seems to have believed), but why should evolution arrange for grammar to come first? Pinker answers by quoting a suggestion of the biologist George Williams: acquiring language enables a small child to understand a parent's warnings – 'Don't play near the fire', 'Don't tease the sabre-tooth'.

Avoiding fires and dangerous animals is one advantage a child can get from language, and cannot get from an ability to sort beads by size or grasp the conservation of volume. If that advantage is the reason why language precedes bead sorting, it does require language to be innate: genes for early language learning would spread in the population because the bearers of genes for late language learning would sometimes end up burned or inside tigers before they were old enough to reproduce. But that does nothing to strengthen the case for nativism, unless the contrary assumption (that language and bead sorting are learned abilities) permits no explanation for the differential timing. It permits an obvious explanation: differential motivation.

A small child does not know what the noises coming out of adults' mouths are, but he can easily see that they matter a lot to adults, that they look like a key to closer interaction with adults – including one adult with whom he has a relationship perhaps more passionately loving than he will ever have with anyone again: his mother. Where, by contrast, is the motive for learning bead sorting? It has no human significance, it is a skill as abstract as algebra. Pinker believes that utterances like 'Don't play near the fire' must have special importance for small children, because he assumes that language is innate. But utterances like 'Who's Mummy's great big boy, then?' may be just as important, or more so.

We have seen that nativists disagree among themselves about Eric Lenneberg's concept of a critical period for language acquisition. Unlike some nativists, Steven Pinker does recognize that the failure of a wild child like Genie to master language need not be ascribed to her having encountered language after the end of the critical period: the lasting emotional scars caused by such an appalling childhood might adequately explain all sorts of intellectual failures. But Pinker quotes a new case, 'Chelsea', whose parallel failure to acquire language can *only* be explained, Pinker believes, as a consequence of lack of exposure during the critical period, because her childhood was happy.

Chelsea was born deaf in a remote rural community in California; at age 32 she was fitted with hearing aids that gave her near-normal hearing, and she has since received language instruction, but she has not learned to construct meaningful sentences. (Chelsea says things like *The small a the hat*, or *Richard eat peppers hot*.) Yet, Pinker says, she grew up 'emotionally and neurologically normal, sheltered by a loving family'.

This case does sound as though it might offer the nativists more support than the harrowing case of Genie. But any case of this kind is inevitably so complicated that we will naturally want to check some of the details before deciding just how weighty the evidence is. There we are out of luck. To supplement his single paragraph on Chelsea, Pinker quotes only a 1989 article by Susan Curtiss, the scholar who earlier documented the Genie case. Whereas Curtiss wrote a book of almost three hundred pages on Genie, her article contains roughly one page on Chelsea (based on an unpublished talk given by N. Dronkers to the annual meeting of a dyslexia society), and leaves many questions unanswered. It is not clear from Susan Curtiss's remarks how Pinker knows that Chelsea's family was a loving one – Curtiss says nothing about that. More important, neither writer gives any clue about how much time elapsed between Chelsea getting the hearing aids and producing sentences like *Richard eat peppers hot*. All told, it seems reasonable to wait for fuller and better particulars before concluding that Chelsea forces us to transform our fundamental beliefs about human nature.

We saw in Chapter 2 that one reason to doubt the significance of a biologically programmed 'critical period' as an explanation for adults' limited success at learning second languages was that it ignored the highly relevant variable of motivation. A small child lives in a world with close horizons: the adults who take care of him are all-powerful sources of authority and love, and if he is given into the charge of a foreign nanny he will soon pick up her language. Someone who has grown to maturity as a member of one society is unlikely, as an adult, to give wholehearted allegiance to another. But Pinker claims that 'recent evidence is calling these social and motivational explanations into doubt'. The research which nativists usually cite in this connection is a study by Jacqueline Johnson and Elissa Newport of English-language proficiency among Chinese and Korean students and staff at a US university. The subjects' scores were correlated with their age on arrival in the USA, and with attitudinal variables which were measured by asking subjects to rate themselves on a 1 to 5 scale on questions such as 'How strongly would you say you identify with the American culture?' Success in learning English turned out to be predicted far better by age on arrival than by the attitudinal variables.

It is common ground that learning gets slower with age, so one would expect age of initial exposure to correlate with language-learning success. But I am sceptical about the way Johnson and Newport measured 'attitude'. When I consider the issue of successful adult second-language learning, I think for instance of the distinguished academic J.P. Stern, born in 1920, whom I knew when I was an undergraduate. I judged his English to be better than mine, although I am a native speaker and he was a Czech Jew who spoke no English until he was 18 (long after the end of Lenneberg's critical period), learning it partly by listening to the amateur orators at Speaker's Corner. He had escaped to Britain from the Nazi occupation of Prague, which had caused his mother to kill herself, put his sister in a concentration camp, and in effect destroyed the world of his childhood. A catastrophe of this order might lead an adult to embrace a new culture almost as unreservedly as a little child accepts a nanny. When an adult goes abroad for work or educational opportunities, keeping in touch with his home country and knowing that it continues to jog along in his absence, I question whether a comparable emotional reorientation will occur, whatever box is ticked on a researcher's clipboard.

Pinker illustrates his belief that 'there seems to be a cap even for the best adults in the best circumstances' by saying that the actress Meryl Streep sounded less than convincing in film roles that cast her as an Englishwoman or an Australian. Apart from the fact that acquiring a different accent in one's own language is a rather separate issue, Meryl Streep was hardly a hapless refugee cut off for ever from a devastated homeland.

## Language mutants from Essex

So far, Pinker's nativist arguments have done no more than develop points which we have already seen put forward by others. Pinker's trump card, though, is something quite different in kind from the evidence we have inspected so far. It is a startling, concrete, 'human interest' story. It has been causing people who were left cold by Noam Chomsky's writings to think that, after all, there must be something in this idea of innate language knowledge. It concerns the discovery – in England, as it happens – of a family of 'language mutants' (as Pinker calls them).

Pinker is not the first of the linguistic nativists to discuss this family, and he was not responsible for the firsthand research – that was done by Myrna Gopnik, who teaches the theory and history of linguistics at McGill University in Montreal. It was she who initially announced the discovery in a 1990 communication to the journal *Nature*. But Pinker was associated with the research more closely than others who have propounded the nativist case – Myrna Gopnik acknowledges his help in her main published account of the topic, and he chaired the meeting of the American Association for the Advancement of Science in 1992 which led to the 'language mutants' becoming a topic of discussion in general interest newspaper columns and radio shows. Pinker's analysis of the evidence in *The Language Instinct* is the fullest airing the material has received in non-specialist publications.

The case concerns a four-generation family who, for the sake of their privacy, are referred to in the literature as the 'KE' family. They live in Essex. In 1994 the oldest member of the family ('the grandmother') was 75; she had five children and twenty-four grandchildren. (Five of the older grandchildren each had one baby son or daughter, but this fourth generation was too young to be included in the study.) The grandmother, and about half her descendants, suffer from a consistent pattern of disability which affects their language, and specifically their control of grammar. The other half of the family members are linguistically normal. (The grandfather had already died when the KE family were first studied, but he is believed to have been normal.)

It is easy to see the significance. The fact that the disability recurs in generation after generation implies a genetic basis. The alternative possibility, that something special in this family's environment has prevented them from learning to use language normally, apart from its inherent implausibility is excluded by the fact that normal individuals were growing up and living alongside affected individuals: for instance, among the children of the grandmother's second son (who was affected), a daughter of 17 was affected but daughters of 18 and 16 (and a son of 15) were unaffected. Yet the disability concerns a core aspect of human language structure, grammar: the aspect which has been central to Chomsky's and other linguistic nativists' arguments, and an aspect that no empiricist will willingly concede as inherited rather than learned.

There is nothing new in the idea that some humans may suffer from disabilities which relate specifically to language structure – as opposed to more general disabilities that affect language structure among other things. (An example of the latter would be dumbness – in the proper sense, rather than the unpleasant American slang sense of 'stupidity'. Someone who is dumb cannot produce grammatical English utterances, but only as a particular consequence of a general inability to utter speech sounds at all, whether as words in grammatical sequences or otherwise.) The phrase 'specific language impairment' has been used for disabilities that relate to language rather than to anything more general. But there has been real doubt even about whether specific language impairments exist, let alone whether they are trans- mitted genetically.

Laurence Leonard looked, for instance, at children with a pattern of speech problems that has sometimes been interpreted as a specific inability to cope with the phonetic structure of words. He found that these children do not produce unusual kinds of mispronunciation which are not heard from normal children – for instance, they do not substitute very different sounds for target sounds, mispronouncing, say, *goat* as *poat*, nor do they swap sounds round in a word, saying, for instance, *tack* for *cat*. All that happens is that the children affected go through the same stages of learning to master sounds and sound combinations as normal children, but at a later age. For instance, the affected children might say *gock* for *block*, simplifying the *bl-* consonant cluster and making it more similar to the [k] sound at the end of the syllable, or they might eliminate the unstressed syllable of a two-syllable word, saying *buh* for *button*. Normal children mispronounce in these ways, too; only they get beyond these errors around age 2, whereas some of Leonard's subjects were over 3 years old. In later work, Leonard cast doubt on whether any of the syndromes discussed in the literature can usefully be described as 'specific language impairment'. A propensity simply to be slow at learning to speak might not worry an empiricist even if it was genetic (and nothing in Leonard's research implied that the disorders he was looking at were inherited).

The language behaviour of affected members of the KE family, as described by Myrna Gopnik, is nothing like what Leonard described. Their disability is lifelong, rather than a stage that they grow out of (Gopnik describes the KE individuals as developing strategies for dealing with it as they grow older, so that it becomes less obvious to outsiders, but this is different from losing the disability). And the behaviour it causes is very different from the kind of behaviour found with normal people on their way to becoming mature language users.

One example is their production of 'nonsense plurals'. A normal speaker of English can put a noun into the plural without consciously thinking about it. In a small number of cases, the nouns are irregular, and learning English involves learning the plural forms on a case-by-case basis: the plural of *child* is *children*, the plural of *foot* is *feet*. In most cases, we use a general rule. The rule as it applies in speech is slightly obscured by English spelling: in writing, *cat*, *dog* and *horse* each 'add an S', but in speech what is added is different in the three cases – an s sound in *cats*, a z sound in *dogs*, and a separate syllable *ez* in *horses*. The choice depends on the sound at the end of the stem: *horses* has an extra syllable because *horse* itself ends in an s sound. Because the rules are general, normal speakers can apply them without difficulty to 'nonsense nouns'. Shown a picture of an imaginary creature and told 'This is a zoop', then shown a picture of several similar creatures and asked 'These are . . . ?', a normal speaker will say 'Zoops' – no problem.

The KE family members with the inherited disability behave differently. To quote Myrna Gopnik writing jointly with her collaborator Martha Crago:

> One adult subject, when given the first item, paused for a long while repeating it under her breath several times and then whispered to herself 'Add an "s".' For the items *sas* and *zash* instead of adding *ez* she simply prolonged the sibilant – *sasss*. Another subject when given the first item, 'This is a wug. These are __ ?', looked totally confused and laughed nervously and responded, 'How should I know?' After some prompting she said 'These are wug.' To the next item *zat* she responded 'These are zacko.' . . . When she was given the third item *sas* she smiled broadly, shook her head yes [presumably Gopnik and Crago mean that she nodded] and responded *sasez*, which she repeated several times. She then added *ez* to all the rest of the items: *zoop* goes to *zoopez*, *tob* goes to *tobez* and *zash* goes to *zashez*.

(The second subject's answers for *sas* and *zash* were correct – if these were real English words, we would spell them *sass/sasses*, *zash/zashes*; but for *zoop*, *tob*, a normal speaker would give a single-syllable plural.)

As Myrna Gopnik, and Steven Pinker, see it, the problem these people suffer from is inability to master general grammatical rules, at least in specific (and basic) areas of grammar. They may know that *books* is the plural of *book*, and indeed may be able to produce *books* when appropriate: but they know that *books* is the plural of *book* in the way that normal speakers know that *feet* is the plural of *foot*, by learning it as an individual case. Consequently, faced with a word they have heard only in the singular, they have no basis for deciding its plural form. Without a rule, all anyone can do is make a wild guess, such as *zacko* as the plural of *zat*.

Another rule these individuals have difficulty with is the rule relating past and present tenses of verbs. The youngest generation studied were at school age, and for many years they had been attending a special school for language-disordered children: Myrna Gopnik studied some of their exercise books. A 10-year-old wrote, on 12 September 1988:

On Saturday I watch TV and I watch plastic man and I watch football. On Sunday I had pork and potato and cabbage.

The teacher corrected each *watch* to *watched*, and on 17 October he got this word right, writing:

On Saturday I got up and I wash my self and I get dress and I eat my breakfast and I watched TV all day and I went to bed.

The teacher corrected *wash, dress, get, eat* to *washed, dressed, got, ate,* and on 28 November he wrote:

On Saturday I got up and I got dressed and I watched Motormouth . . . and I ate my dinner.

Each individual past form is learned as the teacher provides it, but the individual forms are not extrapolated to a general rule for putting verbs into the past tense.

For a nativist, these are just the kinds of disability one would expect to crop up sooner or later. On discovering the KE family's inability to learn grammatical rules, we are told, Myrna Gopnik 'telephoned Chomsky to tell him the good news'.

Myrna Gopnik herself expresses the difference between the affected KE family members and normal speakers in a form that is more radical than the way I put it above. For her, it is not that they know *books* as the plural of *book* in the manner that a normal speaker knows *feet* as the plural of *foot*; rather, words like *books* are 'simply unanalyzed lexical items that include "numerous" in the specification of their meaning'. *Books* for the affected individuals is a word rather like *library*: it refers to a collection of things, and they are the sort of thing one of which is called a *book*, but there is no more connection than that between the two words.

To say that the affected people could not deal with nonsense plurals at all would be too sweeping. We saw that sometimes one of these individuals would get a form correct; for instance, the second subject in the quoted passage got the plural of *sas* right. What Gopnik and Pinker are saying is that, even when they manage to produce the correct answer, they are not drawing on the innate machinery that allows normal speakers to generate such responses effortlessly and unconsciously. Most nativists do not claim that *all* our intellectual abilities are governed by specific innate mechanisms. For instance, many people can do long division; but they have to be formally taught how to do this, they have to think about what they are doing, and they make mistakes at first. Pinker and Gopnik argue that insofar as affected members of the KE family can cope with nonsense plurals at all, they are deploying a painfully learned conscious

skill akin to long division. Notice how one of Gopnik's subjects said 'Add an
s' to herself – normal speakers do not do things like that when using the basic
grammar of their own language. It is more the type of thing you might hear
a schoolboy mutter when challenged to produce the accusative plural of *mensa*.
Pinker suggests that the KE individuals speak like 'a tourist struggling in a
foreign city' – they behave like people who have tried to master a language
after their 'critical period' had terminated, but for these individuals, with
respect to certain aspects of grammar, the critical period never started.

It is undeniable that there is something odd about the KE family. And there
is little doubt that the deficiency, whatever it is, is genetic. The pattern of
inheritance has been studied by geneticists, and classified as 'autosomally
dominant'. But does the nature of the deficiency truly conflict with the view
that language is learned rather than innate?

After Myrna Gopnik had made the KE family famous, they were studied a
second time by a five-person team led by Faraneh Vargha-Khadem, and
representing the Neurosciences Unit of the Institute of Child Health, the
Department of Psychological Medicine at the Great Ormond Street Hospital,
the University of Oxford Experimental Psychology Department, and the
Department of Linguistic Science of the University of Reading. This team's
report was published in the *Proceedings of the National Academy of Science of the
USA* in January 1995. It concludes that the problem with the KE family is not
really language-specific at all. (Vargha-Khadem and Richard Passingham had
published a preliminary statement pointing out that Myrna Gopnik's
description was misleading, as a reply in *Nature* a few months after her original
communication. Steven Pinker does not refer to this; it is not prosecuting
counsel's job to draw attention to a defendant's solid alibi.)

From reading Myrna Gopnik's main publications on the KE family, it would
be easy to imagine that the affected individuals were perfectly ordinary,
average citizens except that they happened to have this special problem about
certain aspects of grammar. But they have many other problems too. Their
pronunciation is defective (they say things like 'bu' for blue, 'able' for table,
and reduce polysyllables to monosyllables or disyllables), and they find it
difficult to name familiar objects – they tend 'to use approximate words, for
example "glass" or "tea" for cup, and "sky" for star'. In some cases they are
'unintelligible and reluctant to offer spontaneous conversation'. Steven Pinker
tells us that 'Most of the language-impaired family members were average in
intelligence.' I do not know what led Pinker to say that (Myrna Gopnik does
not discuss the issue in the articles I have read); the Vargha-Khadem report
shows that it is far from true.

The thirteen affected family members tested were assigned an average verbal
IQ of 75 (the highest individual score being 91), and an average performance
IQ of 86. On performance, the highest individual score was 111 (by definition,
the average for the population at large is 100); on the other hand, the report
notes that six of the affected individuals – just under half of them – obtained
performance IQ scores below 85. Standardly, scores this low are taken to rule

out a diagnosis of specific language impairment, because performance on all sorts of intellectual tasks can be expected to be impaired.

Myrna Gopnik and Martha Crago had carried out some statistical tests of differential performance by affected and unaffected family members on a wide range of language tasks, and they found that the poor performance of the affected members was specific to particular tasks (such as those relating to noun plurals and verb tenses). The fact that deficits seemed to relate to very particular aspects of language structure was one reason why the KE family looked like impressive evidence for innate control of detailed aspects of language structure. But the Vargha-Khadem report involves fuller and more careful statistical testing, and it concludes that Gopnik and Crago were mistaken. The difference between affected and unaffected individuals applies across the board, to almost all aspects of language ability tested – and to other abilities too.

The Vargha-Khadem team tested the affected individuals on ability to execute parallel and sequential actions of a non-linguistic nature, for instance, opening the mouth, sticking out the tongue, and making a noise (parallel), or closing the lips, then opening the mouth, then sticking out the tongue (sequential). The affected individuals performed significantly less well than normal controls (the difference was particularly large on the sequential tests).

The real killer in the Vargha-Khadem report had to do with verb tenses. Recall that, according to Gopnik, past tenses such as *watched* are verbal atoms for the affected individuals: these people may learn such forms case by case as units, but they cannot generate them by rule. When the Vargha-Khadem team tested the affected individuals on verbs, therefore, it came as an 'unexpected feature' of the results (as their report politely puts it) that many of the errors were overgeneralizations. 'Overgeneralization' in this context means treating an irregular verb as if it were regular – if the tester says 'Every day I bring my sister; yesterday I . . . ?', it would be an overgeneralization to respond 'bringed'. An overgeneralization is a type of error that can *only* be produced by applying a general rule (to a case where it should not be applied). If the KE subjects have no ability to operate with general rules for verb tenses, as Gopnik claimed, then this is one kind of mistake they should be quite safe from making.

Yet almost half (41 per cent, to be precise) of the affected individuals' errors on the verb test were overgeneralizations. (Gopnik and Crago probably failed to see such evidence because they only tested two irregular verbs, *went* and *was*; these are so common that people are likely to get them right even if they make mistakes with other verbs.) As the Vargha-Khadem report dryly remarks, the incidence of overgeneralization 'indicates that [the affected group] know more about the rule for English past tense than was previously claimed'.

Evidently there is some sort of genetic abnormality running through the KE family. It gives those affected low general intelligence; among other things, it damages their ability to execute simple sequences of actions. Language is heavily dependent on the ability to execute complex sequences of actions rapidly and accurately, so there is little wonder that the affected KE family

members have a wide range of problems with language. 'Language mutants',
however, they are not.


## The structure of words

Pinker's language mutants took a bit of answering, though in the end the case
fell apart fairly thoroughly. The other house speciality on Pinker's nativist
menu is much easier to deconstruct.

Pinker's *The Language Instinct* is unique among books on linguistic nativism
for the general reader, so far as I know, in devoting quite a lot of attention to
word construction – the way vocabulary is built up from roots and affixes.
Vocabulary is a very accessible aspect of language, and one reason for Pinker
to write about it is simply that many readers are interested in it. We have seen
that Pinker's book is not single-mindedly concerned with data that relate to
his nativist agenda. But in fact Pinker does claim that word structure offers
additional evidence for nativism. There are regularities in word structure: they
are not widely known (style manuals or books on grammar by people without
expertise in theoretical linguistics often get the facts wrong), yet they are there
if you look for them, and 'children's minds seem to be designed with the logic
of word structure built in'.

To begin with, some terminology. Processes of word formation in English
are classified as *derivational* and *inflexional*. Inflexion is when we add a
grammatical ending to the 'dictionary form' of a word to produce the
appropriate form for a particular grammatical context – putting a noun into
the plural by adding *-s* or putting an adjective into the comparative by adding
*-er* are examples of inflexion. Derivation is when we produce a separate
dictionary entry from a simpler form by adding an affix – for instance, adding
*-ism* to *tour* to give *tourism*, a word which will have its own entry in a
sufficiently large dictionary (whereas the largest dictionary would not list the
plural *tours* as a separate word from the singular *tour*). A *root* is a simple form
having no affixes, either derivational or inflexional (e.g. *tour*, or the root
*commun-* of *communist*). A *stem* is a root with or without one or more
derivational affixes; thus *tourist* is a stem – it can occur as a word without
further affixes, but alternatively it can take an additional derivational affix to
make *touristic*, or an inflexional affix to make *tourists*.

There are patterns in the way affixes can be attached to roots; for Pinker,
these patterns are among the aspects of language structure that we seem
instinctively to know more about, as it were, than we have any right to know.

Pinker diagrams words as having an internal tree structure embodying these
patterns, similar to the tree structures that all linguists use to show the assembly
of words into sentences. His first example of a derivational pattern is the rule
that *-ian*, as in *Darwinian*, can attach only to roots, not to stems that already
include a previous affix. That is why *Darwinismian* 'sounds ridiculous'.

Well, it certainly sounds cumbersome. If it was said, it would mean
'pertaining to Darwinism', and we have a well-established convention in

English of using *X-ist* for 'pertaining to X-ism' – why say *Darwinismian* when one could say *Darwinist*? But to say that *-ian* attaches *only* to roots is a bit sweeping. What about *musician*? A *musician* is someone who has to do with *music*, and *music* is what pertains to the *Muses* – so *-ian* is being added to the suffix *-ic*. Or, if you think it is a bit arcane to quote the relationship between *music* and *Muse*, try *academician* – not such a common word as *musician*, but not a particularly rare word either, and everybody knows that *academic* has to do with *academy*.

Pinker seems to be on stronger ground when he goes on to say that derivational affixes cannot be added to inflected words, so that *Darwinsian* ('pertaining to the two famous Darwins, Charles and Erasmus') is 'quite impossible'. But I wonder. There was recently a film called *Heathers*, about a group of girls all called Heather. If someone wanted to coin a word referring to, say, the style of this film, or to people who make a cult of watching the film, I would not be too surprised to find him coming up with *Heathersian*. OK, it strikes me as barbaric, but so do a lot of other things which are routine in the 1990s.

What is going on here is something rather different in kind from what Pinker imagines. It has to do with culture and history, not with biological instinct. The *-ian* suffix is Latin, and the first words incorporating this suffix that were taken into English were Latin words. Later, many *-ian* words that had not existed in Latin were invented by speakers of English and other modern European languages; but people occupying the sort of social roles that licensed them to coin new words for formal, intellectual use knew Latin themselves, and perceived their task as being to model their coinage on a word that *could* have existed in that language, even though it happened not to. While that was the case, there was no possibility of inventing words that added *-ian* to an inflexional ending such as the plural *-s* – thinking in terms of Latin, it is not even clear what it would mean to construct a word like that.

But things have changed. When I went to university in the 1960s, if I could not show that I had passed a substantial Latin exam my application to enrol would have been rejected out of hand. Now, few British students know any Latin at all. In future, people who produce new vocabulary will not be able to conform to Latin models even if they want to, and we shall see more and more 'barbaric' new words like *Heathersian*. Obviously, this has nothing to do with a change in our genetic endowment. It is a cultural change.

Pinker happens to be writing at a time when the tradition of studying classical languages is sufficiently recent that it continues to be a dominant influence on the shape of our vocabulary (after all, most of the words we use were not coined yesterday), and yet it has become sufficiently obsolete that many readers have no personal feeling for the relationship with Latin models which led to the regularities among English *-ian* words. So Pinker can announce that these regularities stem from unconscious biological instinct, and gullible readers may believe it.

What Pinker says about the *-ian* suffix is not in fact his main argument from word structure to nativism, although I have spent some time on it because it is a good example of how the nativists interpret the most contingent, culture-bound aspects of language as innate. More important for Pinker is what he says about the plurals of 'headless compounds'.

In a compound word such as *keyboard*, normally the last element is the 'head' and any prefixed element modifies that head – thus a keyboard is a sort of board, namely one with keys. Some words are exceptional. For instance, a *redcap*, meaning a military policeman, is not a sort of cap, but a sort of person – one who wears a red cap. As Pinker describes it, *redcap* is 'headless'.

The interesting issue is how we form the plural of a compound, if it ends in an element whose plural is irregular. Provided this element is the head, things are straightforward: we use the irregular plural, so *workman* gives *workmen* (not *workmans*). Pinker gets very graphic about the innate linguistic machinery involved: we have a 'percolation conduit' by which information about meaning, and also about things such as plural formation, 'bubbles up' within the tree representing a word's structure from the head element to the node representing the complete word. But what if the last element of a compound is not its head? With a headless compound, the 'percolation conduit' must be 'blocked', to prevent *redcap* being understood as a kind of cap; and in that case the irregular plural rule is blocked too, so speakers fall back on the general rule and say *sabre-tooths* rather than *sabre-teeth* as the plural of a kind of tiger, *tenderfoots* rather than *tenderfeet* for the plural of novice boy scouts, *still lifes* rather than *still lives* as the plural of a type of painting, and so forth.

When I read this, I found myself questioning whether my percolation conduit worked the same way as Pinker's. Would I say *tenderfoots* or *tenderfeet*? I was never in the Scouts, so the question had not arisen for me before. Would I say *still lifes*, or *still lives*? I was not at all sure.

The more you ask yourself what you would say in a case like this, the more confused you get. If you want the answer to be one thing rather than another (because it will suit your theory), the chances are you will find yourself deciding that is what the answer is. Responsible linguistics scholars, in a situation like this, do not ask themselves what they *would* say: they check what other people *have* said or written when using the language in natural, real-life situations rather than responding to linguistic research questionnaires. They search for examples in a corpus, which is the term used for a large collection of computer-readable samples of a language.

I did a quick search for plurals of *-foot* words in the Brown and LOB Corpora, which are standard million-word samples of real-life written American and British English, respectively. There were not many instances (two million words is not a lot for this purpose), but two relevant forms occurred. One writer made repeated references to members of the Blackfoot tribe of American Indians: he consistently called them *Blackfeet*. Another passage concerned various species of geese, including one called the pinkfoot; multiple geese of this species were consistently called *pinkfeet*. Note that neither a Blackfoot nor a pinkfoot is a kind of foot.

Conversely, the number of words ending in *-foots* was zero. (I ignore here the verbal use, as in 'he foots the bill', which is beside the point.) Pleasingly, in case any nativist is inclined to blame substandard British percolation conduits, the two -*feet* examples came from the two corpora: *pinkfeet* occurred in British writing, *Blackfeet* in American.

I do not doubt that Pinker consistently says *tenderfoots, sabre-tooths* and *still lifes*. (As a matter of fact I believe I would say *sabre-tooths* rather than *sabre-teeth* myself, though I think I would probably say *tenderfeet*, if I just talked without reflecting on the linguistics of what I was saying – I shall never know now, because if I ever have occasion to use that word I shall remember this debate.) But that is the point. 'Headless' words are somewhat different from the general run of compounds, and plurals of headless words with irregular final roots are not things for which one is constantly encountering models in others' speech. As a result, some speakers react to their special status by pluralizing them in a special way, others do not, and still others possibly do this for some headless compounds but not for the rest, or pluralize the same word inconsistently on different occasions. We have not got innate machinery forcing all of us to treat headless compounds in the same fixed fashion.

Pinker describes an experiment by the psycholinguist Peter Gordon which aimed to show that children are innately aware of a related constraint on word formation, namely that 'compounds can be formed out of irregular plurals but not out of regular plurals. For example, a house infested with mice can be described as *mice-infested,* but it sounds awkward to describe a house infested with rats as *rats-infested.*' Again, though, the alleged constraint is not a constraint. Stig Johansson has written a whole book on compounds found in real-life English that are formed from plurals, most of which are regular plurals. An example from the LOB Corpus is *fares-cutting,* as in *the smaller European carriers, who have in the past been strong opponents of fares-cutting airlines.* Whatever Peter Gordon's experiment was probing, it cannot have been an innately fixed principle of language. Johansson does find that these compounds tend to be more acceptable to British than to American speakers, which might help to explain Gordon's error; but a finding like this simply underlines the point that we are dealing with a cultural, not a biological issue.

## Mentalese

An issue which Pinker discusses near the beginning of his book but I have deferred towards the end of this chapter, because it strikes me as one of the less interesting elements of the nativist structure of ideas, is the concept of a universal Mentalese language. The suggestion here is that all humans are born knowing one specific language, Mentalese, the same for people everywhere; learning the spoken language of one's society is learning a way to translate between that language and Mentalese.

One reason why this is not a very interesting suggestion is that it converts the nativist manifesto from an empirical, testable theory about how humans function into a purported necessary truth, like 'Nothing can be both red and green all over'. In order to decide whether this last statement is true, you do not go out checking all the coloured objects you can lay your hands on, you just sit in your armchair reflecting on what words like 'red' and 'all over' mean. To concede that we are born knowing an internal Mentalese language, and that learning English or Vietnamese is learning to translate between them and Mentalese, means conceding that we are born with a 'language instinct' in spades. But, according to Pinker, 'if babies did not have a mentalese to translate to and from English, it is not clear how learning English could take place, or even what learning English would mean.' Pinker implies that the reality of Mentalese is as much a matter of conceptual analysis as the impossibility of something being two colours at once.

If Pinker truly believes that, why would he spend 400 pages and more discussing word structure, speech perception, language mutants, aphasia, and all sorts of other *evidence* that is supposed to demonstrate that we have a language instinct? If someone doubts the truth of the statement 'Either there are elephants in Ethiopia or there are not', you would not waste money on airline tickets and tropical clothing in order to go and gather evidence; you would sit him down for a quiet chat about *either* and *not*. (If that did not settle the matter, how would a visit to Ethiopia help?) By marshalling a large and impressive array of empirical observations in support of the language instinct theory, Pinker is in effect admitting that he actually believes it is an empirical theory – one that has to be checked against the facts, not one that can be accepted or rejected just by thinking about what it means.

Pinker is right: linguistic nativism is an empirical claim. I disagree with it, but not because it does not make sense. Logically, it is perfectly possible that human beings could be born with detailed instructions in their genetic code for building and using a language, just as we certainly are born with detailed instructions for building and using hands and eyes. Linguistic nativism is a reasonable idea, it just happens to be wrong. The facts quoted in support of it either do not support it, or are not facts, or are not facts and would not support it even if they were.

There is a nugget of sense lying behind Pinker's argument for Mentalese. Using a computer analogy, Pinker makes the point that we use language to reason with, but it is not plausible that our internal mental representation of statements, which we use in order to draw inferences and reason in other modes, will map in a simple element-by-element fashion into the words with which we express those statements in speech. If we are told that a pipe has burst in the loft and we start talking about how to deal with the burst pipe, it does not seem likely that our reasoning machinery will contain little bits representing 'a' and 'the'. It is more likely that *a burst pipe* will create some new element within a mental model of the house, and *the burst pipe* will manipulate that element somehow after it has been created. (Pinker and I are both talking in the dark here: nobody really has the least idea what is physically going on in the head when we reason, but I agree that whatever goes on is likely to relate in a fairly abstract way to the words of spoken utterances, which are adapted to the necessary linearity of speech and to the fact that speaker and hearer are working with separate models of reality.) It might perhaps be harmless to use the term 'English mentalese' to indicate the hypothetical activities in an English speaker's mental models which are triggered by and which lead to the production of English utterances – though the phrase seems to carry an implication that we know more about this than we do. But Pinker slides in successive sentences from the suggestion that spoken languages have mentalese counterparts to the claim that 'it is likely that they are the same: a universal mentalese'. That is merely assuming what the bulk of his book purports to prove.

I began my discussion of Steven Pinker's book by describing his view of evolutionary biology as more sophisticated than that of earlier nativists. But even there Pinker seems to have fallen prey to the wackiness which infects this corner of the map of scholarship. If human beings *were* all born knowing a single, universal Mentalese language, one might wonder why separate human communities would have developed separate spoken languages. Because he thinks language is mainly innate, for Pinker it is a problem to understand why evolution has not made it wholly innate – how come biology has left the leeway which allowed mankind to develop the minor differences between local dialects that we call English, Vietnamese, Xhosa, and so forth? He has an answer: it was to help us to communicate with one another.

Genomes 'mutate and drift and recombine' when people have children, so:

> Rather than selecting for a completely innate grammar, which would soon fall out of register with everyone else's, evolution may have given children an ability to learn the variable parts of language as a way of synchronizing their grammars with that of the community.

*Huh?* We would be able to communicate quite well if everyone in the world were born with the full range of tacit knowledge needed to speak Scots Gaelic. If communication is as beneficial for survival as Pinker assumes, then any mutation arising in this situation which prevented its bearer from communicating with Gaelic speakers would not spread.

Pinker recognizes that we learn some things, and he recognizes that there can be advantages in the flexibility of learning over the rigidity of innate knowledge. It is fascinating to see the logical gymnastics he goes through to avoid recognizing that languages are learned systems, after getting this close.

## What makes empiricists run

The last few years have seen startling new findings emerge about genetic control of human behaviour. The most remarkable evidence has come from a group at the University of Minnesota who study pairs of identical twins who were reared separately from birth or from early childhood. Identical twins share the same biological inheritance; if they resemble one another in ways that cannot plausibly be attributed to similarities of environment, the only alternative is to suppose that these resemblances are determined by their genes.

It surprises no one that identical twins look alike – we know that anatomy is genetically controlled; and we have known for decades (though some have sought to deny it) that there is a strong factor of heritability in the broad mental feature of intelligence level. The Minnesota team, though, have been finding that behavioural resemblances between separately reared identical twins go far beyond this, to include quirks that no one (if they thought about it at all) would have imagined were inherited. Jerome Burne lists 'such curiously specific things as: being brilliant storytellers, refusing to express controversial opinions, being habitual gigglers, and always wearing seven rings. There was even a pair who always entered the sea backwards and then only to their knees'.

And if behaviour at this level of detail is genetically determined, one would expect to find some detailed patterns of behaviour common to all members of our species, in the same way as much of the detail of our anatomical structure is species-universal, despite individual variation which allows us to recognize our acquaintances. The anthropologist Donald Brown has surveyed ethno-graphic descriptions of the different societies of the world and found that behind the superficial differences there are indeed abundant universal features, from gossip through the use of smiles as a friendly greeting to division of labour by sex and age. I do not doubt that Brown is right to claim that these and many other things are universal, and I expect he is right that at least some of them are universal because genes make people behave in that way (some of them might be parallel responses to common environmental challenges and opportunities).

As Steven Pinker sees it, someone who recognizes genetic control of behaviour in cases like these has little reason to deny the nativist case for language: why admit the role of genes in some areas and resist it in others? But he, and many other linguistic nativists, seem to have little understanding of what makes empiricists run.

Nobody suggests that a person's nature is entirely independent of biology; the idea would be ridiculous. We have always known that our anatomy is almost wholly determined by inheritance. I have never heard of anyone disputing that our urge to eat when our stomachs are empty is built in, not a habit we develop or are taught by parents because it has turned out to work for them. But to many of us there is a clear contrast between features of a human being that seem obviously fixed by inheritance, and features that seem obviously under a person's conscious control, so that resemblance between individuals must be a matter of cultural convention rather than biology. The apparent contrast is a spectrum with two ends – many things are intermediate. But anatomical structure seems to be right over at the biology end of the spectrum; and things to do with thinking, belief, and hence language seem to be right over at the culture end. Moreover, those things which appear to be furthest towards the culture end of the spectrum are things which are central to human beings' sense of self-worth. It matters to us that our ideas and opinions are our own creations – that we choose what to accept and what to reject of our cultural inheritance, and that mentally speaking we are not mere slaves to our biology.

The exact status of various items in the middle of the spectrum is interesting, but less crucial for our general assessment of the nature of Man. Notice that to describe some property of a person as falling in the middle of the spectrum is not just to say that we do not know whether it is biological or cultural: many things are genuinely intermediate. Even a feature that seems most completely biologically determined, say, the possession of two legs, is affected by the environment also. Military or other dangerous circumstances cause some unfortunate individuals to live parts of their lives with one leg, or none. Cooking style might be a good instance of something intermediate on the spectrum: biology gives us a need to take in certain quantities of protein, carbohydrate and various vitamins, but personal choice or cultural co-ordination of many individuals' choices lead to meat being served in slices rather than Chinese-style bite-sized chunks, say.

The Minnesota twins findings come as a surprise, because they show that features which most of us probably took to fall towards the culture end of the spectrum must in fact fall much further towards the biology end. That is unexpected, and interesting in an abstract, scientific sense; but it does not affect things which empiricists have a serious investment in retaining at the culture end. We all have tastes and habits that we have not consciously chosen or cultivated. I do not walk into the sea backwards; but I like the colour yellow and the taste of apples, music does little for me, and I am told I have a habit of pushing my hair back when thinking. In the past, if I had asked myself the question I would probably have supposed that such matters are consequences of things like chance associations in early childhood. Since reading the Minnesota findings, I now guess it is more likely that they are somehow implied by the code sequence in my individual genome; but frankly, my dear, I don't give a damn.

On the other hand, if you tell me that my genes are determining what I believe or how I think, I give a lot of damns. I do not find this either intuitively plausible or at all congenial; if someone tells me that I should believe it, I want to be shown very solid evidence. As we have seen, this is not forthcoming.

That is not to say that some items apparently far along to the cultural end of the spectrum may not involve a measure of biological influence (just as two-leggedness, though largely determined by biology, also has an environmental aspect). It would leave me unmoved to learn, for instance, that biology imposed a degree of sound symbolism on the words a language uses for particular concepts. Pinker believes that it does. He says that 'words that connote me-here-now tend to have higher and fronter vowels than [words] that connote distance from "me": *me* versus *you*, *here* versus *there*, *this* versus *that*', and that words for little things have high front vowels while words for big things have low back vowels: 'English speakers correctly guess that in Chinese *ch'ing* means light and *chung* means heavy.' There is no reason why an empiricist should feel threatened by such facts, if they were true.

But I do not believe that they are. The English words *big* and *small* are the wrong way round; in Chinese 'I' is *wo* and 'you' is *ni*, wrong again. Pinker takes his facts on sound symbolism in the world's languages from a 1958 book by Roger Brown, but Brown's findings do not justify the claims Pinker makes. In the abstract, people do fairly consistently make the same linkages as one another between vowel sounds and concepts like size, but vocabulary in real languages does not conform to those linkages. In the area of human language, in my experience, biology usually leaves it to individual decision and cultural convention to settle even those choices which an empiricist would happily allow biology to pre-empt.

### The Standard Social Science Model

Perhaps some readers have found my remarks on the faith of an empiricist out of place in a book which aims to establish the scientific truth about an important aspect of human life, not to discuss what we might like to be true. But I am not too apologetic, because one of the most enlightening aspects of Pinker's book – it helps to explain not only why he says some of the things he does, but also why other nativists rush to embrace seemingly illogical and unattractive viewpoints – is his discussion of why the nativists want to believe in innate knowledge. Pinker sees nativism as the only alternative to what he calls the 'Standard Social Science Model', or SSSM.

The Standard Social Science Model, as Pinker describes it, is an ideology based on the 'straw man' account of the human mind which we looked at in Chapter 1 – the idea that the mind is like a passive camera film, not only lacking initial content but not possessing the ability to formulate spontaneous conjectures in order to make sense of its environment. According to Pinker, this Standard Social Science Model has dominated intellectual life since the 1920s – it is 'the secular ideology of our age'; 'in the rhetoric of the educated, the SSSM has attained total victory.'

Has it? When Pinker makes statements like these, I am not sure whether he is writing specifically about the USA or more generally. I cannot answer for the USA, but for Britain – a culture closer to North America than most, on a world scale – the claim is completely untenable. It was a cliché of intellectual life for most of this century that education (as its etymology suggests) is about drawing out what is naturally in a young person, as much as about instilling facts – the view that young people are empty buckets to be filled with 'training' has gained currency only in the 1990s. The 1944 Education Act, whatever one may say about its implementation in practice, was explicitly based on a philosophy that children have their own natural bents and need diverse provision; and the same idea had occurred in the 1926 Hadow Report on education. It remains the view of the present Prime Minister. In a *Times* interview of 25 July 1996 John Major said:

> I am speaking of a straightforward matter of common sense . . . If you look at children around this country, there is an infinite variety and they are all individuals. They have different talents and needs; they seek different

opportunities . . . We should have an educational system which is as diverse and original as the children for whom it caters.

John Major was speaking in a context of disagreement with the 'comprehensive' education policy of the 1960s and 1970s, but one could hardly claim that that policy, either, was based on anything similar to Pinker's Standard Social Science Model. I do not believe there has been any time from the 1920s until now when Britons would not have agreed that John Major's view is plain common sense. (Whether they trust a particular party's education policy to deliver is a separate issue, obviously.)

True, there have been social developments which do harmonize with the Standard Social Science Model. Perhaps the most notable is the movement to erase the difference between the social roles of the sexes, after thousands of years when it was taken for granted that such a difference is natural. But that movement began in the late 1960s and has been influential only in the last decade or so – as it happens, just the period when nativist philosophy has been overturning the long reign of empiricist thought. This is opposite to the pattern predicted, if the Women's Movement were a response to trends in thinking about the nature of mind. In reality it is a political movement concerned with the distribution of money and power; highflown philosophical considerations never came into it, that I could see.

The leading names that Pinker associates with his Standard Social Science Model are Chomsky's antagonist B.F. Skinner, together with J.B. Watson and the anthropologist Margaret Mead. To identify these people as responsible for the general tone of intellectual life for seventy years seems comical. I wonder whether Pinker does not himself sense that these names are unsuitable to bear the weight he lays on them. In the world I inhabit, cultured people can be assumed to know of Plato, René Descartes, John Locke, Karl Popper, and to be able to give at least sketchy hints at their respective master ideas. The people quoted by Pinker, with due respect, are hardly in this league.

Quite a lot of people nowadays have heard of B.F. Skinner, as a professor of the science of mind who did not believe in minds. They have heard of him for one reason and one reason only: his role as a target of Noam Chomsky's venom. Every paperback which sets out to explain Chomsky to the general reader includes a description of Skinner's theories, in order to explain that Chomsky said they were wrong; you would look a long way to find someone who has read Skinner's own writings. J.B. Watson is an unknown name except to professional academic psychologists. Margaret Mead is a little better known. Her reputation derives from a description of the society of Samoa, based on nine months' stay in her early twenties, with no previous knowledge of the Samoan language, as a guest of a white family resident on a Samoan island. The description has subsequently turned out to be not just over-romanticized, but a preposterous travesty of the truth about Samoan life.

Can these people really have exerted the influence in North America which Pinker ascribes to them? I would not know; but even if they did, there is no call for the rest of us to intrude on private American grief.

The Standard Social Science Model, as Pinker describes it, is an empiricist view of human nature, but an appallingly crude version of empiricism – not a version that any serious thinker is likely to defend. To react against it by swinging to the opposite extreme and claiming that most of the contents of our minds are built in by biology is itself a crude response, arguing a lack of intellectual suppleness.

The deficiencies of the so-called Standard Social Science Model of mankind are no reason to embrace nativism, since far more reasonable versions of empiricism have long been available and widely held. The nativists are of course free to advocate their point of view for its own sake, independently of the Standard Social Science Model. But what does their advocacy amount to? Apart from the special issue of linguistic universals (to be taken up in Chapter 4), we have now examined the entire range of evidence and arguments deployed in the linguistic nativists' leading works – at least, if there are any further significant points, I have not spotted them. I have attempted in good faith to be thorough. Does this skein of *non sequiturs* and false premisses truly oblige us to see mankind through new eyes?

# 4  Language Structure Turns Queen's Evidence

## Words grow on trees

The one aspect of the nativist case that we have not yet looked at systematically is the argument from language universals. I have kept the best to last. The universal features of human languages do not just fail to support nativism: they show that the converse, empiricist view of human nature is correct.

I introduced the concept of 'language universals' as one of the strands of Noam Chomsky's nativist case (see Chapter 2, subsection 5). That in itself is controversial. Quoting a statement by me that 'Chomsky infers innateness from universality', David Lightfoot (a particularly close associate of Chomsky's) has responded bluntly, 'This is false.' According to Lightfoot, Chomsky's nativism is based solely on 'poverty of the stimulus' arguments (subsection 3) and not on language universals.

If Lightfoot were right about that, the present book could be shorter; I have disposed of 3 already. But it is hard to understand how he can maintain such a position, in view of passages in Chomsky's writings such as those I quoted under 5. When Chomsky claimed in 1975 that 'An innatist hypothesis is a refutable hypothesis', he supported the claim exclusively by discussing refutation in terms of violation of language universals. In an earlier book, Chomsky wrote:

> A theory of linguistic structure that aims for explanatory adequacy incorporates an account of linguistic universals, and it attributes tacit knowledge of these universals to the child . . . Language learning would be impossible unless this were the case.

> Real progress in linguistics consists in the discovery that certain features of given languages can be reduced to universal properties of language . . .

The bulk of empirical research in linguistic theory triggered off by that book, during the thirty years since it was written, has been concerned with refining theories about language universals. Perhaps David Lightfoot felt he could not be too choosy in the means he used to fend off awkward criticism.

To my mind, any interpretation of Chomsky's work which plays down his argument from universals does Chomsky little service. His other arguments dissolve in a cloud of illogic more or less immediately they are soberly scrutinized. The argument from universals is the only one of his arguments that has some serious prima facie force. If all human languages that have been examined turn out to share certain properties which are not mere defining properties of the notion 'language' – if systems are not required to have these properties in order to be counted as languages, yet all human languages do have them nevertheless – then we are obliged to offer some explanation for the universal properties (unless we are willing to postulate a massive coincidence). If no other explanation is available, then explaining them as genetically determined could be a quite reasonable thing to do.

But of course that depends on there being no other satisfactory explanation. I believe Chomsky is perfectly correct in claiming that human languages all share significant structural properties. However, we shall see that there is a very different explanation available for these properties, which accounts for the facts much better than the hypothesis of innate language knowledge would account for them.

When I say that Chomsky is correct in asserting the existence of language universals, that does not mean that all the properties which he or other nativists have claimed to be universal actually are so. Once it became fashionable to believe that biology controls the detailed structure of human languages, one began to find scholars spotting that a few languages they happened to know coincided on some particular structural point and hypothesizing that this must be a language universal, apparently taking very little care to check whether the coincidence did in fact hold good for further languages. Karl Popper enjoined scientists to make risky conjectures; but there is nothing praiseworthy about publishing conjectures when refuting data are already easily available, and scientists are supposed to take the conjectural status of their hypotheses seriously, continuing to search for counterexamples even if none appear at first. Nativists have often made authoritative-sounding claims about language universals when it is clear that the claims could not have survived a minimal attempt to check for counter-evidence.

Chomsky has done this himself. For instance, he makes various statements that seem indefensible about universal restrictions on the meanings of words. He suggests that 'proper names, in any language, must designate objects meeting a condition of spatiotemporal contiguity', and so must 'other terms designating objects'; likewise there are conditions 'that the color words of any language must subdivide the color spectrum into continuous segments', and that 'artifacts are defined in terms of certain human goals, needs, and functions instead of solely in terms of physical qualities'. Chomsky stresses that these are not tautological, self-evident truths but substantial empirical findings:

> there are no logical grounds for the apparent nonexistence in natural languages of words such as 'LIMB,' similar to 'limb' except that it designates the single object consisting of a dog's four legs, so that 'its LIMB is brown'

(like 'its head is brown') would mean that the object consisting of the four legs is brown.

But Chomsky's suggestions are not merely not self-evident truths. They are false – obviously so, in some cases. *Cassiopeia*, or any other name of a constellation, is a proper name which refers to a set of objects about as distant from one another as any things that most people know about; even the apparent adjacency relative to other stars is an illusion depending on the angle at which we happen to see them from the Earth. I do not know of a language which uses a singular noun for the four legs of a dog, but quite a close match is the French word *rouage*, denoting the singular object comprising the wheels of a vehicle. The noun *hardware* denotes a range of artefacts defined by reference to their physical qualities rather than the human 'goals, needs, and functions' they serve, which are extremely diverse. The point about colour terminology sounds too predictable to constitute weighty support for nativism, but according to Noriko McNeill even this is in fact untrue; for instance, some languages use one word for both blue and yellow, and another word for both red and green.

Chomsky once tried in correspondence to answer my point about French *rouage*, saying that it is not a true counterexample because it does not designate 'a scattered object in . . . the sense of the calculus of individuals. Thus, the left half of the front wheel and the middle of the back wheel do not constitute a part of the "rouage".' I could not see the force of this reply. In the first place, in suitable circumstances (that is, if there were any reason to do so) I should have thought Chomsky's pair of wheel segments *would* be counted as part of the *rouage* – I can imagine talking about them as 'the rusty part of the *rouage*', if just those segments were rusty. (Admittedly I, like Chomsky, am not a native speaker of French.) Perhaps more important, Chomsky's published claim did not say anything about 'the calculus of individuals'. He predicted that no language would have a word like 'LIMB' – not that there are limits on what would count as part of a 'LIMB' in languages containing such a word. Many nativists have proposed isolated, individual examples of language universals, such as these of Chomsky's; but proposals of this kind are not very impressive. As Gerald Gazdar and co-authors put it,

> The penalty for failure of such a universal is effectively zero; a new universal saying something carefully hedged to avoid the last known counterexample can be constructed in a moment.

However, there is a coherent 'hard core' of universal truths about grammar in human languages which escapes this sort of criticism. It is not a mere list of disconnected features which might individually be dropped and replaced with new features as fast as counterexamples are spotted. It relates to a system of general organizing principles which control the entire grammatical structure of a language, so that the system stands or falls as a whole. Like any scientific theory, this system makes a statement about human languages which is in principle refutable; but if our current understanding proves to be mistaken this will surely be because it is replaced by a superior but closely related account, as Newton's physics was replaced by Einstein's – it seems almost inconceivable that future observations could lead us just to abandon the theory without replacement.

The hard core universals have to do with the central role of *tree structure* in grammar. Words are organized into sentences by rules which group them into units of different sizes – 'phrases' and 'clauses' – which nest inside one another, so that sentence structure can be diagrammed by bracketing off word sequences, or by drawing trees:

[ [ *To mourn* [ *a mischief* [ *that is* [ *past and gone* ] ] ] ] *is* [ *the next way* [ *to draw* [ *new mischief* ] *on* ] ] ]

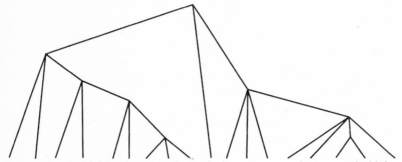

To mourn a mischief that is past and gone is the next way to draw new mischief on

(These alternative ways of depicting grammatical structure are completely equivalent; trees are easier for most people to grasp visually, bracketing is easier to print.)

Sentences have tree structures, and rules of grammar that modify elements of a sentence are always 'structure-dependent', as we saw in Chapter 2: their correct application depends on the tree structure. It is probably not too likely that anyone would ever want to convert the Doge's statement into a question, but if someone did, he would have to shift to the front the verb which is directly attached to the root node – the word *is* at the bottom of the long branch in the middle of the tree:

*Is to mourn a mischief that is past and gone the next way to draw new mischief on?*

It would not do to move the *is* that is located at the bottom of a shorter branch, after the word *that*:

*\*Is to mourn a mischief that past and gone is the next way to draw new mischief on?*

Provided that one expresses it informally rather than technically, this idea about tree structure being at the heart of grammar is not at all new.

Schoolchildren have been taught to map out the structures of sentences using tree-like notation for at least a hundred years, probably longer. It might seem that to say sentences have tree structures is not really to say anything substantial – the only physical reality is a linear string of words; we just choose to impose tree structures on the strings. That is not so. It is perfectly possible, as an abstract exercise, to invent artificial languages with grammars that have nothing to do with tree structure. That is to say, in such a language there are definite rules for assembling words into sentences, so that one could say whether or not any given string of words is a grammatical sequence in the language; but the rules do not imply any grouping of the words into phrases and clauses. It is an empirical claim (but a well-tested one) that human languages all have what are technically called *indexed grammars*, which impose tree structures on their sentences.

Because we all speak such languages, it seems quite natural and inevitable that languages should have this kind of structure. But then it seems natural that we each have two arms and two legs – but an octopus might not see it that way. One of the chief genuine contributions Noam Chomsky has made to science is to show us that tree structuring in grammar is an empirical finding, not a logical necessity. In his early work, Chomsky elaborated a mathematical scheme for classifying different types of grammatical system, and hence different types of language. Languages involving tree structure occupy just one area of the classification; but that area seems to include all the languages which human beings speak.

Ironically, though, having been the first to realize that tree structure in human grammar is a universal feature that is telling us something about how human beings universally function, Chomsky failed to grasp what it is telling us. The universality of tree structuring tells us that languages are systems which human beings develop in the gradual, guess-and-test style by which, according to Karl Popper, all knowledge is brought into being. Tree structuring is the hallmark of gradual evolution.

## The architecture of complexity

The link between tree structuring and evolutionary development was first made by Herbert Simon, a Nobel Prize winner and contributor to many branches of knowledge, in an article on 'The architecture of complexity'. Although the essential idea is quite simple, there are some complications in the way it is worked out which cannot be omitted; I shall have to ask the reader to be patient for a few pages until we return to language and the question of innate knowledge.

Simon begins his article with a parable about two watchmakers, Hora and Tempus. Both make equally good watches, but Hora's business prospers while Tempus's fails. The reason for this has to do with the structure of their respective watches. Each contains roughly the same number of elementary parts – say, a thousand. Tempus must assemble all thousand parts in a continuous operation to produce a solid watch; if he has to put down a partly assembled watch to attend to an interruption, it falls apart into its component pieces and he must begin again from scratch after the interruption. Hora's watches, on the other hand, consist of ten hundred-part sub-assemblies which are solid in themselves; if Hora is interrupted in the middle of assembling the ten sub-assemblies into a complete watch, after the interruption he has to reassemble only the ten sub-assemblies rather than all thousand elementary parts. Each sub-assembly, similarly, is made up of ten independently solid sub-sub-assemblies each containing ten basic parts.

The result is that, when Hora is interrupted, he loses at most eight individual assembly operations performed before the interruption, whereas Tempus may lose anything up to 998 operations; therefore Hora produces complete watches very much more rapidly than Tempus. If each carries out individual operations at the same rate, and if they are interrupted at the same average frequency, say once per hundred operations, then, Simon shows, Hora will complete almost 4000 watches for every one completed by Tempus.

The essential difference between the two kinds of watch is that Hora's watches are hierarchically structured – tree-structured – while Tempus's watches are not. The two designs can be represented abstractly by means of diagrams in which nodes represent units that are stable, or 'solid' as I put it above (that is, capable of enduring as units). I have simplified the diagrams by using threes rather than tens.

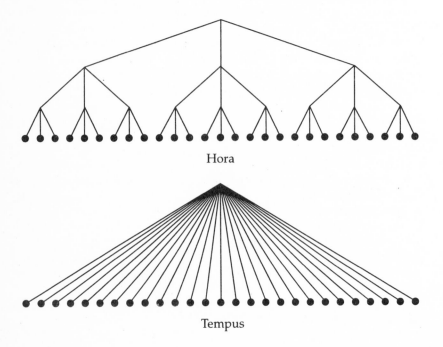

Hora

Tempus

Each tree has a single 'root' node, representing the completed watches, which are stable in both cases, and each tree has the same number of 'leaf' nodes representing the elementary parts from which the watches are constructed, which are stable because they are not made up of smaller parts. Tempus's design has a single non-leaf node (the root node), with a 'span' – number of immediately dominated nodes – of 1000; Hora's design has numerous non-leaf nodes each with a span of ten. Other things (in particular, the number of leaves) being equal, a design with a low average node-span can be produced in a much shorter time than a design with a high average node-span; the difference will increase very rapidly with increase in rate of interruptions.

The point of the parable is that it shows, according to Simon, that complex entities produced by any process of unplanned evolution, such as the Darwinian process of biological evolution, will have tree structuring as a matter of statistical necessity, even if tree structure is not logically necessary to them.

An evolutionary process can be thought of as one in which elementary building blocks are constantly shuffled together in varying combinations, and some particular combinations which happen to be stable – 'fit' is the Darwinian term – survive as units in the shuffling process. ('Shuffling' is represented in the parable both by the watchmakers' actions in bringing parts together and by the interruptions which cause them to fall apart unless they form a stable whole.) In the case of biology, for instance, think of various molecules floating past one another in the 'primeval soup' within which life has been conjectured as beginning, several thousand million years ago. (It has recently been argued that the molecules from which life emerged probably encountered each other on the surface of clay rather than in a liquid soup – for the purposes of Simon's argument it does not really matter.)

The molecules would have constantly come together in diverse chance combinations, and some of these combinations would have fitted together as stable ensembles which then took part as units in the continuing process of shuffling – so that, as time went on, organisms of increasing complexity would make an appearance. (Note, by the way, that the particular threshold beyond which certain quite complex ensembles acquired the ability to reproduce their kind is not very relevant to the present discussion, though in other respects it is all-important. Self-replication is simply one means by which a *type* of organism can endure through time.)

Intuitively it is easy to grasp the idea that a complex organism stands a far better chance of being translated from possibility into actuality if it can be built up in many stages, each of which is independently viable, than if all its many ultimate components have to happen to come together in the right way simultaneously.

It is important to grasp that Simon is *not* saying that tree-structured organisms are necessarily 'fitter' or stabler than organisms with other kinds of structure. Tempus's watches were as good as Hora's, once they were finished. What Simon is saying is rather subtler. Suppose there are two logically possible organisms which are equally complex, in the sense that they are composed of the same number of elementary building blocks, and are equally fit to fill some environmental niche: but one contains tree structuring and the other does not. Then (Simon is saying) it is a statistical certainty that the former will be thrown up by the evolutionary process as a *candidate for survival* long before the latter organism gets a look in.

The important point about the Hora/Tempus parable is not that Hora completes 4000 watches for every one watch completed by Tempus, but that if the two begin making watches at about the same time, Hora can expect to complete his first watch 4000 times sooner than Tempus. If two possible organisms are equally fit, the fact that the tree-structured one is given the earlier chance is quite sufficient to guarantee that the tree-structured rather than the non-tree-structured organism will fill the environmental niche. As evolutionists put it, 'prior arrival pre-empts survival'.

In other words, Simon is arguing that there might well be complex non-hierarchical organisms which would in principle succeed, if given a chance, just as well as the complex tree-structured organisms that are actually found after an evolutionary process has reached an advanced stage; but the nature of the process by which new types of organism come into being guarantees that the non-hierarchical ones will never be given their chance. This cannot fail to remind us of the linguistic nativists' argument that tree structuring is not logically necessary to language, and that one can conceive of systems similar to languages except that their grammar does not involve tree structures; yet no languages of that kind are actually used by human communities.

## Evolution everywhere

Herbert Simon himself is not centrally concerned with language, though it gets a fairly brief mention in his article. (Simon certainly did not write his article in order to undercut linguistic nativism, although the article lends itself to that purpose.) He argues that the tendency of evolutionary processes to yield tree structuring is visible in many different domains.

The obvious example of an evolutionary process is the biological evolution of different anatomical arrangements in animal and plant species, and Simon claims that his principle has explanatory force in that domain. All complex biological organisms are made up of cells, and cells were originally independent organisms. While the biological evolution of body shapes is the best-known example of an evolutionary process, however, it might not seem to be a particularly good example for Simon's purposes – a point which Simon himself does not altogether recognize. In the first place, Simon predicts that complex organisms will have *many* layers of hierarchical structure, yet it is not obvious that familiar biological species contain intermediate levels of structure, in his sense, between the level of cells and the level of complete individuals. Simon writes that 'we find cells organized into tissues, tissues into organs, organs into systems'. But these latter classes of biological component are not descended from independent organisms; there never was a time when the ancestors of, say, circulatory system, respiratory system and skeleton chanced to encounter one another and from then on evolved jointly as a symbiotic unit.

The problem here is that Simon fails to distinguish two rather different processes that can lead to the creation of hierarchical structure. On the one hand, organisms that were previously independent may contract a permanent symbiotic relationship with one another, becoming a single larger organism. If this happens repeatedly, and the units which came together retain some sort of identity within the more inclusive organism, the result is hierarchy of what we might call the 'symbiotic' variety. This is the kind of hierarchy predicted directly by the watchmaker parable. On the other hand, a very salient feature of biological development is that hierarchical structures are created by the repeated splitting and differentiation of what begins as a *single* unit. This is well known in the case of ontogeny (the development of an individual of a species): a man, composed of a billion or more cells, is the outcome of repeated division of a single fertilized egg, and the kind of hierarchy indicated by Simon's 'tissues, organs, and systems' corresponds to the successive divisions into different lines of descent that specialize in different directions.

In this respect, as in many others, 'ontogeny recapitulates phylogeny' – the development of the individual recapitulates the evolution of its species, not necessarily in exact detail but in broad outline. A complex species such as Man has been produced not by the coming together in successively larger aggregates of what were originally a very large number of different kinds of protozoon, but by failure on the part of the descendants of one single-celled ancestor species to drift apart after splitting. We may call this latter kind of hierarchy 'endogenous'; it is much less clear that the watchmaker parable can be used to predict that the products of an evolutionary process must contain endogenous hierarchy, yet that is the type of tree structuring which is most noticeable in biology.

However, at another level of biology than the one just discussed, Simon's predictions have in fact been borne out, in a way that is all the more striking in view of the fact that the relevant biological theories were worked out only after the publication of Simon's article.

To the layman, the cell sounds like a very elementary sort of unit, but this impression is quite misleading. G.G. Simpson stressed that 'if, as must almost necessarily be true short of miracles, life arose as a living molecule or protogene, the progression from this stage to that of the ameba is at least as great as from ameba to man'. In discussing the biological application of his thesis about hierarchy, Simon wrote vaguely that 'well-defined subsystems – for example, nucleus, cell membrane, microsomes, mitochondria, and so on – have been identified in animal cells.' More recently it has come to be widely accepted that the evolutionary history of 'eukaryotic' cells (cells with nuclei, including protozoa such as amoebae, and the cells of all higher organisms) involves a series of cases of symbiosis between previously independent organisms, just as Simon leads us to expect. As Lynn Margulis reconstructs the sequence of events, first an anaerobic host bacterium teamed up with a number of smaller, aerobic bacteria, which developed into the original

mitochondria; then a number of spirochaete-like bacteria attached themselves
to the surface of the resulting organism, evolving into the spindle apparatus
for mitosis; while this ensemble was the ancestor of the animal and fungus
kingdoms, in another line (or lines) of descent it in turn formed a symbiosis
with blue-green algae to produce the kingdom of plants.

Once the symbiotic relationships became established, the partners developed
in such a way that they ceased even potentially to be independent organisms;
one cannot remove a mitochondrion from a eukaryotic cell and grow it as an
isolated bacterium. There is no analogue for this in the watchmaker parable –
cogwheels and the like remain what they are and do not develop
spontaneously. But this point does not damage the force of Simon's argument;
it means merely that we must understand him to be predicting that the
products of evolution will be tree-structured in the sense that they are made
up of components, sub-components, etc., which are *or which descend from units
that once were* independent organisms.

Even the 'endogenous' type of hierarchical structure in anatomy may be
indirectly explicable in Simon's terms. Bodies are the structures which the
nucleotide sequences of DNA build in order to immortalize themselves; the
random shuffling through which evolution continues to occur in multi-celled
organisms is shuffling of gene sequences, not shuffling of bodies. (Gene
sequences are 'shuffled' through mutation, and the splitting and crossing over
of DNA sequences in sexual reproduction.) We do not, in the higher species,
find symbiotic evolution in the sense that a horse which rolls in burrs becomes
the ancestor of a race of horses covered in prickly lumps; but we do find
symbiotic evolution in the sense that nucleotide sequences which have
succeeded in becoming common in a gene-pool are constantly shuffled into
new longer sequences, a few of which themselves turn out to be highly 'fit'
as units.

Simon could be interpreted as saying something like this: logically it is
entirely possible that a highly fit organism could emerge from a reshuffling
which destroyed the unity of the various subsequences of nucleotides already
established as successful ('crossing over' and mutation occur at random with
respect to the 'semantics' of a chromosome); but statistically it is sure that fitter
organisms will only emerge through slight modifications to and new
combinations of nucleotide subsequences which had proved their worth in
ancestor organisms. (This is why it is appropriate to think of the nucleotides
along a chromosome as grouped into 'genes'.)

Furthermore, whether or not Simon's argument succeeds in this way in
making correct predictions about anatomy above the cell level, anatomy is not
the whole of biology. Richard Dawkins finds Simon's principle to be one of
first-rank importance for ethology, the study of animal behaviour. Dawkins
suggests that Simon provides the intellectually satisfying explanation for
abstract characteristics of animal behaviour widely noticed by ethologists
(Dawkins gives a wealth of references), and that this is an achievement
comparable to Darwin's use of the notion of natural selection to account for
the diversity of species.

Thus biological evolution is one domain to which Simon's argument applies, with respect to anatomy at least below the cell level, and possibly above it, and apparently also with respect to behaviour. But there are plenty of 'evolutionary' processes in the world other than Darwinian biological evolution. Simon points out, for instance, that the development of human societies seems to conform rather well to the pattern he predicts.

In the early history of our species, men can hardly have belonged to social groups much larger than the bands of a score or so individuals observed in related species – lack of technology would have ensured that no regular social relationships could be maintained across distances of a hundred miles or more, and one band would have had only sporadic, chance contacts with others. The growth of technology both permitted the emergence of wider social units, by facilitating communication, and provided a motive for such developments, namely taking advantage of greater division of labour. So far as can be inferred from the historical record, the growth of increasingly inclusive social organizations has built up hierarchical systems from smaller to larger, just as Simon suggests. Several extended families group themselves into parishes or similar units, parishes later group themselves into wapentakes, wapentakes into counties, counties into nations, nations into empires.

The precise natures of the units at different levels, and indeed the number of intermediate levels, vary from place to place in the world; that is to be expected. The watchmaker parable gives no reason to predict that evolution-generated hierarchies will be regular, with the same number of branches between each leaf and the root (Simon made the hierarchical structure of Hora's watches regular only in order to simplify the calculation). The parable predicts only that the average span of nodes will be low, and that the pattern will be a true tree structure, with no 'ambiguities of dominance' (i.e. upward branching).

Similarly, Simon points out that social institutions such as commercial firms, universities, and so forth which function independently of specific tiers of government show considerable internal hierarchical structure. Large firms very frequently result from mergers of a number of smaller concerns, which may in turn be the successors to groups of lesser firms again. Simon comments that, in the social sphere as in biology, the units commonly retain their identity as units for periods, often very long periods, after they have lost their independence. Simon refers to the fact that the empire of Alexander the Great resolved itself after his death into some of the same components from which it had earlier been formed. Subordinate firms within a conglomerate often retain an identifiable individuality long after they have lost their independence.

To assert that social institutions show a strong tendency to be hierarchical in this way seems as if it might be a mere truism. But it is not a necessary truth; in some special cases the pattern does not hold, and 'ambiguities of dominance' are found. My own university has a very unusual, 'heterarchical' management structure: but this did not arise through spontaneous evolution, it was imposed as a conscious experiment when the university was brought into being from nothing in the 1960s. In the 1970s, there was a fashion in the industrial world for non-hierarchical structures (it was called 'matrix management'). Examples like this show that hierarchical organization is not a logical necessity, so the fact that it exists almost ubiquitously requires explanation. In industry, Thomas Peters and Robert Waterman suggest that matrix management was not successful in practice (it was 'unfit'); but Herbert Simon gives us a reason to believe that non-hierarchical organization will not occur in gradually evolved social institutions, whether it would work or not.

The development of knowledge, as Karl Popper describes it, is another clear case of the type of evolutionary process to which Simon's argument applies. Popper has been explicit, in books such as *Objective Knowledge*, about the parallels between the development of knowledge in the individual, and the evolution of species in Nature.

The individual tries out ideas, many of which fail to survive the test of correspondence with future experience – they are not 'fit' – but some of which do prove to have staying power. The early ideas will be simple and will relate to narrow areas of experience, but once some of them are established, they can be built on in formulating higher-order, more general ideas to be tested against experience in their turn. One can imagine an infant at an early stage formulating concepts like 'day', 'night', 'playpen', 'cot', as symbols for regularly recurring coherent entities in the chaotic hubbub of sense impressions; after these ideas were available, the child would be in a position to invent an idea like 'bedtime', conjecturing a regular association between being placed in his cot and day giving way to night.

It may be that these specific examples are not well chosen to represent the sort of ideas that an infant will formulate before he speaks – they may well be too advanced, since it is obviously not easy for an adult to reconstruct the mental world of a baby. But the general point is independent of specific examples. If knowledge is developed, as Popper says, by a process of guessing and testing, then by Simon's argument we can expect that elaborate systems of knowledge will have hierarchical – tree-shaped – structuring. This will be so not because it is logically necessary that systems of knowledge must have this structure, but because of the statistical considerations which imply that tree-shaped structures will emerge as candidates for survival far sooner than any others, if alternatives are logically possible. Tree structures will be universal as an empirical finding, and they will identify the process which created them as a Popperian, guess-and-test process.

Because language is one kind of intellectual product in which structure is relatively easily identified, Herbert Simon's argument is particularly convincing in this domain. (Indeed, it seems to me that Simon's argument about the 'architecture of complexity' works better for language than it does for some of the domains which he himself used as illustrations.) When language was first developed by our remote ancestors, Simon's argument implies that they would have begun by speaking in the way that Derek Bickerton's Seth spoke at 21 months: in one-word sentences. Then, after a period when sequences of sentences like 'Get.' 'Apple.' or 'Wash.' 'Baby.' had quite often proved useful when uttered in succession, the sequences might be perceived as units – 'Get apple', 'Wash baby' – and a grammatical rule would have come into existence, defining a way of building up an utterance out of separate words. Initially perhaps the mental rule producing 'Get apple' would be separate from the rule producing 'Wash baby', but as people spotted regularities in the respective ranges of words which were useful in the two positions of such utterances, they would begin to work with classifications corresponding to 'verb' and 'noun'.

It would be rash to try to fill in details of this hypothetical process whereby grammatical structure might gradually emerge from an initial one-word-sentence stage. Anything one tried to say in detail would be wholly speculative. The linguistic nativists claim that human language ability depends on innate mechanisms in the brain, but they make no attempt to specify what those mechanisms are like. There is no reason for me to give hostages to fortune by trying to penetrate further into the unknowable prehistory of mankind's intellectual life than the nativists try to penetrate into the currently unknowable operations of the mind.

But the general point is straightforward. If languages were created through a process of gradual Popperian guess-and-test development, then Simon's argument implies that their grammar will be based on tree structuring, if it is possible for grammar to be based on that sort of structure. Sentences will organize words into nested hierarchical structures, and rules of grammar which modify sentences will treat the tree constituents as units – they will be 'structure-dependent'. My picture of how grammar could have arisen from simple single-word utterances may be very broad-brush and vague – it could hardly be otherwise; but in terms of prima facie plausibility it surely beats Bickerton's and Chomsky's picture of one individual child suddenly having the whole thing ready-made.

The empiricist picture of human nature implies that language will originally have been created as a system full of hierarchy and structure dependence; and it has similar implications for the way that individuals in successive generations reconstruct for themselves the linguistic systems which their elders are using. Until we have learned our mother tongue to the point where our elders can use it to transmit their knowledge to us directly, all the knowledge each of us creates, including our mastery of our parents' language, is developed by Popperian guessing-and-testing; so we must build up our understanding of our mother tongue hierarchically. Even if the system we were trying to master were not really characterized by tree structure, we would try to impose tree structure on it in our attempts to make sense of it. But for human languages this is not a problem. Today's children try to impose tree structure on the languages they learn; and the tree structure is there, because the languages were created by previous generations who also worked by guessing-and-testing.

So far as I know, Herbert Simon was the first person to point out this intimate connection between evolutionary development and hierarchical structure. Perhaps the implication for the growth of knowledge should not come as a surprise, though. We have known for a long time that when Eve first acquired knowledge, it came in the form of a tree.

## Trees and nothing but trees

At this point, the reader may feel that I have cheated. I have explained why gradual evolutionary processes have a strong tendency to produce tree structures, and I have pointed out that Popperian, guess-and-test knowledge development is an evolutionary process. But, the reader may object, Darwinian biological evolution is also an evolutionary process – indeed it is the most obvious example. So it might seem that my explanation for the language universals is no more compelling than the nativists' explanation. They say that biological evolution has led to a body of innate linguistic knowledge which is shared by all members of a species; I am saying that languages are products of cultural development, and are reconstructed by individuals through a Popperian process of guessing and testing. *All* these processes are the kind to which Simon's argument applies, so all of them equally predict tree structuring in language. The fact that we observe tree structuring leaves the debate between empiricists and nativists exactly where it was.

That is wrong. If the individual members of a biological species share elaborate inherited properties created by biological evolution, we expect that hierarchical structure will be one aspect of the shared properties – but that will be the least of what there is in common. All humans share a hierarchical structure, comprising a bony skeleton of a certain intricate shape, a heart and a system for circulating blood of certain composition, a nervous system of a particular type, and so forth. All rose bushes share a hierarchical structure comprising roots, branches with thorns, leaves of a particular shape, and so forth. If someone asked 'What properties do rose bushes share that enable us to recognize them as rose bushes?', it would be ridiculous to answer 'They are hierarchically structured.'

If knowledge of language were innate in humans as a product of biological evolution, human languages ought to share a mass of common properties so specific and concrete that someone discussing language universals would never think of mentioning hierarchical structure, just as someone explaining how to recognize rose bushes would not bother to mention such an abstract property. Even if there were some differences among the dialects spoken by separate communities (just as some rose bushes have more branches and larger leaves than others), we would expect to find that a specification of human language universals looked more like a description of an individual language. It would tell us things like: the word for 'sun' universally begins with *s* and ends with *n*, perhaps with dialect variation in the vowel; the adjective universally goes before the noun, not after it; single-syllable adjectives and two-syllable adjectives ending in -*y* take endings (such as English -*er*, -*est*) to form their comparative and superlative, other adjectives prefix separate words (such as English *more* and *most*), and so on.

But the nativists' theories of language universals contain nothing as concrete as this. Properties of this sort are *not* universal among human languages. (The rule about adjectives going before nouns rather than after is widely shared, but – provided a language has 'adjectives' and 'nouns' – there are only two possible orders, so obviously many languages must coincide. There are plenty of languages like French that use the opposite rule.)

If languages were originally created as cultural developments, and are reconstructed by young children as an individual intellectual achievement, then they will all have tree structuring because Popperian knowledge development is an evolutionary process; but, beyond that, they will have only such shared properties as occur by chance, or through the mechanisms of cultural transmission. Individuals in each generation will reconstruct an approximation to their elders' language, but with minor differences because a child's data will not uniquely determine his elders' system. Where separate human communities once spoke the same language but have spent many generations out of contact, their languages may be recognizably related but will contain large differences. If communities have never been in contact and developed languages independently, there will be no common features shared by their languages (other than the abstract features to do with tree structuring, which will always appear in languages used by creatures who have to discover knowledge rather than inheriting it). If an individual baby is separated at birth from its biological parents and reared by speakers of a different language, it will reconstruct an approximation to the language it hears – it will not be influenced by the language which its biological parents speak.

The pattern we observe is precisely the pattern predicted, if human beings inherit no knowledge of language and have to reconstruct their elders' language system as one of their first research projects. It is just the opposite of the pattern predicted, if human beings have innate knowledge of language.

## Chunks and islands

The linguistic nativists I have been discussing would, I am sure, not agree that gradual knowledge development is a sufficient explanation for the universal features of language. They often write as though they have found universal properties in whatever aspects of language they have looked at – not just universal tree structure in grammar, but many different universal features at every linguistic level, so that what a linguistics expert can say about the structure shared by all human languages is not so different from what a botanist can say about the structure of all rose bushes.

However, in this area we need to take more than normal care to distinguish hype from reality. The writings of the nativists contain airy hints about the wealth of language universals they could cite in evidence, if space permitted. If one tries to pursue those hints, though, the substance is often elusive.

We have already seen how Chomsky's hints about universal constraints on the meanings of words turned out, when one thought about them, to be simply mistaken. In the early years of linguistic nativism, scholars such as Roman Jakobson and Morris Halle made large claims about universal structuring in the pattern of sounds used in speech, going far beyond what could be predicted from the physical facts about human vocal organs and the acoustic signals they generate. To discuss phonetic issues in detail would be unduly technical for a book like this one, but I have described elsewhere how some of the most central claims were in due course dropped – silently, so that unwary readers may have failed to notice how far the base of evidence for nativism had shrunk; while other claims that were never withdrawn can easily be refuted.

I believe that all the properties which are common to different human languages are adequately explained by reference to the empiricist account of knowledge development outlined above, and to the common features of physical reality which confront speakers of any language. (It is no doubt true that every human language has at least one word meaning 'sun', but this is easily explained by pointing out how significant the sun is in the life of every human community. We do not need to invoke an innate predisposition to create a word meaning 'sun'.)

Checking whether all language universals are indeed adequately explained in these ways is not a straightforward thing to achieve, because theories of universals in linguistics are a moving target, changing year by year. That is no criticism: sciences are supposed to develop, not stand still.

What I shall do in the rest of this chapter is to check the references to language universals in the new-wave nativist writings which we have already looked at from other points of view. These books are recent, so the picture of linguistic theory they present should be up to date; and their aim is to convince the uncommitted reader, so it is reasonable to assume that they have chosen the most impressive pieces of evidence available, even if they cannot survey the field exhaustively.

Almost the first example of a language universal cited by Steven Pinker is the structure dependence of grammar rules, which we have already dealt with. His example of an 'impossible' structure-independent rule is that 'no language forms questions by reversing the order of words within a sentence, like *Built Jack that house the this is?*' Actually Pinker has got this example subtly wrong: if human languages *could* use reversal to form questions, and if English were such a language, the question would reverse the order found in the statement – it would run *Built Jack that house the is this?*, not . . . *the this is?* But in a way this minor muddle just reinforces Pinker's point: sentence reversal is an utterly unnatural grammatical operation, so people make mistakes when they try to do it.

Pinker (and Chomsky) are quite right to say that a rule like this is unnatural, but they have missed the reason why it is unnatural. Because we are not born with an understanding of the world built into us, we have to learn by mastering the structure of small chunks of experience, and going on to treat these as units when mastering the structure of larger chunks. Learning how to ask questions is a sentence-level aspect of language learning, so the only bits and pieces of language we can easily manipulate when we learn how to ask questions are the chunks out of which sentences are built. Compare the problem of learning how to drive to a distant town. If someone asks me how to drive from Brighton to Birmingham, I will explain in terms of chunks like 'Follow the signs to the M23', 'Turn on to the London Orbital clockwise', 'Take the M40 exit westbound'. Someone who learns these elements can manipulate them to produce a recipe for getting back from Birmingham to Brighton, by changing the order of the chunks and making simple modifications, for instance, replacing 'clockwise' with 'anticlockwise'. But each of these chunks of behaviour is made up of lower-level chunks, for instance, in order to 'follow the signs to the M23' one has to execute actions like 'get in the car', 'start the car', 'drive to the road junction', and each of these in turn is made up of still lower-level chunks: to 'start the car' one has to 'select neutral', 'insert the key in the ignition', 'turn the key', and so forth. When someone is working out how to turn a Brighton-to-Birmingham recipe into a Birmingham-to-Brighton recipe, he does not take these lower-level chunks into consideration; if he had to do that, there would be so many different elements to juggle that no one would ever find his way home.

A question rule like 'Reverse the order of the words in the statement' looks as though it ought to be straightforward to apply, because what we see on the page is the linear sequence of words – we do not see the chunks into which they group. But, psychologically, a rule like that would create the same sort of problems for a speaker that a driver would have if, in order to retrace a route between two towns, he had to start thinking about the relative ordering of turning the ignition key and selecting neutral (and all the many other elementary actions into which the various high-level chunks can ultimately be decomposed).

In other areas of psychology these concepts seem to be well understood. It is only in linguistics, so far as I know, that people implicitly call them into question by arguing that tree structuring and structure dependence are universal properties requiring special explanations.

One reason for this may be that our practice of reducing speech to writing encourages us to contemplate utterances as something like the sequences of lowest level behavioural units into which they are ultimately decomposed. Words, and even letters (corresponding to something like individual gestures of the vocal organs), are visually salient on the page; larger grammatical units are scarcely indicated in writing at all. In other fields of human behaviour, there is nothing like this – someone who thinks about the problem of driving between two towns is not immediately confronted with a standard representation of the driver's behaviour in terms of long lists of actions at the 'turn the ignition key' level, so nothing distracts attention from the psychologically relevant chunks of behaviour.

Another reason for linguists to see structure dependence as problematic, though, is that in certain respects it can seem that grammar is *not* limited to operating with chunks at one level at a time. Some individual grammatical operations seem to manipulate units simultaneously at very different levels, as if people discussing navigation found it natural to say things like 'Take the London Orbital clockwise, then grasp the gearstick with your left hand'.

Take a question like 'Who did Alan think Barbara wished Charles to meet?' The question is about something that Alan thought. What Alan thought was something about a wish of Barbara's. Barbara's wish was about Charles meeting somebody; and the identity of that somebody is what is in question. In other words, the sentence would be given a structure resembling the following:

[ Who did [ Alan think [ Barbara wished [ Charles to meet . . . ] ] ] ]?

– where *Who* at the beginning is an invitation to the hearer to fill in the gap at the end. Among the linguistic nativists there has been a strong tradition of describing this sort of grammatical situation by saying that the word *who* is moved out of its logical position after *meet* into its surface position at the beginning; the sentence is said 'underlyingly' to have a structure more like:

[ Alan thought [ Barbara wished [ Charles to meet who ] ] ]?

– and this is converted into the *who*-first sequence by a 'transformational rule'. If one thinks about grammar this way, then it is difficult to maintain the position that grammatical operations can manipulate only chunks at their own level. Questioning is a sentence-level function, yet in order to turn the statement into a question we have to shift a word, *who*, which is an element of the *Charles to meet* chunk, which is itself an element of the *Barbara wished* chunk, which is in turn an element of the *Alan thought* chunk. If we can do this sort of thing without difficulty, then perhaps we do after all need to ask why we cannot have a rule that forms yes/no questions by reversing the word order of corresponding statements.

But we should not be misled by metaphors that people use for talking about grammar. Nothing really 'moves' when we ask, 'Who did Alan think Barbara wished Charles to meet?' We do not first construct the sentence on a mental blackboard in the other order, and then shift the word *who* around before reading it off. We just say *who*, then *did*, then a chunk expressing a proposition which contains somewhere an information gap to be filled. In this case, that chunk consists of *Alan*, then *think*, then a chunk that itself expresses a proposition which contains an information gap; and this chunk in turn consists of *Barbara* and *wished* and the expression of a proposition containing an information gap. The rule that English questions can consist of a *who* or *what* chunk and a proposition-containing-an-information-gap chunk, and the recursive rule that a proposition-containing-an-information-gap chunk can consist of a subject, a verb, and a proposition-containing-an-information-gap chunk, are themselves ordinary rules which involve only relationships among chunks at a particular level.

One of the real advances in grammatical theory, since linguistic nativism first started to be influential, was the development by Gerald Gazdar, Geoffrey Pullum and their collaborators of the theory of *Generalized Phrase Structure Grammar*. Among other things, Generalized Phrase Structure Grammar shows how grammatical phenomena which used to be described using rules akin to 'take the London Orbital clockwise and grasp the gearstick' can instead be described in a scientifically precise and insightful fashion which does not imply that any individual grammatical rule mixes levels in this way.

Nativists describe grammatical tree structures as containing 'islands' from which no words can be moved by grammatical rule; one of their arguments for innate knowledge is that the islands are the same from language to language, even though there seems to be no particular logic to them. Ray Jackendoff gives a clear version of this argument. Consider the strange and rather artificial statement:

> Sam said Harold thought the teacher had told us that Fred would get Susie to kiss Oscar last Tuesday.

Even though this has a highly intricate grammatical structure, we can question Oscar's identity, replacing his name with 'whom?' and moving that to the beginning:

> Whom did Sam say Harold thought the teacher had told us that Fred would get Susie to kiss last Tuesday?

It is a silly question, and no one would ever ask it; but if someone *did* ask it we could understand what they were asking, at a pinch. But now consider the shorter and more straightforward statement:

> General Washington ate kippers and toast for breakfast.

If we could query *Oscar* in the previous case, logically we ought to be able to query *toast* in this case and ask:

> What did General Washington eat kippers and for breakfast?

Yet the reader will surely agree with Jackendoff that this question is unnatural, in a way in which the previous question was not. The nativist explanation is that it violates a 'syntactic island constraint': with certain exceptions, rules are not allowed to move elements out of co-ordinations (constructions which link units using words like *and*). The 'Whom did Sam say . . .' question was cumbersome and implausible; but *whom* was not moved out of a syntactic island, so it worked. The 'What did General Washington eat . . .' question is shorter and logically more reasonable – it expresses a question we 'ought' to be able to ask; but it is unnatural because it violates an innate constraint. There is a style of questioning in which the question word is left in its logical position, for instance in quiz shows – 'For $64,000, Mr Van Doren, Benjamin Disraeli was leader of which political party?' In this style, the question about Washington's breakfast is perfectly acceptable and understandable:

> On the morning of 4 July 1776, General Washington ate kippers and what for breakfast?

The same question has been asked; but in this style of questioning nothing is moved, so the island constraint remains inviolate.

Once we cease to think in terms of grammar 'moving' elements around, though, the picture changes. The generalization violated by the 'What did General Washington eat . . .' question becomes the generalization that co-ordinations – *X and Y* constructions – always link like with like. We can say, for instance:

The doctor who Kim worked for and Sandy relied on died.

The sequences *Kim worked for* and *Sandy relied on* are both examples of a sentence-with-a-noun-phrase-missing, so they can be co-ordinated. But we cannot say:

The doctor who Kim worked for and Sandy relied on Lee died.

Here, *Kim worked for* is a sentence-with-a-noun-phrase-missing, as before, but *Sandy relied on Lee* is a sentence with nothing missing; so the two sequences cannot be conjoined. In the unnatural question 'What did General Washington eat kippers and for breakfast?' the word *and* is linking *kippers* on one side with nothing at all on the other, which violates the generalization even more obviously.

While the restrictions were expressed in terms of islands which limit movement, it might have appeared reasonable to say that the restrictions were so arbitrary that their universality could only be the result of shared genetic inheritance. On the other hand, it is far less plausible to say that a rule that words such as *and* link like with like is 'unlearnable' and therefore must be innate. Co-ordination is virtually by definition the joining together of grammatically equivalent units. It does not seem at all arbitrary or surprising that no language allows people to say things like *X and*, or *and X*, where something is linked to nothing. Only the misleading tradition which saw the phrase *kippers and* as really, 'underlyingly', *kippers and what* made it seem as though one ought to be able to ask a question like that.

When people first encounter a nativist argument like Jackendoff's, based on the idea that logically we 'ought' to be able to utter some sentence which it is clear no one would ever use in practice, they often obscurely think that the argument does not *feel* very weighty – surely there must be something at fault in the logic which says that such sentences ought to be normal? But when the nativist challenges them to identify the logical flaw, they cannot put their finger on it. So they concede, almost despite themselves, that the nativist explanation has to be accepted. According to that explanation, the example would be all right so far as the rules of the English language are concerned, but those rules are overridden by genetically based constraints which have no particular logic to them, and which just arbitrarily forbid certain grammatical configurations from occurring in *any* language.

However, Gerald Gazdar and his co-creators of Generalized Phrase Structure Grammar have provided the analysis which justifies people's obscure feelings that the 'impossible' examples are 'obviously impossible' – so that their impossibility does not need an explanation in terms of genetic constraints.

Gazdar has analysed the universal principles which nativists identify as controlling aspects of grammar such as co-ordination (for co-ordination the universal constraints are actually more complicated than I have discussed here), and he has shown that in a grammatical framework where elements do not move, the principles are implied by absolutely fundamental, truly self-evident axioms. For instance, one of the central Generalized Phrase Structure Grammar axioms is the *Foot Feature Principle*, which is stated as a formal requirement on grammatical tree diagrams. What the Foot Feature Principle really means could be partly expressed as follows:

> When a whole contains a part which has a missing element of a certain sort, the whole itself has a missing element of that sort, unless the missing element is crucial to the way the part fits into the whole.

In itself this is an entirely general truth – it has nothing in particular to do with language, or even with human cognition more generally. So, for instance, if a field contains a mineshaft – a column of missing ground – then the parish which includes the field contains a mineshaft; but when a jigsaw piece has an indentation of some particular shape, and completes a jigsaw which had a protrusion matching the indentation, the finished jigsaw does not itself have a missing indentation.

The theory of Generalized Phrase Structure Grammar is couched in terms of exact mathematical formalisms (as it needs to be, in order to yield precise, testable predictions); and the chain of reasoning by which the observable island constraints follow from the fundamental axioms is a subtle one, which is why people confronted with arguments like Jackendoff's usually cannot put their finger on what is wrong with the claim that we 'ought' to be able to ask the question about Washington's breakfast. However, once one grasps what the Generalized Phrase Structure Grammar axioms really mean, it is no longer tempting to explain the linguistic constraints in terms of innate cognitive machinery. If principles as general and obvious as the Foot Feature Principle, as I have glossed it above, account for the 'island' phenomena, then those phenomena can lend no support to the nativist point of view.

Steven Pinker offers what looks like a variant of Jackendoff's argument, based on a different 'island constraint'. Pinker's impossible example is:

> *That's the guy that you heard the rumour that Mary likes.

If we could say this, it would refer to a rumour (which you have heard) that Mary likes some guy, call him Mr X, and the sentence is saying that that man over there is this Mr X. But we cannot say it.

The standard nativist description of the situation is that there is an arbitrary (but universal) constraint which makes a full or reduced clause modifying a noun into an 'island'. Pinker's example would be derived from a structure containing the sequence:

> the rumour [that Mary likes the guy]

– where the bracketed sequence is a relative clause modifying *rumour*, hence an island; so shifting *the guy* out of this clause, to make it the complement of *that's*, violates the island constraint.

With Jackendoff's example, the constraint relating to co-ordination did seem to be valid, though the nativists' description in terms of prohibiting hypothetical 'movement' made it sound more arbitrary than it really is. In the case of Pinker's example, on the other hand, we have known for more than twenty years that the alleged constraint does not exist. Dwight Bolinger pointed out in 1972 that sentences which nativists describe as violating this constraint sometimes work and sometimes do not. For instance, we cannot say:

*It's the front door that I know the man at

(meaning, the man I know is the one who is at the front door), but (assuming *Jordan's* is the name of a company) we *can* say, in natural and informal speech:

It's Jordan's that I know the people at.

Each sentence would equally violate the constraint Pinker alludes to – *the front door*, or *Jordan's*, would be described as 'moved' out of a reduced relative clause, *(who is) at the front door* or *(who are) at Jordan's*, modifying the respective nouns *man* and *people*; but one is good and the other is bad. The difference relates not to abstract grammatical structure, but to more 'human', practical considerations. Being people 'at Jordan's' is a genuine characteristic of the persons in question – they are Jordan's employees, the link with the company is a significant identifying property of those people. Being at the front door is just a temporary location, it is not part of what makes a man who he is. As the medieval schoolmen would express it, being a Jordan's employee is part of someone's *essence*, being at the front door is an *accident*. If a sentence brings a property into focus as a device for picking out a person or thing to which the property applies, then we assume that the property chosen will be reasonably essential to that person or thing.

That is why Pinker's example is bad. Being a person such that the hearer heard the rumour that Mary likes that person is in no sense an essential part of anyone's identity. Since the identifying property referred to is not a sensible, 'essential' property, it gives the hearer no help in unpicking the grammar of the example: the hearer could equally well take *the rumour that Mary likes* as a phrase meaning 'the rumour which Mary likes', and be left wondering how that constituent fits into a reasonable statement. On the other hand, another example grammatically fairly similar to Pinker's is:

That's the guy that the police hold a warrant that allows them to spy on.

In terms of pure grammar this example involves the same alleged 'forbidden movement' as Pinker's sentence, and in other respects is rather more complicated. Yet the reader may agree that (while very clumsy) it sounds better than Pinker's example. Being someone such that the police have a warrant allowing them to spy on him comes much closer to being an 'essential' property of a person: it tells us something about the person, whereas the analogous wording in Pinker's sentence tells us only about what you heard.

But now, if we express the universal constraint in terms such as 'identifying descriptions which have to be linked to distant parts of a sentence in order to make sense of it should refer to properties that are reasonably essential to the entity identified', this sounds much less arbitrary and in need of explanation.

It seems more predictable that languages which grew up as real-life expressive media, rather than artificial academic constructs, would naturally find it efficient to conform to such a constraint. Explanations in terms of genetically inherited cognitive processing machinery appear attractive only because the nativists' insistence on describing the facts in terms of abstract grammatical structure (even in cases where this is known not to be the relevant issue) makes the facts appear more arbitrary than they really are.

### True and false universals

Although the tree structuring and structure dependence we have been discussing is central to Pinker's case for nativism (as it is for Chomsky's), structure dependence is not quite Pinker's first example of a language universal. The very first study he discusses is the research carried out by Joseph Greenberg on universals of word order. Greenberg approached the issue of language universals in a very empirical spirit: he looked at a large range of languages from diverse areas of the world and asked what generalizations could be made about word order. Greenberg was not himself interested in the idea that language universals might reflect innate linguistic knowledge, and the findings he came up with do not harmonize well with that idea: many of them are statistical rather than absolute.

Greenberg found, for instance, that:

> In languages with prepositions, the genitive almost always follows the governing noun, while in languages with postpositions it almost always precedes.

Prepositions are words like *on, through, in*. In some languages, words with these meanings follow rather than precede the noun to which they relate, in which case they are called 'postpositions'; a language with postpositions uses turns of phrase like 'mountain on', 'kitchen in', rather than 'on the mountain', 'in the kitchen'. So Greenberg is saying that if a language uses phrases like 'on the mountain', the betting is that it will use phrases like 'book of John'; if it says 'mountain on', it will probably say 'John's book'. (English is an unusual case: we have alternative orderings for the genitive construction, one using *of* and one using apostrophe-s. Most languages have just one ordering.)

If language universals reflected innate knowledge, one would not expect to find them applying in a statistical fashion, with exceptions. (For the universal quoted, Norwegian is an exception: it has prepositions but genitive-before-head noun order.) It is easier to interpret some of Greenberg's universals as residues of the gradual process of cultural development by which subtle modern languages emerged from cruder beginnings. When languages first found themselves needing to express the sort of space and time relationships for which English uses prepositions, it is plausible that they would often have initially treated these as a kind of genitive relationship. That is, 'on the mountain', 'in the kitchen', would have been conceptualized as something like 'mountain's top', 'kitchen's inside'. In some languages these constructions differ only marginally even now, though in European languages such as English the differentiation is rather complete. If prepositional phrases and genitive constructions often began as a single linguistic construction, then even after they grew apart one would expect the ordering commonly to remain parallel, though the accidents of language history might happen occasionally to change one construction in an individual language and leave the other alone.

So a lot of what Greenberg says seems if anything to damage rather than support the nativist case. It is not obvious why Pinker uses Greenberg's study to lead off his discussion of language universals, except that the concreteness of Greenberg's approach is perhaps reassuring for readers who find the nativists' own grammatical analyses off-puttingly abstract in style.

The Greenberg universal which Pinker writes most about, namely that subjects precede objects in almost all languages, is one of the least satisfactory of Greenberg's findings, because it assumes that we can identify 'subjects' and 'objects', in any language, in some way that is independent of word order: it is not at all clear that we can. In the context of English and other European languages we think of the subject as the element with which the verb agrees, but this is a provincial definition not suitable for discussing 'subject' as a universal notion; there are plenty of languages in which verbs do not inflect at all, and when verbs do inflect it is not always in order to mark 'agreement' with a noun phrase. (On the other hand, even in English we cannot define 'subject' as 'doer of the action'; there are many cases, for instance, 'John was killed', 'John can see the light', where the subject is 'done to' rather than 'doer'.) Edward Keenan has attempted to answer this objection by arguing that the notion 'subject' represents a constellation of separate properties, most of which tend in most languages to be shared by one noun phrase in each clause, which is thereby identified as the subject. To my mind Keenan does not really solve the problem of circularity. Some of the properties in his constellation, for instance, that of being the topic of the discourse, are properties which we might expect a priori to apply to the first element of a sentence, so that saying that subjects precede objects may be close to tautologous.

The nativists' books discuss other types of language universal as well. For instance, Pinker spends some time on the idea, which has been a cliché of theoretical linguistics for more than thirty years, that our innate language-processing machinery cannot handle sentences that include 'multiple central embeddings', such as 'The malt that the rat that the cat killed ate lay in the house'. A sentence like this is described as involving multiple central embedding, because it contains a construction (the relative clause *that the rat that the cat killed ate*) which is not adjacent to either end of the sentence, and which in turn includes a construction of the same grammatical category (the relative clause *that the cat killed*) centrally located within itself. Ever since George Miller and Noam Chomsky discussed the allegedly problematic status of such sentences in 1963, even linguists not particularly well disposed towards the nativists have accepted that human beings cannot cope with multiple central embedding, so that it does not occur in practice.

But they have not looked. The fact is that we *do* cope with it, frequently. For instance, here is a sentence from a published academic article about linguistics written by a Canadian:

The only thing that the words that can lose -d have in common is, apparently, that they are all quite common words.

This is a multiple central embedding in precisely the same sense as Pinker's sentence about the malt and the rat. Who cannot understand it? I logged multiple central embeddings which I encountered over a period, and I found them cropping up again and again: in *The Times* and in the *News of the World*, in writing for adults and in writing for children, in a student essay and in spoken utterances.

Explaining the unacceptability of multiple central embeddings by reference to innate linguistic machinery is like saying that swifts do everything (even sleep) on the wing, in order to explain why they have no feet. It is a pleasant idea, and for a long time simple folk believed it was so. But in hard fact, swifts have got feet. (And they do sometimes touch down.)

Derek Bickerton relates innate linguistic knowledge to universal structural principles of the lexicon. All words in any human language fall into hierarchical relationships, he says, so that a *spaniel* is a kind of *dog* (*dog* is the 'superordinate' term for *spaniel*), a *dog* is a kind of *mammal*, and so forth. Bickerton identifies this as an empirical finding: logically there could be languages in which not all words had superordinates, but human languages are not that kind of language.

All right, then, what is the superordinate term for *carpet*? I cannot think of any obvious word that includes *carpet* and is more general (unless one goes all the way to a word like *thing* – if that counts, Bickerton's statement about human languages seems fairly empty). Perhaps some people would say that *carpet* is a special case of *furniture*, but I would not think of a carpet as a piece of furniture myself. If this counterexample does not work for you, I predict that you will be able to find some other word which has no superordinate in your usage. People use words differently.

With the language universals discussed so far, it has been fairly clear what it means to say that they apply to a language (except perhaps for the one about subjects before objects), though in many cases they turn out not to apply to all languages – in some cases they may not apply to any language. There are other things which nativists identify as language universals, though, where it is quite hard to see what it could mean for a language not to obey them. For Derek Bickerton, one of the most significant aspects of innate linguistic knowledge is 'argument structure'. The *arguments* of a verb are the items that play essential roles in the activity depicted by the verb – elements like the subject, direct object, indirect object. Bickerton says that argument structure is the one area of foreign-language learning where

we never make mistakes, indeed our success is so complete we probably never realize how effortlessly we are 'learning'. . . . If a foreign language has a verb that means 'sleep', we can be sure it will have only one obligatory argument. If it has a verb that means 'beat', that verb will have two, and if it has a verb that means 'give', that verb will have three. . . . Argument structure . . . is universal.

Well, of course: because, if the foreign verb has more than one obligatory argument, we will not translate it as 'sleep'. In learning a foreign language we do often make mistakes about vocabulary. Suppose someone with limited German and no dictionary to hand comes across the word *unterstützen*, and a friend who speaks only German tries to gloss it by saying that, for instance, it would cover the action of someone who uses his money to keep a poor student or elderly parent afloat. That makes *unterstützen* sound like 'contribute' or 'donate', so can one say *ich unterstützte ihm 1000 Mark*? No, you cannot say that; you have to say *ich unterstützte ihn*, full stop. Then it cannot be 'contribute' or 'donate' – and in fact it means 'support'. Having the same range of arguments is part of what it means to say that a foreign verb and an English verb are synonyms. What Bickerton is telling us is that we know, effortlessly and unerringly, that words which mean the same are words which mean the same.

### Which way to the X-bar?

The new wave of linguistic nativists discuss a further class of universal grammatical properties, relating to the system of grammatical notation called *X-bar theory*. This concept was not part of the original case for nativism. It stems ultimately from a brief suggestion published by Noam Chomsky in 1970, but it became a major component of the nativists' view of language structure only after the publication of a 1977 book by Ray Jackendoff. Among the nativists of the new wave, X-bar theory has now become a crucial aspect of their conception of innate language knowledge.

Essentially, the theory says that there is more in common to the sentence structures found in different languages than merely the fact that they are tree-shaped. The trees always have a predictable, standard patterning. For instance, a word of a given part of speech, say a verb, will always be separated by the same number of branches from the node representing the most inclusive sentence constituent for which that is the 'head' word.

That sounds as though X-bar theorists were describing regularities that no one had previously noticed in the structures which linguists used to depict sentence grammar. It was not like that: the tree structures which linguists drew before the invention of X-bar theory did not have these regular patterns, but the theory says that the old trees ought to be replaced by trees drawn in the new style. Clearly, this makes sense only if the new notation implies testable predictions, not implied by the old notation, about observable matters of fact. Otherwise, advocating the theory would just mean expressing an aesthetic preference for one particular method of recording grammatical structure. So although Derek Bickerton and Steven Pinker both lay emphasis on the universal applicability of X-bar notation, whether this tells us anything at all about innate knowledge depends on what observable facts count as evidence for or against X-bar trees. What hypothetical observations would make the notation *in*applicable?

This is not an easy question to answer. One careful assessment of X-bar theory, by András Kornai and Geoffrey Pullum, concludes that the theory has few, if any, potential falsifiers – no hypothetical observations would count as evidence against it, in other words, the decision to use it really is just an aesthetic preference.

Still, Kornai and Pullum may have overlooked something, or they may have examined versions of the theory which differ subtly from those assumed by the nativist writers. (It is common in linguistics that a theory with a single name is really a family of related theories which differ in the predictions they make. That is no criticism; as already said, science is expected to progress, not remain static, so it is a good thing for theories to develop, provided they develop in the direction of yielding larger ranges of testable predictions about observable evidence – provided the family of theories constitutes a 'progressive problemshift', in Imre Lakatos's terms.) We ought to check what evidence the new-wave nativists themselves quote as supporting X-bar theory.

The books mention several points. Steven Pinker comments that one consequence of innate X-bar structure is that the arguments of a verb, such as direct and indirect object, must occur closer to the verb than its 'adjuncts' (elements that add extra information but are not essential, for instance, phrases saying when or where the action occurred): 'we can say *gave the documents to the spy in a hotel*, but not *gave in a hotel the documents to the spy*'. Since arguments and adjuncts are related as essence and accident, respectively, it does not seem too surprising that what is essential is commonly placed closer than what is accidental to the thing they both apply to. But it came as news to me, when I read Pinker's book, that English has a fixed rule about it. Again, though, let us not waste time debating what people *can* say, when it is easy to check how they *do* use the language.

It took very little time to disprove Pinker's statement from the million-word Brown Corpus of American English, because the second sentence in that corpus (taken from a news story in the *Atlanta Constitution*) is a counterexample:

> The jury further said in term-end presentments that the City Executive Committee, which had over-all charge of the election, 'deserves the praise and thanks of the City of Atlanta' for the manner in which the election was conducted.

The direct object of *said*, representing what was said, is the long nominal clause which begins *that the City Executive Committee . . .* and runs to the end of the sentence at *. . . was conducted*: this is an argument of *said*. On the other hand, *in term-end presentments* is an adjunct – it explains where or how the jury said what they did. (Incidentally: no, I do not know what presentments are either – but I am sure that if I lived in Georgia it would make perfect sense.)

In this case, the reason why the argument is further from the verb than the adjunct is because the argument is much longer. English (though not every language) has a strong tendency to get the short elements of a clause out of the way first, and defer 'heavy' elements to the end. Cases of this sort were extremely common in the corpus I searched. But length is not always an issue. Consider this sentence from an adventure novel:

I kept circling the block hoping to see, from the street behind it, the rear of the hall.

Again *the rear of the hall* is direct object of *see*, hence an argument, while *from the street behind it* is an adjunct of direction. Perhaps the novelist chose this order because the alternative, 'I kept circling the block hoping to see the rear of the hall from the street behind it', could carry a suggestion that the narrator had seen the rear of the hall from other places and now wanted to see it from the street – in fact, he was searching for any way to catch a glimpse of it. This is the kind of consideration which a careful writer will constantly be weighing up, consciously or unconsciously, in order to tweak his wording into the clearest, most persuasive possible sequence. It is odd to find as skilful a writer as Steven Pinker imagining that such matters are fixed by mechanical rules laid down in our genes. At any rate, they evidently are not.

Derek Bickerton tells us that X-bar theory explains why certain grammatical elements are obligatory and unomissible, while others are optional. In a noun phrase, for instance, a head noun is obligatory though subordinate elements such as *the* are optional. Or again, according to Bickerton the immensely distinguished American philosopher Willard Quine was 'baffled' at the fact that every sentence has to have a tense: X-bar theory dissolves Quine's bewilderment, by predicting that tense is obligatory as an innate language universal.

In English, though, head nouns do *not* seem to be obligatory in noun phrases. We have it on the highest authority, for instance, that 'ye have the poor always with you': the obvious way to describe the phrase *the poor* is as a noun phrase which includes the specifier *the* and the modifying adjective *poor*, but lacks a head noun. Phrases of this pattern are not rare in English, or in other languages. What would refute Bickerton's claim about heads being obligatory, if this does not?

As for tense, there are entire languages in which the ordinary grammatical concept of 'tense' gets no purchase. Chinese has no grammatical category of tense, unless that term is used in such a broad sense that it is hard to imagine what kind of language could possibly refute Bickerton's claim.

It might be that Bickerton has simply overlooked phrases like *the poor*, and the existence of tenseless languages. Much more likely, I believe, he and other X-bar theorists know about these things, but interpret their theory in such a way that it is not refuted by them. The significance of X-bar theory seems to lie more in suggesting that linguistics has entered a 'degenerating problemshift' phase, like Marxism after the Russian Revolution, than in helping to support the nativist view of Man.

Whether or not the predictions of X-bar theory are borne out, they cannot be understood unless we know what we mean by traditional part-of-speech names like 'noun' and 'verb'. For Ray Jackendoff this in itself is an important part of our innate knowledge of language. Universal grammar 'stipulates that a language contains a class of *nouns*', and it 'stipulates that there is a class of *verbs*'; 'children don't have to figure out that there are such things as nouns and verbs that fit into hierarchical tree patterns'.

This one I cannot contradict. That does not mean that all the traditional parts of speech are identical from language to language. For instance, some languages have no separate class of adjectives (in those languages adjectives translate into words that behave like verbs). Nor do the classes 'noun' and 'verb' always closely resemble the English word classes with those names. English and other European languages make an important distinction between two sorts of noun: 'countable' nouns like *dog, belief* (we can say 'two dogs', 'three beliefs') versus 'mass' nouns like *milk, seaweed* (we have to identify the units we are counting and say things like 'two pints of milk', 'three strands of seaweed'). In many Pacific Rim languages, on the other hand, all nouns are mass nouns: in Chinese, 'two dogs' translates into a phrase that might be glossed 'two *tiao* of dog', where *tiao* is a measure like *pint* or *strand* – one *tiao* is a quantity or segment of dog containing exactly four legs, one head and one tail. Still, I will admit that personally I do not know of any language to which the categories 'noun' and 'verb' cannot be applied in some shape or form. Jorge Luis Borges invented a fictional planet, Tlön, whose languages contained no nouns – instead of saying 'The moon rose above the river', an inhabitant of Tlön said something like 'Upward behind the onstreaming it mooned'. But I have never heard of a real language like this.

Even so. 'All languages have nouns and verbs.' It does not seem a lot, does it, on which to base a radically novel vision of the nature of the human mind?

And there is no more. We have now surveyed everything that these nativist writings say about language universals. No doubt there are other points which they omitted for lack of space. But they are not likely to be better points, otherwise the nativists would have used them and left out the points we have looked at.

Linguistic nativists have the virtue of tenacity, and I have little doubt that some of them will respond to this book along the lines 'OK, perhaps some of our past examples were ill chosen; but here is a new bunch of arguments for innate linguistic knowledge – what do you say to *them*?' The nativists are good at describing shared linguistic properties in terms which make their rationale unobvious and hence make the genetic explanation seem plausible to the layman (remember the island constraints); and I personally shall probably not say anything in response to the new arguments. I have other and more positive work commitments; there is a limit to the amount of time I can spend on refuting nativism. But the reader should look at things this way. We have now examined the cream of more than three decades of nativist arguments, and we have seen what they add up to. At this late date, how likely can it be that there is anything solider to be pulled out of the bag?

Steven Pinker himself has suggested that nativist arguments do not amount to much. In a posting on the electronic LINGUIST List (posting 9.1209, 1 September 1998), after the hardback edition of this book had appeared, he wrote: 'I agree that U[niversal] G[rammar] has been poorly defended and documented in the linguistics literature.' Yet that literature comprises the only grounds we are given for believing in the language universals theory. If the theory is more a matter of faith than evidence and reasoned argument even for its best-known advocate, why should anyone take it seriously?

To sum up this chapter: yes, there are some universal features in human languages, but what they mainly show is that human beings have to learn their mother tongues from scratch rather than having knowledge of language innate in their minds. Apart from the properties which lead to that conclusion, languages are just different (except that they probably do all contain nouns and verbs). I rest my case.

# 5   The Creative Mind

## Mind and brain

Earlier chapters have described the view of human nature which this book aims to defend. They have offered a picture of human languages as part of Man's culture, rather than part of our biology. We have looked at the linguistic nativists' attacks on that view, from the 1960s onwards. We have seen how insubstantial those attacks have been; and we have seen that some of the very evidence cited by the nativists to bolster their case actually supports the contrary view, that languages are wholly cultural constructs.

There remains a final objection to be met. I have presented the Popperian view of human nature, which sees the individual as making original though fallible conjectures and testing them against objective reality, as the common-sense, default view which most people would naturally accept unless they had good evidence that it was wrong. As an assessment of the outlook of the average man in the street who has no investment in any particular ideology, I believe that is broadly fair; but of course this proves nothing. The fact that an opinion coincides with the average man's common sense is no guarantee of truth – consensus opinions have certainly often been wrong. Since I began to advocate the Popperian view in print against the nativists almost twenty years ago, it has repeatedly been put to me that it must be rejected because it is incoherent. Human beings are only machines, although they are remarkably subtle and complex machines. Any machine can only produce some fixed, definable range of outputs, even if the range is very large; the idea that people create truly original ideas does not really make sense. Full information about the mechanisms of the human mind *must* imply what mental products human beings are capable of developing or mastering – what possible scientific theories or artistic genres it is open to us to construct, and what languages we could possibly speak. We are a long way off acquiring such full information, but, in principle, nativism must be right.

The first thing to notice about this line of argument, which I have mainly encountered in face-to-face discussion (though I shall quote some published expressions of it below), is that it is quite different from – and incompatible with – the nativist arguments put forward in the writings we have been looking at. Noam Chomsky, Derek Bickerton, Ray Jackendoff and Steven Pinker argue that the observable *evidence* points to nativism being correct. They quote a mass of different kinds of data which, they believe, can all be explained if we assume innate knowledge, and are difficult to explain without that postulate. It would be inconsistent to argue that there is observable evidence in favour of a given opinion, and also that the converse of that opinion is senseless or incoherent. If the evidence strongly suggests that smoking causes cancer, that implies that, logically, smoking might not cause cancer – otherwise, observable evidence would be irrelevant. Chomsky and the other leading linguistic nativists hardly ever claim that their opponents' views are incoherent. (We have seen occasional claims of that sort, notably in connection with the 'Mentalese' concept, but they are not typical.)

So arguably it is not necessary to answer the incoherence objection. In addition, I hesitate to do so, because explaining why it is misguided requires us to consider ideas that are very different in kind from the ideas we have looked at so far; they are more abstractly philosophical, and therefore perhaps less congenial to many readers. In previous chapters I was able to cover many points with a reasonably light touch, because I could quote chapter and verse in the notes for readers who wanted to follow up the detail. With the present topic, we are getting to frontiers-of-human-understanding stuff: if I handle it at all, I must spell the details out myself, and therefore I must write relatively densely.

Nevertheless, in conversations about linguistic nativism with fellow academics I have so often found myself pushed away from the specific, concrete issues about language structure and linguistic behaviour towards talking about how human beings can coherently be described as creatively original that I believe this book would not be complete if it ignored the question. Many readers would assume that I had not discussed it because it was a gaping hole in my argument which I was incapable of filling.

To say that human minds have an ability to be original, or creative, is to say that they engender ideas which fall outside any range that could be predicted by studying past ideas, or by possible study of mental mechanisms. If minds were physical entities – if talk about a person's mental life were really talk about an aspect of his brain functioning – then there could be no creativity in this sense. Physical objects work by physical law, so for any physical mechanism, no matter how complex, there is a fixed range of possible future behaviours, which in principle could be specified explicitly. The range may be very large and diverse (it may be infinitely large), but its boundaries are definite.

The position adopted in this book is that conscious human minds are not physical entities. Talking about minds is not a way of talking about high-level aspects of brain functioning. Minds and bodies are different and separate things which act on one another.

Together with the neurobiologist Sir John Eccles, Sir Karl Popper wrote *The Self and Its Brain* to reassert the classic philosophical stance of *interactionism*.

A person's mind uses his brain to control his body and hence act on the physical world, and to monitor the environment, as an aircraft pilot uses the cockpit with its instrumentation to monitor and control the aeroplane. The word 'pilot' is not just an abstract way of talking about aircraft cockpits. It is not the case that as the structure of aircraft cockpits is made increasingly subtle and complex, from the stick-and-string era at the beginning of mechanical flight through to the serried ranks of indicators and controls in a high-performance present-day plane, pilots eventually come into being as an automatic spin-off from the degree of cockpit complexity. Pilots are a different sort of thing from cockpits; and minds are a different sort of thing from brains.

Minds are not a topic open to scientific theorizing. Popper has urged that when subjects can be studied scientifically, it is desirable that they should be; but he stresses at the same time that there are real and important topics to which the scientific method does not apply. Morality is one obvious case: there are things it is right to do and things it is wrong to do, but scientific research will not tell us which is which. Minds are another.

For much of the twentieth century it has been more fashionable to believe that everything can be reduced to physics. A. J. Ayer argued that insofar as statements about morality are not scientific, 'they are not in the literal sense significant, but are simply expressions of emotion which can be neither true nor false'. Materialist philosophers such as J. J. C. Smart have argued that mental phenomena are identical to physical phenomena.

But on a longer timescale this is just one point of view, and not a very usual one. On the mind/body issue, Descartes' dualism – his assertion of the fundamental distinctness of conscious minds and physical matter – was an aspect of his thought that proved to have much more staying power than his belief that our ideas are innate. ('Dualism' refers to the belief that mind and matter are two ultimately distinct substances; the converse belief, that minds are reducible to one aspect of bodies, is called 'materialism' or 'monism'.) Classically, dualism was not one of the issues dividing nativists and empiricists – M. R. Ayers refers to dualism as a 'system of thought that Locke a little hesitantly shares with Descartes'. In the 1990s the dualist view is receiving fresh impetus through the work of David Chalmers of the University of California, Santa Cruz.

The advent of the computer has made a real change to the way we think about intellectual creativity. It forces us to appreciate that, if the human mind is genuinely creative, it cannot be a physical structure.

Before the computer, it was easy to avoid noticing that thinking about minds as just an aspect of brains was not compatible with the idea that minds innovate in unpredictable ways. Even if equating minds with brains implied that minds can do only what physical machines of some kind can do, brains were certainly mechanisms that were immensely more complicated than any machines which mankind had designed and understood, and their products were correspondingly far more diverse than those of any artificial machines; this great diversity was a much more noticeable thing than the fact that ultimately there must be fixed bounds to the diversity. The leading philosophical argument for dualism was an argument about *consciousness*; people felt that consciousness did not seem to be the kind of thing that could be brought into being by a particular arrangement of matter. Intellectual creativity was less central to the argument.

Computers, though, have made us familiar with the idea of surveying with ease the exact boundaries of domains that contain immense (but finite) diversity. Before the computer, one could speak loosely of personal names, say, being 'endlessly' diverse – of course educated people knew the difference between mathematical infinity and very large finite quantities, but this was an abstract, bloodless awareness and in many circumstances it would have felt pedantic to insist on the difference. Now, someone with access to an appropriate electronic database can press a few buttons and within seconds see a list of, say, all current British personal names containing more than three Qs, if there are any. It casts a new light on the distinction between innovation within fixed but wide boundaries and truly creative, boundary-breaking innovation. Any physical machine can be innovative only in the former sense. If the human mind is innovative in the latter sense, it cannot be a physical machine.

Within the literature of linguistic nativism, it happens that this issue has been obscured by the fact that Noam Chomsky chooses to use the word 'creative' in a rather unusual way. He often claims that his nativist account of human mental functioning attributes 'creativity' to human beings. Yet, in the terms of the previous paragraph, Chomsky is claiming that human beings can innovate only within fixed boundaries. Indeed, as we saw in Chapter 1, the tendency of Chomsky's writings is to urge that the fixed boundaries are not even all that wide. Humanity may already have run out of new art-forms. The range of possible human languages may be not merely definable in terms of fixed rules but actually finite – all the different languages which any human community could ever learn to use might in principle be listed and defined in something like a manual one could pick up and hold.

In Chomsky's terms, a simple automaton like a speak-your-weight machine would not be 'creative', because it has only one mechanical response available to any one simple stimulus (a particular weight standing on its platform); but a computer program like, say, John McDermott's expert system R1, which designs effective configurations of computer hardware components, ought to be called 'creative' because its outputs are drawn from a large and diverse range and depend on a complex internal knowledge base and fairly subtle interactions with the human user. Yet of course the range of possible outputs from R1 is rigidly fixed, though it may be large. R1 will never surprise us in the fashion that an original painter or composer may surprise us.

There is no copyright in words. But the difficulty about Chomsky's use of 'creative' to refer to individually unpredictable innovations within fixed boundaries is that it leaves no obvious English word free for the deeper, boundary-breaking sense of 'creativity'. When I have discussed this issue before, particularly in my 1979 book *Liberty and Language*, I have found that commentators with a background in linguistics tend to be reluctant to recognize that there is a real distinction here that should not be obscured.

More philosophically minded commentators take my point. The philosopher Mary Warnock, for instance, sees Chomsky's use of the word 'creative' as 'misleading if not positively fraudulent'. Perhaps we need not go further than 'misleading', but Chomsky's usage does cause a regrettable confusion. My own use of 'creative' in the following pages will always refer to the 'boundary-breaking' sense.

## Popper a nativist?

Of course, the reader may be wedded to a materialist concept of mind himself. The nativists' insistence that intellectual innovation occurs not only within fixed boundaries but boundaries which are quite narrow means that the present book has a message which even a convinced materialist may find acceptable. If human minds are machines built from matter, then there must be some specifiable boundaries to their range of potential products, but materialism alone gives us no reason to assume that the boundaries are narrow. A computerized, mechanical language-processing system could be set up to use the kind of structure-independent question-forming rule which Chomsky says is unnatural for human beings. A materialist concept of mind, with no further premises, certainly does not in itself yield a prediction that there can be only finitely many humanly learnable languages. Materialist-oriented readers could therefore read this book as demonstrating that the facts of human language give us no reason to suppose that human intellectual creativity is constrained any more tightly than would be implied by the bare fact that the mind is a highly complex machine of some unknown design. The linguistic nativists argue that far more specific, restrictive constraints can be seen to apply. This book has refuted those arguments.

Nevertheless, the author's own position is not materialist. The view I am actually defending is that languages, like other examples of human culture, are the result of individuals producing fallible but innovative ideas in the attempt to make sense of and to master their environment, and that individuals are able to participate in the development of culture because we have minds which are genuinely creative: minds are not machines whose outputs are drawn from a fixed and predictable range. Is there anything incoherent in this view?

If critics object that one's beliefs are empirically mistaken, one defends them by examining the objective evidence. If the criticism is that one's ideas are incoherent (and if the criticism does not go away after one restates the ideas two or three times in different wording), the only real method of defence is to point to more distinguished thinkers who have shared the same views. It is very understandable that readers will not want to accept that something makes sense just because the present writer says it does. But there are thinkers whose reputations are less easily dismissed who have said so too.

For some time it seemed to me self-evident that Karl Popper was one of those thinkers. To my surprise, this turned out to be a controversial claim.

Some people have argued that Popper's true position is virtually the opposite of the one I attribute to him.

Ultimately this does not matter for my thesis; if Popper was ambiguous about creativity, we shall see that others have been unambiguous. Nevertheless, it is worth looking in some depth at just what Karl Popper's position was. His intellectual principles are in other respects so central to the picture of human nature advocated in this book that, if they diverge in one respect, we need to be explicit about this. And careful study of the ambiguities in Popper's statements about creativity will be a way of becoming clearer in our own minds about that concept.

At one level, Popper is supremely a philosopher of creativity. In a long essay on Popper's œuvre, the American philosopher W.W. Bartley has written:

> The basic theme of Karl Popper's philosophy is that something can come from nothing.
>
> It is not surprising that such an idea should meet incomprehension and stark resistance, for it opposes the dominant watchwords of our philosophical tradition:
>
>> There is nothing new under the sun.
>> Nothing can be created or destroyed.
>> *Ex nihilo nihil fit.*
>
> The chief ideas of Popper's philosophy all relate to the basic theme that something can come from nothing. Scientific theories introduce new forms into the universe and cannot be reduced to observations . . . The future is not contained in the present or the past . . . There is genuine emergence in biology. Value cannot be reduced to fact. Mind cannot be reduced to matter. . . . the products of consciousness are not determined.

However, after reading critics' objections to my discussion of Popper's view of creativity in earlier writings, I must give some ground. The truth seems to be that, like many thinkers who have written in depth about complex subjects over a long period, Popper was not entirely consistent. His views developed, and at some periods contained contradictions. Popper's various readers, myself included, have tended (in a very human fashion) unconsciously to fasten on those remarks which coincide with our own views and to overlook the less pleasing quotations.

Let me be careful about the issue I am dealing with. I am not concerned with the question whether human thought or action is deterministic – which is an issue that often seems to get confused with the issue I am discussing. It is quite conceivable that human beings might be indeterministic in the sense that it was impossible to predict what particular thought would occur to them or how they would behave in any particular situation, yet their thoughts and actions might always be drawn from a fixed, antecedently specifiable range. Chomsky sees the situation in very much that way. I am taking it for granted that we are not deterministic with respect to *individual* thoughts and actions;

the question I am considering is whether our ideas are deterministic even in the far weaker sense of being drawn from fixed, enumerable ranges of possibilities. My own view (and the view which I originally took to be Popper's) is that we are not deterministic even in this weak sense; a person will sometimes produce an idea which does not belong to a range of potential ideas that could have been predicted on the basis of ideal, complete knowledge of that person as he was before he produced the idea.

As already suggested, a common reaction to my previous writings on this topic has been the claim that Popper does not see human beings as mentally creative in this sense. This has often been allied to the suggestion that Popper does not hold this view, because no one could (or at least no one but Sampson could), since it is incoherent or otherwise inadmissible a priori. Thus, for instance, Robert Lees quotes my definition of a creative phenomenon as 'one which constantly escapes the bounds suggested by its past history, so that any testable prediction about it will be falsified (unless it just happens to remain unrefuted by accident)', and Lees comments, 'some readers may regard this quotation as close to gibberish' – though he adds a remark which possibly implies that Lees does not himself share this judgement. Again, James Hurford says that 'a serious philosopher of mind must believe that it is possible to say something about the mind, whereas S[ampson]'s "creative view" is essentially the conviction that nothing can be said about the mind.' Or, to give one more example, Anthony Storr comments that 'Sampson writes: "Some people find the notion that minds engender ideas out of nothing unacceptable *a priori*." I am one of those people.'

Deferring for the moment the question of Popper's position, why do these writers suggest that the notion of mental creativity is a priori unacceptable? I believe there are two reasons. The less important of these is spelled out by Hurford: he summarizes the thesis of my *Making Sense* in the words 'There can be no "science of mind" which is able to specify a way in which no human will think in the future' (I accept that as a broadly fair summary), and he comments that this thesis 'is in principle neither falsifiable nor verifiable, because it contains too many negated existential quantifiers'. If my thesis of mental creativity had been offered as an empirical scientific hypothesis, this would be a rather damning criticism; but I tried to avoid suggesting that the thesis has this status. As I had pointed out in the earlier *Liberty and Language*, it is an example of another sort of statement which philosophers of science recognize as having an important role to play in human understanding: what John Watkins calls a 'haunted-universe doctrine'.

The a priori objection to mental creativity which I believe looms larger than this one in many people's minds is that, as we have seen, creativity implies dualism. Even when I have given papers criticizing the nativist account of language to audiences of linguists, who might be expected to be more interested in the aspects of the argument that deal with observable facts about languages than in the philosophical underpinnings, people have often been very quick to say that my alternative to the nativist account might sound superficially attractive but it will not do, because it requires dualism and people are much more confident that dualism is wrong than they are about any of the detailed differences of opinion between the linguistic nativists and myself.

But to treat dualism as intellectually incoherent really would be to dismiss a vast swathe of the world's leading thinkers as woolly minds. They may be, but the case would require argument, not just a brief allusion to currently fashionable opinion. As Popper says, what he calls 'promissory materialism' – materialism which claims not that the reduction of mental to physical language has already been achieved (which it has certainly not) but that it will ultimately be achieved – is

> a peculiar theory. It consists, essentially, of a . . . prophecy about the future results of brain research . . . This prophecy is baseless . . . The opinion of researchers who . . . started as identity theorists, but ended as dualists . . . is ignored . . .

Popper has been criticized for his readiness to embrace dualism. John Beloff argues that both he and Sir John Eccles 'underestimate . . . the enormously powerful case for materialism' – though this does not mean that Beloff believes Popper and Eccles's position is untenable, he is writing as an ally warning them not to underestimate the strength of the opposition. The kinds of evidence to which Beloff alludes are neurological phenomena that I am not qualified to comment on; I must leave that aspect of the debate to the likes of Eccles. But anyone who agrees that empirical scientific evidence, such as the things Beloff mentions, provides good support for the materialist view of mind demonstrates that he does *not* see the dualist view as inadmissible on a priori grounds (as some of my own critics seem to suppose it is).

The philosopher Hilary Putnam has pointed out that linguists are too ready in this area to rule out ideas which they disagree with as 'logically impossible'. Stanley Jaki has offered an impressive historical survey of the way in which, again and again, purported arguments for materialism have begged the question.

My alternative to the nativists' account of the nature of human mind and human learning is surely at least logically coherent. But am I right in taking it to coincide with Popper's view?

On this issue my most explicit critic has been James Hurford. He has quoted me as contrasting the 'creative view of mind' which I aim to defend with the 'limited view of mind' which was the (possibly tendentious) name I gave to the view that rejects mental creativity:

> 'Limited minders' include Plato, Kant, Descartes, and Chomsky. In contrast, 'the . . . creative view . . . is represented . . . by . . . Popper' . . . [Sampson] largely extrapolates Popper's view of mind from his philosophy of science; but he finds no non-contemporary philosophers to set up as 'creative minders'. This is not surprising, since a serious philosopher of mind must believe that it is possible to say something about the mind, whereas S[ampson]'s 'creative view' is essentially the conviction that nothing can be

said about the mind [this is the passage quoted above] . . . A debate which can have participants only on one side is no debate.

Hurford's point about my 'extrapolating Popper's views from his philosophy of science' suggests that I may be misrepresenting Popper; and later in his review Hurford returns to this charge. He quotes me as 'attribut[ing] to the mind "the ability to create ex nihilo"', and comments:

> I cannot reconcile . . . this with what Popper calls 'the fundamental theorem': 'All acquired knowledge, all learning, consists of the modification (possibly the rejection) of some form of knowledge, or disposition, which was there previously, and in the last instance of inborn dispositions.'

Hurford continues: 'I find a strong contrast of emphasis between S[ampson]'s account of Popper's position . . . and Popper's own words.' Hurford quotes a passage in which I paraphrase what I take to be Popper's view as follows: 'we may genetically inherit some ideas, but we produce many more, and the new ideas are not predictable from or related in any simple way to the innate ideas', and Hurford contrasts this with the following passage from Popper:

> If it were not absurd to make any estimate, I should say that 999 units out of 1,000 of the knowledge of an organism are inherited or inborn, and that one unit only consists of the modifications of this inborn knowledge; and I suggest, in addition, that *the plasticity needed* for these modifications is also inborn.

Now, of these two passages of Popper's quoted by Hurford, which occur on the same page of a single essay, the one about all learning consisting of the modification or rejection of earlier knowledge and ultimately of inborn dispositions is only a restatement of Popper's frequent point that the growth of knowledge is a dialectic process, which I do not want to dispute. The claim that new ideas are produced in response to problems that have arisen with old ideas, rather than just popping up apropos of nothing in particular, does not in any way contradict the suggestion that the formulation of new ideas is a creative act. What matters is not why we produce new ideas, but whether the ideas produced are genuinely new.

But the second passage, about 999 out of 1000 units of knowledge of an organism being inborn, and the plasticity needed for the modification represented by the thousandth unit also being inborn, does indeed make Popper sound very Chomskyan. It is difficult not to interpret this passage as saying something like

> the bulk of our knowledge is genetically inherited, so that when an individual appears to be 'learning' all that is really going on is that he is becoming consciously aware of aspects of his mental organization that were present in unconscious form from the beginning; and although our genetic endowment leaves some minor aspects of an adult's knowledge freely variable, it does fix the range of possible values for the variable aspects of knowledge, so that when these variables are filled in through the individual's interaction with

his environment he is only selecting one among a set of possibilities given in advance rather than inventing genuinely novel beliefs.

The linguistic nativists could scarcely ask for a better pupil.

Moreover, this passage is not the only one suitable to Hurford's purpose. Popper makes other remarks which sound, if anything, even more Chomskyan – though the really telling examples I have found both come from the same essay that Hurford quoted, 'Two faces of common sense', in which Popper, like Chomsky, is concerned to refute a passive, *tabula rasa* view of learning – what Popper calls the 'bucket theory of the mind'. Thus Popper writes:

> As children we learn to decode the chaotic messages which meet us from our environment . . . Learning to decode the messages which reach us is extremely complicated. It is based on innate dispositions. We are, I conjecture, innately disposed to refer the messages to a coherent and partly regular or ordered system . . . our subjective knowledge of reality consists of maturing innate dispositions . . . we learn the decoding by *trial and error elimination* . . .

Again, he writes:

> The *tabula rasa* theory is pre-Darwinian: to every man who has any feeling for biology it must be clear that most of our dispositions are inborn, either in the sense that we are born with them (for example, the dispositions to breathe, to swallow, and so on) or in the sense that in the process of maturation, the development of the disposition is elicited by the environment (for example, the disposition to learn a language).

This latter passage, admittedly, might be read as saying only that we have an innate disposition to learn some language, without any detailed information about the structure of language being inborn. We saw on p. 25 that Popper believes in nativism in that very weak sense (though I do not). But the statement that 'our subjective knowledge of reality consists of maturing innate dispositions' does seem to mean that the individual, detailed components of our knowledge of language (or of any other complex aspect of reality) are themselves built in from the start as a range of inborn possibilities, so that the active role of the mind would be limited to choosing a strategy for carrying out the trial-and-error process which winnows out those of the innate ideas that do not fit experience. In his *Autobiography*, Popper writes that

> a 'trial' or a newly formed 'dogma' or 'expectation' is largely the result of inborn *needs* . . . I do not of course deny that there may also be an element of personal ingenuity present in the formation of trials or dogmas, but I think that ingenuity and imagination play their main part in the *critical process of error elimination*.

The mind is active, in other words, in the sense that an enterprising grocer may be active, scurrying round to find just the right tin to suit a shopper's tastes, but hardly in the sense that an artist is active when he creates an art object different in kind from anything the world had known before.

All this seems very comparable to the linguistic nativists' view of mental activity. Consider Chomsky's statement:

> As a precondition for language learning, [the child] must possess, first, a linguistic theory that specifies the form of the grammar of a possible human language, and, second, a strategy for selecting a grammar of the appropriate form that is compatible with the primary linguistic data.

Again:

> A child who is capable of language learning must have . . . some initial delimitation of a class of possible hypotheses about language structure . . . [and] . . . a method for selecting one of the . . . hypotheses . . . compatible with the . . . data.

In a note, Chomsky adds that

> it might very well be true that a series of successively more detailed and highly structured schemata (corresponding to maturational stages, but perhaps in part themselves determined in form by earlier steps of language acquisition) are applied to the data at successive stages of language acquisition.

There is a difference between Chomsky's account of learning and the account I have suggested by the quotations I have just excerpted from Popper. For Chomsky, the strategy for finding the correct hypothesis is itself biologically determined: his grocer is an automaton who selects a particular item from the shelves quite mechanically in response to the data which the customer enters at his console, while Popper's grocer exercises 'ingenuity and imagination' in seeking out the item that will make the shopper happy. But both Chomsky's and Popper's grocers, apparently, are no more than grocers: what they can sell is limited to the '57 varieties' that their supplier provides. True, Popper concedes that 'there may . . . be an element of personal ingenuity' in the formation as well as in the choice of hypotheses; but this reads like a reluctant concession.

## Popper and emergence

However, other passages in Popper's writings read very differently. Consider, to begin with, remarks that occur just a few paragraphs earlier than the passage just quoted in the *Autobiography*:

> critical thinking may consist not only in a rejection of any particular trial or conjecture, but also in a rejection of what may be described as a deeper conjecture – the assumption of the range of 'all possible trials' . . . What characterizes creative thinking . . . seems to me often the ability to break

through the limits of the range – or to vary the range – from which a less
creative thinker selects his trials.

A natural way to interpret this passage, surely, is to interpret Popper as saying
that the mind is indeed an artist rather than a grocer. Much of the time the
mind is a hack artist producing stereotyped responses to stereotyped stimuli:
yet another captain of industry commissions yet another boardroom portrait,
and what he gets is no more than a numerically distinct example of a familiar
genre. But from time to time experience poses a novel, unexpected problem,
and the mind can rise to the challenge by formulating genuinely novel
conjectures: episodes of real creativity punctuate an otherwise humdrum
artistic career.

Now I appreciate that a sceptical reader could well argue that I am
misinterpreting Popper, and that the passage just quoted is perfectly compatible
with the grocer view of the mind. The concept of 'breaking through the limits
of the range of possible trials', it might be said, should be understood in the
following way. The supermarket containing the hypotheses which a person
uses in order to meet the challenges posed by experience is an enormously
large one, and the numerous lines of goods it stocks are kept not just in the
shop itself but in a series of store-rooms at different distances from the shop.
All this is true of each individual branch of the supermarket chain we are
talking about, but the branches differ with respect to how much trouble their
respective managers will take when a customer who has unusual wants
appears. At some branches, if the shopper is not happy with what she sees on
the open shelves the manager will unlock store-room after store-room and
fetch out goods which no one has ever bought before. At a lot of other branches,
the manager either has no key to the store-rooms or perhaps he is just lazy, so
if the shopper is not happy with what she can see that is too bad: the manager
either avoids noticing her and hopes she will go away, or else he forces some
packet on her which is not really what she requires. The stock in the store-
rooms just gathers dust year after year.

This way of contrasting creative and uncreative minds would still leave
Popper's view rather different from Chomsky's. Chomsky is hostile to the idea
that individuals might differ in the extent to which they can exploit their innate
structures of knowledge. He often asserted, for instance, that the various
members of a speech community, whether highly intelligent or educationally
subnormal, are virtually indistinguishable in their degree of mastery of the
grammar of their language (though so far as I know he never gave evidence
for this startling claim, and we saw in Chapter 2 that he eventually withdrew
it). Nevertheless, if Chomsky means his theory of learning as selection among
inborn hypotheses to apply not just to language acquisition but to scientific
progress, then it seems he would be forced to accept a model something like
the one I outlined in the preceding paragraph, in order to explain the fact that
Albert Einstein succeeded in formulating the theory of special relativity while
many other people could not even understand it once it had been formulated.
And, more important, even the picture of the mind as including nearer and

further store-rooms is still a picture which treats the set of possible hypotheses as determinate. If this is how we are to interpret Popper's remarks, then what he calls a 'creative mind' is not actually creating novel products – those products already exist in unconscious, potential form in the minds of dull individuals, and no genuinely new idea is ever formulated (unless by biological mutation).

However, if it is possible to interpret Popper's remarks in the *Autobiography* this way, it is much harder to impose a similar interpretation on passages in *The Self and Its Brain* where Popper explicitly allies himself with the philosophers of emergence. Thus, Popper writes:

> One of the oldest of philosophical dogmas is summed up by the saying . . . 'There is no new thing under the sun'. In a way, this is also implied by materialism . . . Materialists hold – or held – that matter is eternal and that all change consists in the motion of bits of matter, and in the consequent changes of their arrangements . . . The view that there is no new thing under the sun is, in a way, involved in the original meaning of the word 'evolution': . . . evolution meant originally the unrolling of what is there already: what is there, *preformed*, is to be made manifest . . . Today some of us have learnt to use the term 'evolution' differently. For we think that evolution . . . has produced new things: *real novelty* . . . The usual materialist and physicalist view is that all the possibilities which have realized themselves in the course of time and of evolution must have been, potentially, preformed, or pre-established, from the beginning. This is either a triviality . . . or a mistake.

It happens that Popper is here discussing the evolution of new kinds of form in the universe, rather than of new kinds of knowledge within an individual mind. But it would be implausible to suggest that Popper's belief in evolutionary emergence does not extend to the emergence of novel hypotheses within the individual. In earlier writings Popper repeatedly makes it very explicit that he sees the growth of knowledge within the individual as continuous in its logical nature with the evolution of species – 'From the amoeba to Einstein, the growth of knowledge is always the same: we try to solve our problems, and to obtain, by a process of elimination, something approaching adequacy in our tentative solutions.' If the individual human were limited to a preformed range of potential hypotheses while Nature were capable of producing real novelty, little of this logical continuity would survive. In any case, Popper does briefly allude to 'development' as well as 'evolution' in the passage quoted, and elsewhere he makes it clear that his point about the emergence of real novelty is indeed intended to apply to individual thought. For instance, he objects to physical determinism on the ground that 'It . . . destroys . . . the idea of creativity. It reduces to a complete illusion the idea that in preparing this lecture I have used my brain to create *something new*.'

It is also true that the last sentence in the displayed quotation above suggests that the preformation idea might be true as a 'triviality'; but it is clear that Popper does *not* mean that it is trivially true that the range of all possible future forms can be predicted by physical law: what he goes on to say is that it is trivially true that nothing will emerge which *violates* physical law, but that this does not imply that one can specify the range of all possible forms *compatible* with physical law. (At this point, however – and also in the passage quoted at the end of the last paragraph – Popper unfortunately seems to fall foul of the confusion I mentioned earlier about prediction of individual events v. prediction of classes of all possible events; he writes as if denial of emergent evolution implies that 'the future is and always was foreseeable, at least in principle', but if foreseeing the future means saying which particular elements among a range of possibilities will actually be realized on given occasions then of course there is no such implication.)

Later in *The Self and Its Brain*, Popper goes on to write:

> The idea of 'creative' or 'emergent' evolution . . . is very simple, if somewhat vague. It refers to the fact that . . . new things and events occur, with unexpected and indeed unpredictable properties; things and events that are new, more or less in the sense in which a great work of art may be described as new.

Popper recognizes that there is an 'intuitively appealing' argument against this idea, which he spells out as follows:

> If something new seems to emerge in the course of the evolution of the universe – a new chemical element . . . or a new compound molecule, or a living organism, or human speech, or conscious experience – then the physical particles or structures involved must have possessed beforehand what we may call the 'disposition' or 'possibility' or 'potentiality' or 'capacity' for producing the new properties, under appropriate conditions. In other words, the possibility or potentiality of entering into the new combination or structure, and the possibility or potentiality of producing thereby the apparently unpredictable or emergent new property, must have been there before the event . . .

Popper considers this argument, and rejects it. Rightly or wrongly, he does not believe that all the potentialities of a thing belong to it before the thing manifests them. 'We can admit that the world does not change in so far as certain universal laws remain invariant. But there are other important and interesting lawlike aspects . . . that do change, depending on the changing situation . . . There can be invariant laws *and* emergence . . .' Passages like these, together with the repeatedly drawn parallel between natural evolution and the evolution of knowledge within the individual, surely point unmistakably to the conclusion that (when he wrote them, at least) Popper did not hold a view akin to the nativists' view of hypothesis formulation.

## The possible and the real

Taken as a whole, then, Popper's writings do seem ambiguous on this question. Perhaps we might try to approach the 'real' Popper (assuming that there is a consistent view lurking behind these apparently contradictory passages) along another path: by looking at what Popper has to say about the work of other writers whose belief in genuinely creative emergence was less equivocal than his. Because, whatever else may have been right or wrong in the remarks of Hurford's that I quoted earlier, Hurford is utterly mistaken in suggesting that creativity in the strong sense is a newfangled concept never previously advocated.

Indeed, if Pinker and other linguistic nativists are serious in their call for the intellectual world to retrace a wrong turning it took in the 1920s, then logically they really ought to be urging us to return to the concept of emergence. Philosophically, the opening decades of the twentieth century were soaked in the ideas of creativity or emergence in the strong sense. These ideas were advocated, for instance, by Samuel Alexander and Conwy Lloyd Morgan in England; by J.C. Smuts in South Africa; and, perhaps most notably, by the Frenchman Henri Bergson.

Popper's writings contain only occasional brief references to Alexander and Lloyd Morgan, though when he does refer to them his remarks are usually favourable. About Bergson, on the other hand, Popper says quite a lot, as we shall see in a moment.

Bergson's thought displays a striking range of parallels with Popper's. One link between them is that it was from Bergson that Popper borrowed the key term 'Open Society'. But many of the themes of Popper's evolutionary epistemology, too, are prefigured in Bergson: the notion that intellectual development within Man is a continuation and transcendence of physical evolution within lower species; the notion that the newborn child begins with inherited ideas but uses his intelligence to move beyond them (Bergson in *Creative Evolution* uses the same example as Popper of an innate expectation, namely the expectation of being fed at a nipple – admittedly the example is a rather obvious one); the notion that intellectual advances are evoked by problems, often practical problems; the notion that perception is not a passive function like photography but an active, selective function which is controlled by reference to the organism's problem situation; the dualist notion that a self uses its brain as an instrument (for Bergson, it is an instrument for filtering out useless memories) – all these are key ideas for both thinkers. The one leading idea in Popper for which I have not myself noticed parallels in Bergson is the demarcation criterion for science, but Imre Lakatos has claimed that this too was developed by Popper from ideas of 'the Bergsonians'.

Bergson is not always the clearest of writers. Intellectual styles change; it would be naïve to expect a scholar of one period to conform to the conventions of discourse usual almost a century later. But if there is one point on which Bergson is unequivocal, it is that he believes in creativity in the strongest possible sense of the term. Consider, for instance, his essay 'Le possible et le réel', which is concerned as he says in the first sentence with 'the continual creation of unforeseeable novelty which seems to take place in the universe'. (Translations from this essay are my own.) Bergson contrasts inert matter, whose behaviour is wholly governed by invariant physical laws, with Man who has the power of creating 'radical novelty'. We are:

> Craftsmen of our lives, even artists when we wish, we continually work at moulding the material supplied to us by past and present, by heredity and circumstances, into a shape that is unique, novel, original, unforeseeable like the form which a sculptor gives his clay.

Bergson is well aware that his point of view is commonly resisted. He argues that it is a characteristic of the human intellect to interpret change as the successive occupation by reality of different points in a fixed logical space of possibilities. But, according to Bergson, it is an error to imagine that the question 'What is possible?' has an answer independent of the question 'What is?'

The most telling passage in the essay describes how Bergson was asked by a journalist during the First World War for his views on the future of literature after the War.

> '. . . How do you envisage the great dramatic work of the future, for instance?' . . . I replied: 'If I knew what the great dramatic work of the future would be, I would write it.' [Compare Popper's remark, 'If there is such a thing as growing human knowledge, then we cannot anticipate today what we shall know only tomorrow.'] I could see that [the interviewer] thought of the future work as being already at that time locked up in some sort of cupboard of possibilities; because Philosophy and I were old friends, I was deemed to have been given by her the key to the cupboard. 'But', I said to him, 'the work you speak of is not yet possible.'

> 'Certainly it must be possible, since it will become actual.'

> 'No, it isn't possible. At most I will concede to you that it *will have been* possible.'

> 'What do you mean by that?'

> 'It's simple enough. Let a man of talent or genius appear and create a work: it is then real, and by the same token it becomes retrospectively or retroactively possible . . .'

> . . . The idea, immanent in most philosophies and natural to the human mind, of possibilities which would become realities via an acquisition of existence, is . . . pure illusion.

Bergson goes on to argue that the word 'possible' is ambiguous:

> *Hamlet* was no doubt possible before it became real, if this is understood to mean that there was no insurmountable obstacle to its realization. In *that* sense, we call 'possible' whatever is not impossible; and clearly this non-impossibility of a thing is a necessary condition for its becoming real. But the 'possible' in that sense has no element of the virtual, of the ideally pre-existent.

The almost theological flavour of Bergson's discussion of the nature of possibility contrasts with the concreteness of Popper's manner of philosophizing. But Bergson's idea of the real creating the possible is surely very comparable with Popper's suggestion that 'the first emergence of a novelty such as life may change the possibilities or propensities in the universe . . . newly emergent entities . . . create *new fields of propensities*, as a new star creates a new field of gravitation'. And the remark by Bergson about possibility in the usual sense being something more than non-impossibility might be compared with Popper's statement: 'There can be invariant laws *and* emergence; for the system of invariant laws is not sufficiently complete and restrictive to prevent the emergence of new lawlike properties.' In his emergentist moods, Popper is extremely Bergsonian.

As I have suggested, Popper's mood has not always been so emergentist. Likewise, he has not always been equally Bergsonian; and what he has *said* about Bergson at different times is remarkably diverse.

In his early book, *The Logic of Scientific Discovery*, Bergson is mentioned just once, while Popper is explaining that he is interested in the logic by which scientific hypotheses are tested rather than in how testable hypotheses are formulated. Popper writes: 'my view of the matter . . . is that there is no such thing as a logical method of having new ideas . . . My view may be expressed by saying that every discovery contains "an irrational element", or "a creative intuition", in Bergson's sense.' This harmonizes with Popper's attitude to creativity in *The Self and Its Brain*. But if we come forward in time to *The Open Society and Its Enemies*, which I think contains more references to Bergson than any other of Popper's works, we find a very different tone. When he acknowledges the loan of the term 'Open Society', Popper comments that his use of the term differs from Bergson's, and this difference is 'due to a fundamentally different approach to nearly every problem of philosophy' – surely a remarkable judgement in view of the parallels I drew attention to earlier. Later, again in connection with the political idea of the Open Society, Popper attributes to Bergson 'a somewhat hysterical . . . acceptance of change as real, essential and welcome' – again a surprising remark to come from the man who was to become the leading philosophical advocate of 'scientific and industrial progress'. In his second volume Popper notes with approval that many philosophers are beginning to lose interest in Hegel, but he makes an exception of 'the "evolutionists"', and he explains in a note that 'I have in mind the various philosophies of "evolution" or "progress" or "emergence" such as those of H. Bergson, S. Alexander, Field-Marshal Smuts or A.N. Whitehead' (but not, apparently, of K.R. Popper).

The mention of Hegel may be the key to Popper's hostility towards Bergson in *The Open Society and Its Enemies*. Not only in the last passage quoted but also in the earlier one about 'hysterical acceptance of change', Popper links Bergson with Hegel – Popper describes Hegel and Bergson as the two chief representatives of an 'evolutionary mysticism' which he sees as characteristic of the nineteenth century. In the years around 1940 when Popper was writing *The Open Society*, he saw Hegel as not merely an intellectual opponent but as a philosophical progenitor of Nazism, and it may be that political passion led Popper into near-automatic rejection of the thought of anyone whose ideas seemed to be related to Hegel's. But if this essentially irrational influence was operative, it lasted much longer than the war. As late as in the *Autobiography* (which, according to the acknowledgements page of the Fontana edition, was written between 1963 and 1969) Popper described Bergson as 'utterly wrong in [his] theories'.

The reason why Bergson is referred to at all in this passage, though, is because Popper wants to concede that Bergson was 'right in [his] intuition': Popper has found it desirable in his own theories to posit something sufficiently close to Bergson's *élan vital* to require this nod of acknowledgement. And this is the latest point, as far as I have seen, where Popper makes any blanket condemnation of Bergson's ideas. His subsequent references, in *Objective Knowledge* and *The Self and Its Brain*, grow steadily friendlier and take issue with Bergson only on a specific topic which has little relevance to our current theme.

Indeed, in the penultimate paragraph of *The Self and Its Brain* we find Popper describing the role of animals in biological evolution as 'creative in an almost Bergsonian sense'. If it were not for the word 'almost' (which could mean anything or nothing), this remark would seem to take the notion of creativity further than Bergson takes it, because Bergson draws a sharp distinction between Man and even the most intelligent of other animal species: 'in the animal, invention is never anything but a variation on the theme of routine . . . in man alone, [consciousness] sets itself free.'

## Was Eve a material girl?

If Popper's attitude to Bergson could be used as an index to his views on intellectual creativity, we might see Popper as having moved away from emergentism in the middle of his career to return to it in later decades. But of course we cannot assume that the one attitude can be read off so straight-forwardly from the other. Even though Bergson may be pre-eminently the philosopher of emergence, this may not have been the most important component of Bergson's thought for Popper – and indeed, Popper's references to Bergson mainly allude to his concept of the *élan vital*, which is a rather separate issue.

The other point which strikes me as possibly relevant as an indirect indicator of Popper's views on creativity – since what he says directly seems so equivocal – is his attitude to mind/body dualism. We have seen that mental creativity in the radical sense entails dualism: if the mind were nothing more than an aspect of the physical nervous system, then the range of its potential future products would follow from the laws of physics and it could not be creative. The reverse implication does not hold: one could be a dualist without believing in radical creativity, as, for instance, was Descartes. Nevertheless I would suggest that if we find Popper committed to mind/body dualism this might tend to imply that he believes in a creative mind. The reason I say this is because, if he did *not* believe in mental creativity, it is not clear what his dualism would 'buy' him, as it were. There does seem to be a widespread intuitive presumption in favour of materialism as the 'default' view of the mind/body relationship – I know I feel it, and I doubt if Popper was immune; so one is not likely to embrace dualism unless one has some good reason for doing so. If creativity in the radical sense is part of Popper's model of the mind, this gives him a motive for being a dualist, and, as I say, if that motive is not operative I do not know what other motive he has. (It may be said that Popper was not just a dualist but a 'trialist'; he distinguished 'three worlds', namely World 1 of material things, World 2 of minds and World 3 of objective products of mental activity. But the distinction between Popper's World 3 and Worlds 1 and 2 is not very relevant here, I think – what matters for our purposes is how separate Popper saw his Worlds 1 and 2 as being.)

Unfortunately, dualism, too, seems to be an issue on which Popper turns out to be somewhat equivocal.

Consider, for instance, what he says in various essays collected in the volume *Objective Knowledge*. In the opening paragraph of 'On the theory of the objective mind', first published in 1968, he straightforwardly says, 'Western philosophy consists very largely of . . . variations on the theme of body–mind dualism . . . The main departures from this . . . were attempts to replace it by some kind of monism. It seems to me that these attempts were unsuccessful.' In 'Of clouds and clocks', originally a 1965 lecture, Popper writes: 'like Descartes, I propose the adoption of a dualistic outlook' (he goes on to say that his dualism is a dualism of 'states' or 'events' rather than of 'substances', but I do not understand this distinction clearly enough to know what to make of that). Earlier in the same chapter Popper stressed that his position was more extreme than that of Samuel Alexander, a leading emergentist: Alexander was prepared to accept that all physical events including human behaviour were in principle predictable by deterministic physical laws, while Popper insisted that not even physical events can be wholly predictable because they are often influenced by mental events which are not lawlike in the same way that physical events uninfluenced by mental events are – I am paraphrasing Popper here, but I think I am representing him fairly and his position does seem to be clearly dualistic.

Yet these essays occur in the same book as the piece 'Two faces of common sense', which yielded the quotations that seemed to speak most clearly *against* the view that Popper is an emergentist; in fact the 'Two faces' paper was originally delivered as a lecture a few years later than the pieces I have just quoted, in 1970. Also in the same book, but dating from a few years earlier (from 1961, in fact) is 'Evolution and the tree of knowledge', in which Popper stresses that the kind of dualism which attracts him at that point, and which 'strongly resembles a mind–body dualism', is nevertheless 'compatible with the most radical forms of mechanistic materialism' – in which case I would have thought it was unnecessarily confusing to call it dualism at all.

Well, however equivocal he may have been in the 1960s, later in his life (the reader may feel) there is no doubt what Popper's position was: the mind/body dualism of *The Self and Its Brain* is stated as uncompromisingly as one could ask.

So I thought when I read it. Yet even here the situation turned out to be less straightforward than it first appears. After the publication of my book *Making Sense* in 1980, Popper wrote to me. In general, he was very favourable to the thesis of my book and in particular to my discussion of creativity, but he singled out for criticism just one of the comments I made about him, and not one that I had supposed to be at all controversial: it was the footnote in which I mentioned, in the context of Popper's description of monism as a baseless prophecy (cf. p. 144 above), that John Beloff had made 'cautionary remarks about Popper's forthright dismissal of monism'. Popper did not feel that he had done anything like this. He responded: 'I am unaware of the fact that I have dismissed monism. I certainly have argued against both materialism and panpsychism. But I have not "dismissed" them . . . your remark seems to me not to capture my attitude towards the difficulty of the problem.' Popper's wording in *The Self and Its Brain* looked pretty forthright to me; but if after that he was still keeping his options open on the question of monism v. dualism, then I feel bound to agree that James Hurford was right in saying that I exaggerated the extent to which Popper was committed to the notion of mental creativity in the radical, emergentist, non-Chomskyan sense.

In the end, perhaps the best clue to Popper's attitude is provided by a remark in the *Autobiography*: 'It is my opinion that most investigations into the psychology of creative thought are pretty barren.' Popper always insisted on distinguishing clearly the logical question of how an idea should be assessed from the psychological question of how an idea is produced as a candidate for assessment. I suspect that Popper was equivocal about the nature of idea production because he simply did not accept that this is an interesting or important question, relative to the questions that arise about idea assessment. In another letter, he wrote, 'I do not think that the question of whether a metaphysical monism is correct is an important question,' which tends to confirm this interpretation.

But, finally, I must say that if Popper felt that way I believe he was quite wrong. Popper was a man of his generation. The issue of whether new ideas are freely created, or drawn from an enormously large but genetically fixed repertoire of potential ideas, may have seemed an utterly insubstantial, theological question before the computer made us vividly familiar with the idea of huge domains that nevertheless have rigid boundaries and before the linguistic nativists showed us that the genetically fixed repertoire account entails important practical as well as theoretical consequences for scientific and political life. The scientific and political implications that follow from the nativists' point of view strike me as contrasting about as sharply as can be with Sir Karl Popper's ideals. (I have analysed the political implications of nativism in my *Liberty and Language*.) So I do not believe that we can continue to sweep this question under the carpet. If we support Popper's academic and political liberalism, we must be serious about intellectual creativity.

The Popper whose views harmonized with the early-twentieth-century emergentists, who believed that a man can use his brain 'to create *something new*', is the Popper we should follow on this topic. And the linguistic nativists cannot criticize the emergentist view as incoherent. They use empirical evidence to argue for their idea of innate boundaries to intellectual innovation: which means they must recognize that the contrary idea is equally admissible a priori.

We have dealt with the nativists' empirical evidence in preceding chapters. If the question is to be settled on the basis of evidence rather than conceptual analysis, then the evidence of language points towards creativity, not genetic constraints. Eve was not just a material girl: she had imagination. What reason remains to deny it?

# 6  Conclusion

Over the last thirty years, linguistic nativism has become one of the great academic success stories of the twentieth century. When the movement began, the general intellectual climate was wholly out of sympathy with its central ideas and initially greeted them with something close to derision. But attitudes changed very quickly. Large numbers of influential thinkers from a wide range of disciplines became converts, and began to hail the movement as one of the most significant postwar contributions to the advancement of knowledge – as they continue to do today.

Yet readers who have kept company with me this far will perhaps agree that the contrast between what appears to have been achieved and what has actually been achieved is breathtakingly large. It is hard to imagine a clearer illustration from academic life of the fable of the emperor's new clothes. Indeed, the gulf between hype and reality is *so* wide in this case that some readers may wonder whether I have been playing fair. Have I perhaps deliberately omitted to discuss good nativist arguments which the average reader is likely to overlook unless they are explicitly drawn to his attention, or intentionally misrepresented nativist theories as asserting obvious falsehoods when I know that the writers really meant something less foolish and less easily refuted?

In the circumstances, these suspicions would be understandable. But I assure the reader, if he will accept my assurance, that I have been as fair as I know how. If there have been lapses from proper standards of scholarship in this debate, they have not been on my side. Obviously it is possible that I have myself overlooked or misunderstood elements in the nativists' writings; but I sincerely believe that the nativists' case is as I have depicted it, and is every bit as thin as I have described it. I have been studying this material for most of the thirty-odd years it has been produced. No one could avoid overlooking some details, but I doubt that I have missed anything crucial enough to make the difference between rejecting the nativist point of view and accepting it.

In this situation one cannot fail to ask: what went wrong?

If people had embraced nativism because they believed that the contrary view was ultimately incoherent, one could respect that judgement, although I believe it is mistaken. But the linguistic nativists did and do not argue that way. They say that nativism must be accepted as the best explanation of the observable evidence. Yet the empirical case for nativism is not just flawed but insubstantial, based on palpably inadequate evidence and argument. How can a system of ideas like this have succeeded in capturing the intellectual allegiance of so many educated people?

I believe there is no one answer to this. Many independent factors happened to come together and reinforce one another in promoting linguistic nativism.

Some things were accidents of history. Initially, the nativist movement gained massive early exposure because its founder also happened to be the leading intellectual opponent of the United States engagement in Vietnam, at a period when that war was the hottest issue on American campuses for both moral reasons and reasons of self-preservation.

At the same time, the late 1960s and 1970s were a period when the academic discipline of linguistics found a new market in providing professional training for teachers of English as a Foreign Language. University linguistics departments, which had been small and 'non-vocational', expanded to receive large numbers of foreign English-language teachers who came to Britain and other English-speaking countries partly in order to immerse themselves in the English language, but partly also to gain professional accreditation. The nativist style of language analysis was relatively appealing to these people. Because nativism focused on language universals rather than on the quirky individual features of particular languages, in practice nativist textbooks discussed mainly English-language examples; and the nativist emphasis on the facts of language acquisition was grist to the mill of professional language teachers.

Then again, this was a period when knowledge of other languages among the student population of the English-speaking world was diminishing. In Britain up to the 1960s, someone embarking on an undergraduate degree programme in an arts faculty would normally already know two or three classical and/or modern languages fairly well; but patterns of secondary education changed. The less someone knows about languages other than his own, the easier it is for him to believe that the various languages of the world are virtually dialects of a single language.

The years around 1970 were also a period when the university system expanded massively in a very short period. Large numbers of people were recruited into the university teaching profession over a few years, and having entered the profession of course they stayed; so an over-representation of whatever intellectual trends happened to be 'hot' just then was locked into the system. It could have been anything; unfortunately it happened to be linguistic nativism. And the expansion made the academic world less interested in puncturing intellectual pretension. While university education remained a small-scale, élite activity, undergraduate training in arts subjects was largely about assessing argument and winnowing intellectual wheat from chaff; education was centred on one-to-one tutorial discussion, and exams were an infrequent distraction. The move to a mass higher education system meant that undergraduate study became more of a production line in which all student work is 'continuously assessed' and marks are earned by summarizing what the textbooks say. Time constraints on both students and teachers discourage the cultivation of educated scepticism at the undergraduate level, so intellectual fashions get an easier ride than they should and once did.

Noam Chomsky's early theorizing got a particularly easy ride, because it was largely based on a manuscript that was not publicly available. His intellectual reputation rested for many years chiefly on the slim 1957 volume *Syntactic Structures*, which outlined a novel, formal approach to the analysis of grammar, but omitted much of the detail. The omissions were justified via repeated references to a far longer, unpublished work, *The Logical Structure of Linguistic Theory*. At the time this seemed less like selling a pig in a poke than one might suppose, because it was known in the profession that many copies of this manuscript were in circulation; authors of linguistics articles would sometimes demonstrate their well-connected status by citing it briefly, so readers had a sense that *some* people could check Chomsky's claims even if they were not in a position to do so themselves. *The Logical Structure of Linguistic Theory* was eventually published, in 1975; at which point it became clear that it fell far short of redeeming the IOUs issued by *Syntactic Structures*. The mathematical formalisms were sometimes clumsy and strictly meaningless. More important, what looked in *Syntactic Structures* like the central, most convincing piece of evidence for Chomsky's grammatical theory (the English rule of 'Affix Hopping') turned out in terms of the more explicit statement of the theory in *The Logical Structure of Linguistic Theory* to be a counterexample to it. (Affix Hopping could not be formulated as a 'transformational rule'.) However, by 1975 the terms of the debate had changed. *Syntactic Structures* had achieved its aim of awakening interest in Chomsky's ideas; discussion had come to focus on conceptual issues of nature and nurture, rather than on formal properties of grammatical rules, and many participants were not qualified to judge Chomsky's mathematics. Very few people studied *The Logical Structure of Linguistic Theory* in detail, once it became possible to do so.

Personalities and attitudes are relevant. The 1960s were a time of youthful rebellion against the staid assumptions of the older generation, and in its early years nativist linguistics had an air of irreverence and fun. An academic Young Turk would circulate a paper with a title and example sentences that were jokey or obscene, illustrating a theory that tapped into the hidden machinery of human thought (or claimed to): that had to beat solemn, scholarly studies of phoneme systems in the languages of distant corners of the Commonwealth. Furthermore, professional assumptions in academic life were changing. In Britain into the 1960s, university teachers often had independent incomes; even when they did not, they had no sense of needing to prove themselves. One could make a successful, well-respected career out of undergraduate teaching alone; writing and research were optional extras, carried out for their own sake. Nowadays, everybody depends on a salary, and academics, like everyone else, are required to compete and enhance the standing of their departments and institutions in the league tables; research is the prime currency of academic competition. When a generation attuned to playing intellectual games to win encountered an earlier generation who assumed that everyone was on the same side, it is obvious which was likely to conquer. In the early years of linguistic nativism, academics with more seniority often expressed surprise as well as sadness at the 'eclipsing stance' adopted by the new men.

Increasingly, one encounters suggestions that some of the linguistic nativists not only play to win, but play dirty. A recent review article by Geoffrey Pullum accuses Noam Chomsky and some other nativists of seriously falsifying the intellectual record in their attempt to win the debate. Esa Itkonen, too senior an academic to be personally affected, has put into print what has often been whispered: American linguists not yet established in their careers, he claims, are afraid to voice disagreement with nativism publicly for fear of damaging their chances of academic employment.

The older generation of academics had their own besetting sins, one of which was pomposity. The leaders of the nativist movement were terrific rhetoricians, and several people who went into the lists against their theories in the early years were out-argued so energetically that they ended up looking rather foolish. There is no knowing how many others who might have resisted the tide of nativism, seeing this, decided to devote their efforts to other research areas and avoid the risk of being made to look an idiot in public.

In the 1990s, the public mood has changed again. Suddenly, many educated people seem to have lost the relish for following interesting ideas with an open mind wherever they may lead. Society is showing signs of reverting to an almost medieval acceptance of intellectual authority, from which dissent is seen as morally objectionable. In public affairs, the new orthodoxy of Political Correctness is far less tolerant of contrary views than the older 'progressive' orthodoxy of socialism ever was in its heyday. When an American academic finds herself vilified as a racist for contradicting the claim that Aristotle stole his ideas from Africans, reason seems to be at a low ebb. Critics of linguistic nativism sometimes seem likewise to meet responses whose tone suggests that their criticism is not just ill founded but ought not to have been voiced or published.

If this mood were to deepen, one might begin to wonder whether it was worth arguing against wrong ideas, however clearly mistaken they were. The 'postmodernist' ethos openly elevates modishness above rationality, and I cannot deny that nativism is more fashionable at present than empiricism. But one can only trust that these attitudes are an unrepresentative passing phase, and that the world does remain open to reasoned argument.

Perhaps the most important point keeping the nativist hegemony in being is that, to be blunt, there are more jobs in nativism than in empiricism. If people believe that we inherit a rich structure of mental machinery which determines many details of intellectual life, then there are careers to be made from teasing out the exact nature of different areas of this innate structure. Many academics are earning their livings this way. If, conversely, people believe that culture is freely invented and not dependent on biology, then in one sense there is far less for researchers to study. One can investigate the structures of languages – and the other cultural practices of various societies – for their own sake, as anthropologists and anthropologically oriented linguists did in the 1950s and before. But doing this leads to no insights about inbuilt mental machinery common to all human beings, including the taxpayers who are keeping the researchers afloat. This kind of study is fascinating and intellectually well worth doing, but it is never likely to be easy to 'sell' to the general public (and perhaps is not likely to appeal to such a wide range of academics). If members of the profession sense these negative consequences of a return to empiricism, little wonder that they instinctively avoid noticing how flimsy the nativist case is.

But none of these are worthy reasons for maintaining the life-support system of a moribund theory of human nature. And, although the implausibility of nativism might be bad news for some academics who got caught up in a thirty-year-old tide of fashion and lack the flexibility to retool intellectually, for everyone else it is very good news.

All of us, surely, would rather be what most of us have supposed we are: creatures capable of coming to terms with whatever life throws at us because of our ability to create novel ideas in response to novel challenges – able to take the best ideas and ways of life of our predecessors and build on them, generation after generation. Who would not prefer this picture to that which portrays biology as allotting to the human mind a range of available settings, like a fully featured washing machine or video recorder, and allows us to select the optimum intellectual setting to suit prevailing conditions? The former concept of Man is far nobler. The evidence suggests that it is also more accurate.

Eve was not a born know-all. She was a good learner. She initiated a process of self-education which we continue to participate in today. Provided we do not adopt social arrangements that artificially stifle it, there is no reason for that education process ever to come to an end.

# Notes

References to works by Noam Chomsky, Karl Popper and the present author use short titles; full bibliographical details are given in the lists on pp. 178–9. Except where otherwise noted, references to Derek Bickerton, Ray Jackendoff and Steven Pinker relate to the following books:

D. Bickerton, *Language & Species*, University of Chicago Press, 1990.

R.S. Jackendoff, *Patterns in the Mind: Language and Human Nature*, Harvester Wheatsheaf, 1993.

S. Pinker, *The Language Instinct: The New Science of Language and Mind*, William Morrow (New York), 1994; my page references are to the Penguin edition, 1995.

Bibliographical details in the following notes omit place of publication, except where the list of publisher's offices does not include London and the place does not form part of the publisher's name.

## Chapter 1   Culture or Biology?

Page  4. The term 'rationalism' is sometimes used as a synonym for what I call 'nativism'. But 'rationalism' is ambiguous, which is why I prefer not to use it: it often refers to reliance on reason rather than emotion, which is another matter entirely.

4. Whitehead, 'footnotes to Plato': *Process and Reality: An Essay in Cosmology*, Cambridge University Press, 1929, p. 53.

4. Plato, 'what we call learning': *Phaedo* 72e, trans. Hugh Tredennick.

4. Descartes, 'all those [ideas] which': letter to Mersenne, 22 July 1641; *Œuvres*, ed. C. Adam and P. Tannery, 13 vols, Vrin (Paris), 1964–74, vol. III, p. 418.

5. Descartes, 'the child does not acquire them later': letter to X, August 1641; *Œuvres*, vol. III, p. 424.

5. Plato, 'the truth about reality is always': *Meno* 86a-b, trans. W.K.C. Guthrie.

5. Innate knowledge of Boat Race results: Plato might defend himself by saying that the only things we 'know' are eternal truths, like the ratio of

diagonal to side — he should not be interpreted as saying that we innately know race results, because facts like that are too contingent and uncertain to qualify as 'knowledge' at all. But that would only dig him in deeper. Since Einstein showed that gravity affects geometry, it has turned out that the ratio of diagonal to side of a square is not exactly √2: this is not the eternal truth it seemed. On the other hand, a race result which depends only on before and after among two events is unaffected even by relativistic physics.

Page   5. Plato, 'will behave in the same way': *Meno* 85e.

6. Locke, 'How comes [the mind] to be furnished?', 'He that attentively considers': *An Essay Concerning Human Understanding*, first published 1690; Everyman edition, ed. J.W. Yolton, 2 vols, Dent, 1961, Book II, §§1.2, 1.6. Locke responding to Descartes: see p. 88ff. of R.I. Aaron, *John Locke*, 3rd edn, Clarendon Press (Oxford), 1971.

7. Joos, 'languages could differ ... without limit': M. Joos (ed.), *Readings in Linguistics*, American Council of Learned Societies (New York), 1957, p. 96.

8. Chomsky, 'grammar grows in the mind': *Rules and Representations*, p. 134. Martian might see all humans as speaking one language: 'Linguistics and cognitive science', p. 26.

9. Chomsky, 'an intelligible explanatory theory': *Reflections*, pp. 24–5.

10. Chomsky, 'Mockery of conventions': *Reflections*, p. 125.

10. Jackendoff, Universal Musical Grammar: F. Lerdahl and R.S. Jackendoff, *A Generative Theory of Tonal Music*, MIT Press (Cambridge, Mass.), 1983.

10. Chomsky uses the phrase 'tacit knowledge' but is not wedded to it: *Reflections*, pp. 164–5.

11. Chomsky the most-quoted living writer: S. Targett, 'A rebel with an endless cause', *Times Higher Education Supplement*, 23 June 1995, p. 17.

11. Putnam and Goodman debating Chomsky: 'Symposium on innate ideas', *Boston Studies in the Philosophy of Science*, vol. III, The Humanities Press (New York), 1968, pp. 81–107; reprinted in J.R. Searle (ed.), *The Philosophy of Language*, Oxford University Press, 1971.

11. Chomsky's anarcho-syndicalism: see, e.g. *Problems of Knowledge and Freedom*, pp. 47–55.

11–12. Chomsky on Cambodian massacres: e.g. in *After the Cataclysm* (co-authored with E.S. Herman), Spokesman (Nottingham), 1979. Chomsky's flirtation with the neo-Nazi movement, which seems to be more widely known in Continental Europe than in the English-speaking world, is analysed e.g. by W.D. Rubinstein ('Chomsky and the neo-Nazis', *Quadrant*, October 1981, pp. 8–14), and in more detail by Werner Cohn (*The Hidden Alliances of Noam Chomsky*, Americans for a Safe Israel (New York), 1988). I have described Chomsky's extraordinary response to mildly critical remarks of my own on these aspects of his writings in my 'Censoring 20th-Century Culture: the case of Noam Chomsky' (*The New Criterion*, October 1984, pp. 7–16; and see subsequent letters to the Editor from Chomsky and myself, January 1985, pp. 81–4).

12. Peretz, Chomsky 'a fool': 'Washington diarist', *The New Republic*, 3–10 January 1981.

12. Chomsky, 'I hate experiments': V. Mehta, *John Is Easy to Please*, Secker & Warburg, 1971, p. 209.

Page 13. Acclaim for Pinker's *Language Instinct*: quoted from cover of Penguin edition.

14–15. Locke, broadly the same dialectic of guesswork and testing: for Locke's view of the role of hypotheses, see L. Laudan, 'The nature and sources of Locke's views on hypotheses', *Journal of the History of Ideas* 28.211–23, 1967; revised version in I.C. Tipton (ed.), *Locke on Human Understanding*, Oxford University Press, 1977.

15. Popper began as a philosopher of science: see his *Logic of Scientific Discovery*, *Conjectures and Refutations*. Popper and Adler: *Conjectures and Refutations*, p. 35.

16. Knowledge comes both from inside us and from external reality: Popper's account of knowledge development is often called 'critical rationalism', which is another reason why it would be confusing in this book to use 'rationalism' for what I call 'nativism'. Popper believes we have an innate power of reasoning, but not innate knowledge.

17. Popper, baby has innate expectations: *Conjectures and Refutations*, p. 47.

17. Goodman, 'mind ... in motion from the start': *Fact, Fiction, and Forecast*, Bobbs-Merrill (Indianapolis), 2nd edn, 1965, p. 87.

17–18. Lakatos, progressive and degenerating problemshifts: 'Falsification and the methodology of scientific research programmes', in I. Lakatos and A. Musgrave (eds), *Criticism and the Growth of Knowledge*, Cambridge University Press, 1970.

18. Chomsky, 'The question whether ... The doctrine that ...': *Reflections*, pp. 131–2.

20. Lynda Snell: overseas readers who do not know who Lynda Snell is are doomed to miss this reference, alas. Let us just call her a figment of the British national imagination.

21. Cohn, Chomsky's footnotes: *The Hidden Alliances of Noam Chomsky* (see above), p. 2.

## Chapter 2   The Original Arguments for a Language Instinct

24. Chomsky, 'I would like to suggest': *Rules and Representations*, p. 134. 'our systems of belief': *Reflections*, pp. 7–8. 'There aren't any': V. Mehta, *John Is Easy to Please*, Secker & Warburg, 1971, p. 191. We should assimilate our account of cognition to our account of physiology: e.g. *Reflections*, pp. 9–10; *Rules and Representations*, p. 33ff.

25. Chomsky, gives blessing to others' theories about biological determination of vocabulary: e.g. *Topics*, p. 13.

25. Popper, 'The capacity to learn a language': *The Self and Its Brain*, p. 48.

26. Chomsky, language an 'organ': e.g. *Rules and Representations*, p. 39. 'Knowledge of language is normally': *Language and Mind*, p. ix. 'Mere exposure': 'Explanatory models', p. 529.

27. Chomsky, 'given an input': Review of Skinner, p. 564. 'Grammar ... acquired by virtually everyone': *Reflections*, p. 144. Quotes de Cordemoy: *Cartesian Linguistics*, p. 109. 'there seems to be a critical': *Language and Responsibility*, p. 98. 'There is reason to believe': *Aspects*, p. 206.

27. Lenneberg on critical periods: *Biological Foundations of Language*, Wiley, 1967.

Page 27. Chomsky, 'a young child of immigrant': Review of Skinner, pp. 562–3. Discusses 'Genie' case: *Rules and Representations*, p. 57.

28. Chomsky, 'it is clear that the language': *Reflections*, p. 10. 'The native speaker has acquired': *Language and Mind*, p. 23. 'we cannot avoid being struck': *Language and Mind*, p. 68. 'many children acquire': *Aspects*, pp. 200–1. 'the grammars that are in fact': *Language and Mind*, p. 69. 'To a very good first approximation': *Reflections*, p. 144. 'every child … acquires knowledge': *Logical Structure*, p. 30.

29. Chomsky, 'we discover a substantial system': *Language and Mind*, p. 69. 'appl[ies] to a string of words': *Language and Mind*, p. 51.

30. Chomsky, 'It is easy to imagine': *Language and Mind*, p. 51. 'all known formal operations': *Problems of Knowledge and Freedom*, p. 30. 'There is no a priori reason': *Language and Mind*, p. 52. 'proper names, in any language': *Aspects*, p. 29.

30. Fodor, innate limitations on possible concepts: *The Language of Thought*, Crowell (New York), 1975, especially pp. 59–64. I have spelled out the fallacies in Fodor's argument: my *Making Sense*, pp. 22–6.

30–1. Chomsky, only finitely many grammars: *Government and Binding*, p. 11.

31. Chomsky, 'Children make many errors': *Rules and Representations*, pp. 43–4. 'It surpasses belief': 'Principles and parameters', p. 62. 'It is certainly true': Royaumont Symposium, pp. 114–15. 'Think for example of the capacity': *Rules and Representations*, p. 38.

32. Chomsky, 'Work of the past years': *Reflections on Language*, p. 8.

32. Broadbent, Chomsky's approach 'much more interesting': *In Defence of Empirical Psychology*, Methuen, 1973, p. 189.

32. Ape language experiments, how successful: see E. Linden, *Apes, Men, and Language*, Penguin, 1974; H.S. Terrace, *Nim*, Columbia University Press (New York), Morningside edn, 1986; articles in Part 2 of N.A. Krasnegor *et al.*, eds, *Biological and Behavioral Determinants of Language Development*, Lawrence Erlbaum, 1991; J. Wallman, *Aping Language*, Cambridge University Press, 1992. Herbert Terrace, who directed what seems to have been the fullest and most careful experiment, concluded that it did not settle one way or the other whether an ape can learn a human language, and that the question could only be answered by research on a larger scale than anyone is likely to undertake in the foreseeable future.

32. Chomsky, 'even the most elementary properties': *Rules and Representations*, p. 261. 'Note that if it were discovered': *Rules and Representations*, pp. 260–1.

34. Chomsky, 'it seems easy enough to make': *Rules and Representations*, p. 102.

35. Chomsky, 'There is no absolute sense': *Reflections*, p. 157.

36. Chomsky, 'Though [knowledge of physics], too': *Reflections*, p. 157. Language acquisition ability diminishes 'at a relatively fixed age': Royaumont Symposium, p. 37.

36. Dulay, second-language learning success: Heidi C. Dulay *et al.*, *Language Two*, Oxford University Press, 1982.

36. Lenneberg, second-language learning involves only non-innate features: *Biological Foundations of Language*, Wiley, 1967, p. 176; retardation of physical maturation goes with retardation of language acquisition: p. 132.

Page 37. Biology controlling qualitative as well as quantitative aspects of learning: my *Liberty and Language*, p. 152.

37. Genie: Susan Curtiss, *Genie: A Psycholinguistic Study of a Modern-Day 'Wild Child'*, Academic Press, 1977; quotations from pp. 9, 209.

37. Bickerton, no emotional damage: *Language & Species*, University of Chicago Press, 1990, p. 116.

38. Lenneberg, 'Do the time limitations … ?': *Biological Foundations of Language*, Wiley, 1967, p. 176.

38. Bruner, 'any subject can be taught': *The Process of Learning*, Harvard University Press, 1960, p. 33.

38. Motherese of better quality than Chomsky supposed: Susan Ervin-Tripp, 'An overview of theories of grammatical development', in D.I. Slobin, ed., *The Ontogenesis of Grammar: A Theoretical Symposium*, Academic Press, 1971, pp. 191–4.

38. Adults give infants graded language lessons: see papers in Catherine E. Snow and C.A. Ferguson (eds), *Talking to Children: Language Input and Acquisition*, Cambridge University Press, 1977.

38–9. Mothers not ideal language teachers: N. Hornstein and D. Lightfoot (eds), *Explanation in Linguistics*, Longman, 1981, p. 11, quoting Elissa Newport, H. Gleitman and Lila R. Gleitman, 'Mother, I'd rather do it myself: some effects and non-effects of maternal speech style', in Snow and Ferguson (see previous note).

39. Pinker, 'babies prefer to listen to Motherese': p. 279.

39. Valian, 'Any acquisition theory will have to come to terms': 'Logical and psychological constraints on the acquisition of syntax', in Lyn Frazier and Jill de Villiers (eds), *Language Processing and Language Acquisition*, Kluwer (Dordrecht), 1990, p. 120.

40. Hornstein and Lightfoot, 'People attain knowledge': *Explanation in Linguistics*, Longman, 1981, p. 9.

41. Chomsky, 'you can easily live your whole life': Royaumont Symposium, pp. 114–15. Belief that each child encounters evidence 'strains credulity': *Reflections*, p. 213.

41. Pullum, review of poverty-of-data argument: 'Learnability, hyperlearning, and the poverty of the stimulus', *Proceedings of the 22nd Annual Meeting: General Session and Parasession on the Role of Learnability in Grammatical Theory*, Berkeley Linguistics Society, 1996, pp. 498–513.

41. Chomsky's claim repeated by Marcus and Pinker: G.F. Marcus, 'Negative evidence in language acquisition', *Cognition*, **46**: 53–85, 1993; Pinker, pp. 40–3.

42. Chomsky, 'A person might go through': Royaumont Symposium, p. 40.

43–4. Argument from poverty of data defended against self-defeat: S.P. Stich, 'Can Popperians learn to talk?', *British Journal for the Philosophy of Science*, **32**: 157–64, 1981; Hornstein and Lightfoot, *Explanation in Linguistics*, Longman, 1981, pp. 9, 25.

45. Popperian philosophy of science explains how linguists can judge examples ungrammatical despite encountering only positive examples: pp. 54–5 of Marcus, 'Negative evidence in language acquisition' (see above) list many writers who have seen lack of negative evidence as problematic; Chapter 4 of my *Form of Language* discusses in detail how

Popperian methodology enables a description of a language to be derived from a finite corpus of examples.

Page 45. Linguists exploiting instrumental data: for instance, J.A. Fodor, T.G. Bever and M.F. Garrett, *The Psychology of Language: An Introduction to Psycholinguistics and Generative Grammar*, McGraw-Hill, 1974, p. 329ff.

46. Chomsky admits that intelligent/educated people know their mother tongue better: Royaumont Symposium, pp. 175–6.

47. Labov, differences between individuals' grammaticality judgements: 'Empirical foundations of linguistic theory', in R. Austerlitz (ed.), *The Scope of American Linguistics*, Peter de Ridder Press (Lisse), 1975, p. 90ff.

47. Stich, rough equivalence: 'Can Popperians learn to talk?' (see above), pp. 159, 163.

48. Sampson, logical fallacy in Stich's argument: 'Popperian language-acquisition undefeated', see especially pp. 65–6.

48. Languages lacking large numbers: J.H. Greenberg, 'Generalizations about numeral systems', in J.H. Greenberg (ed.), *Universals of Human Language*, Stanford University Press, 1978, vol. III, p. 256.

48. Thomson, modern concept of infinity: 'Infinity in mathematics and logic', in P. Edwards (ed.), *The Encyclopedia of Philosophy*, 8 vols, Collier-Macmillan, 1967, vol. IV, p. 183.

49. Chomsky, developments such as number system 'far transcend': *Rules and Representations*, p. 38. 'Were it not for': *Rules and Representations*, p. 46.

49. Price, empiricists did not think the mind passive: *Thinking and Experience*, Hutchinson, 1953, p. 199 n. 1. Price continued: 'It is the Rationalist Mind, if either, which is the passive one, or at least the lazy one, equipped from the start with a complete outfit of basic ideas.'

50. Chomsky, 'Opposition to idealization': *Language and Responsibility*, p. 57.

51. Chomsky, language acquisition 'can be conceptualized as ... instantaneous': *Reflections*, p. 15. 'then we would expect to find': *Reflections*, p. 121.

52. Chomsky, 'We might, more realistically': *Reflections*, p. 119.

52. Bloomfield, 'there is no hour or day': *Language*, Holt (New York), 1933, p. 46.

52. Whitney, 'We realize better': *The Life and Growth of Language*, 5th edn, Kegan Paul, Trench, 1885, p. 25.

52–3. Popper, scientific theories will develop indefinitely: see e.g. his *Logic of Scientific Discovery*, §85, and *Conjectures and Refutations*, Chapter 10.

53. Chomsky, 'Linguistic theory is concerned primarily': *Aspects*, p. 3. Assumption 'of critical importance': *Rules and Representations*, pp. 24–5.

54. Emile Durkheim, social facts: *Les Règles de la méthode sociologique*, 1895, translated as *The Rules of Sociological Method*, 8th edn, Collier-Macmillan, 1964.

54. Chomsky, 'People are so constituted': *Rules and Representations*, p. 25. 'hopelessly implausible': *Rules and Representations*, p. 26. 'quite absurd': *Rules and Representations*, p. 117.

55. Chomsky, 'Specific arguments with regard': *Rules and Representations*, p. 213.

Page 57. Liberman, discrete categorization of continuous phonetic variables: A.M. Liberman *et al.*, 'Perception of the speech code', *Psychological Review*, **74:** 431–61, 1967; see pp. 442–3.

57. Vowels distinguished by formants: see e.g. P. Ladefoged, *Elements of Acoustic Phonetics*, University of Chicago Press, 1962, p. 92.

57–8. Lieberman and Laitman, distinctive vocal-tract shape in Man: P. Lieberman *et al.*, *The Speech of Primates (Janua Linguarum, series minor, 148)*, Mouton (The Hague), 1972; Lieberman, *Uniquely Human: The Evolution of Speech, Thought, and Selfless Behavior*, Harvard University Press, 1991, Chapter 2; J.T. Laitman, 'The evolution of the hominid upper respiratory system and implications for the origins of speech', in E. de Grolier, ed., *Glossogenetics: The Origin and Evolution of Language*, Harwood Academic Publishers, 1983.

58. Dart, cultural acceleration: 'On the evolution of language and articulate speech', *Homo*, **10**, 154–65, 1959.

58. Lieberman, 'these phonetic differences are sufficient': 'On the nature and evolution of the biological bases of language', in E. de Grolier (ed.), *Glossogenetics*, pp. 101–2.

58. Kuhl and Miller, chinchilla speech perception: 'Speech perception by the chinchilla: voiced-voiceless distinction in alveolar plosive consonants', *Science*, **190:** 69–72, 3 October 1975; for a convenient summary and discussion, see Joanne L. Miller, 'Speech perception', in D.N. Osherson and H. Lasnik (eds), *An Invitation to Cognitive Science, Vol. I: Language*, Bradford Books/MIT Press, 1990, p. 81ff. I have seen an attempt by Alvin Liberman to defend his version of linguistic nativism against the chinchilla experiments, but as a defence it powerfully evokes the image of the drowning man clutching at straws (see A.M. Liberman, 'Discussion paper' in S.R. Harnad, H.D. Steklis and Jane Lancaster (eds), *Origins and Evolution of Language and Speech (Annals of the New York Academy of Sciences, Vol. CCLXXX)*, New York Academy of Sciences, 1976, p. 721). Recently, a group at Cornell University have published findings even more striking than Kuhl and Miller's on categorical perception of sound by an insect species, and they conclude that 'categorical perception may be a basic and widespread feature of sensory systems, from humans to invertebrates': R.A. Wyttenbach *et al.*, 'Categorical perception of sound frequency by crickets', *Science*, **273:** 1542–4, 13 September 1996.

59. Ohala, women do not have low larynx: 'The frequency code underlies the sound-symbolic use of voice pitch', in Leanne Hinton, Johanna Nichols and J.J. Ohala (eds), *Sound Symbolism*, Cambridge University Press, 1994, p. 338.

60. Berlin and Kay on colour terminologies: *Basic Color Terms: Their Universality and Evolution*, University of California Press, 1969.

60. H.A. Gleason, Jr, *An Introduction to Descriptive Linguistics*, revised edn, Holt, Rinehart & Winston, 1969.

61. Conklin on Hanunóo: 'Hanunóo color categories', *Southwestern Journal of Anthropology*, **11:** 339–44, 1955; reprinted in D.H. Hymes (ed.), *Language in Culture and Society: A Reader in Linguistics and Anthropology*, Harper & Row, 1964.

62. Berlin and Kay report a handful of exceptions: *Basic Color Terms*, pp. 44–5. Treatment of Homeric Greek: pp. 70–1.

Page 62. Gladstone tabulated Homer's colour words: *Studies on Homer and the Homeric Age*, Oxford University Press, 1858, vol. III, pp. 457–99.

63. Berlin and Kay ambivalent about foreign loans: p. 6. 'plan to obtain more data': pp. 41–2. Focal points match regions of greatest sensitivity: G.A. Collier, review of Berlin and Kay, *Language*, **49:** 245–8, 1973.

63–4. Dark-skinned people less sensitive to blue light: M.H. Bornstein, 'Color vision and color naming', *Psychological Bulletin*, **80:** 257–85, 1973.

64. McNeill on traditional Japanese colour terms: 'Colour and colour terminology', *Journal of Linguistics*, **8:** 21–33, 1972.

## Chapter 3   The Debate Renewed

65. Chomsky, 'It is perfectly safe to attribute': *Language and Mind*, p. 83. Language emerged as evolutionary saltation: *Language and Mind*, p. 62.

66. Bickerton, Seth's speech: pp. 165–6.

67. Bickerton, sudden flip: e.g. p. 171. 'Ifu laik meiki': pp. 120, 169.

68. Bickerton, *They wen go up there*: p. 169. (According to Bickerton's *Roots of Language*, Karoma (Ann Arbor, Michigan), 1981, p. 26, in Hawaiian Creole *wen* and *bin* – the latter presumably from English 'been' – function as phonologically determined alternative forms of the same tense-marking item.) Protolanguage: pp. 118, 122ff. 'The evidence ... indicates': p. 190. 'an event, presumably a mutation': p. 165.

69. Mitochondrial DNA research: see M.H. Brown, *The Search for Eve*, Harper & Row, 1990.

70–3. Bickerton, discussion of Russenorsk sample: pp. 121–2.

72. Bickerton, language 'not even primarily a means of communication': p. 5.

73. Bickerton, 'immense gulf': p. 177.

74. Brugmann, 'Originally people spoke only': *Griechische Grammatik*, 3rd edn, C.H. Beck'sche Verlagsbuchhandlung (Munich), 1900, p. 552 (my translation).

74. Hermann, Indo-European subordinate clauses: 'Gab es im Indogermanischen nebensätze?', *Zeitschrift für vergleichende Sprachforschung*, **33:** 481–535, 1895.

74. Paul, early hypotaxis: *Prinzipien der Sprachgeschichte*, 5th edn, Max Niemeyer (Halle an der Saale), 1920, p. 145.

74. Jackendoff, 'the earliest written documents': p. 32.

74. Ong, hypotaxis a product of literacy: *Orality and Literacy: The Technologizing of the Word*, Methuen, 1982, pp. 37–8.

75. Bickerton, delay between emergence of language and effect on technology: cf. pp. 175–6 and p. 140.

76. Bickerton on Bertrand Russell: pp. 13–14. Language may be 'terminally dysfunctional': p. 253.

77. Jackendoff, critical period for sign language: p. 123. Innate mechanisms useful only to deaf implausible: p. 97.

77–8. Jackendoff, highly informative verbs in Onondaga, Hungarian: p. 94.

78. Jackendoff, 'greater use of simultaneity', 'drawn from the same menu': p. 97. 'The effect is that there are': p. 90. 'language learning ability is switched on', 'What Lenneberg actually proposed': p. 118.

Page 78. Lenneberg, diagrams illustrating critical period: *Biological Foundations of Language*, Wiley, 1967, p. 159.

78. Jackendoff, 'children hav[e] a specialized': p. 125.

79. Jackendoff, a child 'already "instinctively" ... knows': p. 62.

79. Ohala: 'Speech perception is hearing sounds, not tongues', *Journal of the Acoustic Society of America*, **99**: 1718–25, 1996.

79. Pinker, babies learn to make sounds by experiment: p. 266.

79. Jackendoff, 'We even "instinctively" ... attribute': p. 63. Slides from 'compatible' to 'strongly indicate': p. 155.

80. Jackendoff on vision: p. 171ff.

80. Pinker, 'a variety of mental processes': p. 306.

80. Curtiss, only Genie's right hemisphere functioned: *Genie: A Psycholinguistic Study of a Modern-Day 'Wild Child'*, Academic Press, 1977, p. 211ff.

80. Jackendoff, functions of Broca's and Wernicke's areas: p. 150.

80. Pinker, 'no one really knows': p. 311.

80. Jackendoff, 'Why can we think more clearly': p. 27.

80–1. Klima and Bellugi, child questions (discussed by Jackendoff, pp. 108–9): 'Syntactic regularities in the speech of children', in J. Lyons and R.J. Wales (eds), *Psycholinguistics Papers*, Edinburgh University Press, 1966.

81. Jackendoff, deaf children 'construct rules': p. 126.

81. Pinker, history of English: p. 246ff.

82. Cavalli-Sforza, correlations between language and race: 'Genes, peoples and languages', *Scientific American*, November 1991, pp. 72–8.

82. Pinker, contradictory attitudes about loss of semantic distinctions and slang: p. 400. 'For example, a banal': p. 401.

83. Pinker, 'any native speaker recognizes', *sram* 'illegal': pp. 173, 181. George Bush lacks a full deck: p. 329.

84. Pinker, 'Language is not a cultural artifact': p. 18. Compares language to elephant's trunk: Chapter 11.

85. Pinker, 'A bit of arithmetic shows': p. 151. 'The child, constrained by Universal Grammar': p. 288.

86. Australian mother-in-law languages: R.M.W. Dixon, *The Languages of Australia*, Cambridge University Press, 1980, p. 58ff.

86. Pinker, Karin Stromswold's data: p. 272.

86. Braine, 'other one spoon': 'On two types of models of the internalization of grammars', in D.I. Slobin (ed.), *The Ontogenesis of Grammar: A Theoretical Symposium*, Academic Press, 1971, pp. 160–1; quoted by Pinker, p. 281.

87. Bickerton, *Roots of Language*: Karoma (Ann Arbor, Michigan), 1981.

87. Shirai and Andersen, Motherese contains relevant evidence: 'The acquisition of tense-aspect morphology: a prototype account', *Language*, **71**: 743–62, 1995.

87. Heath, lack of baby talk: *Ways with Words*, Cambridge University Press, 1983; quoted by Pinker, pp. 40, 279.

87. Pinker, working-class speech highly grammatical: p. 31. 'the rest of the child's mental development': p. 289.

88. Pinker, 'flummoxed by no-brainer tasks': p. 276.

88. Piaget, innate programming of non-linguistic mental achievements: for instance, a fairly unambiguous statement on conservation of liquid volume is in *On the Development of Memory and Identity*, Clark University Press (Barre, Mass.), 1968, p. 17ff.

Page 88. Williams, children warned by parents: *Adaptation and Natural Selection: A Critique of Some Current Evolutionary Thought*, Princeton University Press, 1966, pp. 15–16. Although it is from George Williams that Pinker borrows the idea that understanding spoken warnings of fatal dangers was significant in human evolution, Williams himself does not imply that our genetic endowment includes specific linguistic knowledge. Williams merely suggests, very tentatively, that the value of being able to understand and remember warnings could have been what led Man to develop high general intelligence.

88. Pinker, compares Genie and Chelsea cases: pp. 292–3.

89. Curtiss on Chelsea: 'The independence and task-specificity of language', in A. Bornstein and J. Bruner (eds), *Interaction in Human Development*, Erlbaum (Hillsdale, N J), 1989, pp. 119–20.

89. Pinker, 'recent evidence is calling': p. 290.

89. Johnson and Newport on factors predicting second-language proficiency: 'Critical period effects in second language learning: the influence of maturational state on the acquisition of English as a second language', *Cognitive Psychology*, **21**: 60–99, 1989.

89. J.P. Stern: information on his life from his obituary, *The Times*, 21 November 1991, p. 20.

90. Pinker, 'there seems to be a cap': p. 290. 'language mutants': p. 432, n. 48.

90. Gopnik on KE family: Myrna Gopnik, 'Feature-blind grammar and dysphasia', *Nature*, **344**: 715, 19 April 1990; Myrna Gopnik and Martha B. Crago, 'Familial aggregation of a developmental language disorder', *Cognition*, **39**: 1–50, 1991.

91. Leonard querying specific language impairment: 'Phonological deficits in children with developmental language impairment', *Brain and Language*, **16**: 73–86, 1982; 'Is specific language impairment a useful construct?', in S. Rosenberg (ed.), *Advances in Applied Psycholinguistics, vol. I: Disorders of First-Language Development*, Cambridge University Press, 1987.

93. Gopnik telephoned Chomsky with the good news: S. Targett, 'The bad language carriers', *Times Higher Education Supplement*, 29 March 1996, p. 18.

94. Pinker, 'a tourist struggling': p. 49.

94. KE language deficiency autosomally dominant: J.A. Hurst *et al.*, 'An extended family with a dominantly inherited speech disorder', *Developmental Medicine and Child Neurology*, **32**: 352–5, 1990.

94. Vargha-Khadem reinvestigation: F. Vargha-Khadem and R.E. Passingham, scientific correspondence, *Nature*, **346**: 226, 19 July 1990; F. Vargha-Khadem *et al.*, 'Praxic and nonverbal cognitive deficits in a large family with a genetically transmitted speech and language disorder', *Proceedings of the National Academy of Sciences of the United States of America*, **92**: 930–3, 1995.

94. Affected KE individuals have defective pronunciation, etc.: Hurst *et al.* (see above).

94. Pinker, 'Most of the language-impaired family': p. 324.

96. Pinker, 'children's minds seem to be designed': p. 146. *Darwinismian* 'sounds ridiculous', *Darwinsian* 'quite impossible': p. 135.

98. Pinker, headless words, percolation conduits: pp. 142–3.

98. Brown and LOB Corpora: http://www.hd.uib.no/icame.html.

Page 99. Gordon, compounds not formed from regular plurals: 'Level-ordering in lexical development', *Cognition*, **21**: 73–93, 1986; quoted by Pinker, pp. 146–7.

99. Johansson, compounds formed from plurals: *Plural Attributive Nouns in Present-day English (Lund Studies in English, 59)*, Gleerup (Lund), 1980; for British/American differences, see Johansson's p. 110. (Most phrases discussed by Johansson are written as separate words rather than hyphenated, but this does not mean that they are not compounds; as Pinker points out, p. 133, the test of compoundhood is where the stress goes in speaking, not the way we write.)

100. Pinker, 'if babies did not have a mentalese', 'it is likely that they are the same': p. 82. Pinker also suggests, p. 416, that something like an innate Mentalese must be postulated in order to escape Nelson Goodman's 'gruebleen paradox'; but see Popper, *Realism and the Aim of Science*, p. 67ff., and W.W. Bartley III, 'Eine Lösung des Goodman-Paradoxons', in G. Radnitzky and G. Andersson (eds), *Voraussetzungen und Grenzen der Wissenschaft*, Mohr (Tübingen), 1982.

101. Pinker, 'Rather than selecting for': p. 243.

102. Burne, specific behaviour shared by twins: 'A twin peek at family fortunes', *The Times*, 26 January 1993, p. 15. The Minnesota team have published their findings in T.J. Bouchard, Jr, *et al.*, 'Sources of human psychological differences: the Minnesota study of twins reared apart', *Science*, **250**: 223–8, 12 October 1990.

102. Donald Brown, anthropological universals: *Human Universals*, McGraw-Hill (New York), 1991.

103. Pinker, 'words that connote me-here-now', 'English speakers correctly guess': p. 167. Roger Brown on sound symbolism: *Words and Things: An Introduction to Language*, Collier-Macmillan, 1958, Chapter 4. (Incidentally, Pinker misspells the Chinese word for *heavy*, but this was Brown's error, not Pinker's own.)

104. Pinker, 'secular ideology of our age', 'in the rhetoric of the educated': pp. 406–7.

104. Philosophy of the 1944 Education Act: see e.g. R. Peers, *Fact and Possibility in English Education*, Routledge & Kegan Paul, 1963, pp. 39–40. Hadow Report: see e.g. B. Simon, *The Politics of Educational Reform 1920–1940*, Lawrence & Wishart, 1974, p. 232.

105. Mead on Samoa: Margaret Mead, *Coming of Age in Samoa: A Psychological Study of Primitive Youth for Western Civilisation*, W. Morrow (New York), 1928; Mead's account a travesty: D. Freeman, *Margaret Mead and Samoa*, Harvard University Press, 1983.

## Chapter 4  Language Structure Turns Queen's Evidence

107. Lightfoot, 'This is false': review of my *Liberty and Language*, *Journal of Linguistics*, **17**: 160–73, 1981.

107. Chomsky, 'An innatist hypothesis is a refutable hypothesis': Royaumont Symposium, p. 80. 'A theory of linguistic structure that aims': *Aspects*, p. 27. 'Real progress in linguistics': *Aspects*, p. 35.

108. Chomsky, 'proper names, in any language', etc.: *Aspects*, p. 29. 'there are no logical grounds': *Aspects*, p. 201 n. 15.

Page 109. McNeill, non-contiguous colour terms: 'Colour and colour terminology', *Journal of Linguistics*, **8**: 21–33, 1972, pp. 30–1.

109. Chomsky, *rouage* not a counterexample: letter to the author, 19 April 1977.

109. Gazdar *et al.*, 'The penalty for failure': G. Gazdar, E. Klein, G. Pullum and I. Sag, *Generalized Phrase Structure Grammar*, Blackwell (Oxford), 1985, p. 3.

111. Indexed grammars: J.E. Hopcroft and J.D. Ullman, *Introduction to Automata Theory, Languages, and Computation*, Addison-Wesley, 1979, pp. 389–92.

111. Chomsky, a mathematical scheme for classifying grammar types: e.g. 'Formal properties of grammars'.

111ff. Simon, 'The architecture of complexity': *Proceedings of the American Philosophical Society*, **106**: 467–82, 1962; reprinted in H.A. Simon, *The Sciences of the Artificial*, MIT Press, 1969. Parts of my discussion of Simon's ideas appeared previously in *Making Sense*.

115. Simpson, 'if … life arose as a living molecule': *The Meaning of Evolution*, Yale University Press, 1949, p. 16.

115–16. Margulis, symbiotic origin of eukaryotic cells: *Origin of Eukaryotic Cells*, Yale University Press, 1970.

116. Dawkins, Simon's principle important for ethology: 'Hierarchical organization: a candidate principle for ethology', in P.P.G. Bateson and R.A. Hinde (eds), *Growing Points in Ethology*, Cambridge University Press, 1976; cf. also H.H. Pattee (ed.), *Hierarchy Theory*, George Braziller (New York), 1973.

118. Peters and Waterman, matrix management unsuccessful: *In Search of Excellence*, Harper & Row, 1982, pp. 306–8.

121–2. Jakobson and Halle, universal sound structuring: R.O. Jakobson *et al.*, *Preliminaries to Speech Analysis*, 1952, 6th printing, MIT Press (Cambridge, Mass.), 1965; A.N. Chomsky and M. Halle, *The Sound Pattern of English*, Harper & Row, 1968. Jakobson's and Halle's claims dropped or refuted: my *Schools of Linguistics*, pp. 118–25, 190–8.

122. Pinker, 'no language forms questions by reversing': pp. 233–4.

124. Generalized Phrase Structure Grammar: G. Gazdar, E. Klein, G. Pullum and I. Sag, *Generalized Phrase Structure Grammar*, Blackwell (Oxford), 1985.

125. Syntactic 'islands': this concept was introduced by J.R. ('Haj') Ross, in a thesis which was widely circulated in 'semi-published' form under the title *Constraints on Variables in Syntax*, 1968; it was published in the full sense as *Infinite Syntax!*, Ablex (Norwood, N J), 1986. Jackendoff's version of the 'island' argument: pp. 76–80.

126–7. Gazdar *et al.* explain constraints: *Generalized Phrase Structure Grammar*, Blackwell (Oxford), 1985, p. 177.

127–8. Pinker's 'island constraint' example: p. 221. Bolinger's account in terms of essential v. accidental properties: '*What did John keep the car that was in?', *Linguistic Inquiry*, **3**: 109–14, 1972.

129–30. Greenberg, universals of word order: 'Some universals of grammar with particular reference to the order of meaningful elements', in J.H. Greenberg (ed.), *Universals of Language*, MIT Press, 1963; quoted by Pinker, pp. 233–4.

130. Keenan, language-neutral definition of subject: 'Towards a universal definition of "subject" ', in C.N. Li (ed.), *Subject and Topic*, Academic Press, 1976.

Page 130. Pinker, we cannot handle multiple central embedding: p. 205. Miller and
          Chomsky on multiple central embedding: G.A. Miller and A.N. Chomsky,
          'Finitary models of language users', in R.D. Luce *et al.* (eds), *Handbook of
          Mathematical Psychology*, vol. II, Wiley, 1963.
   131. I logged multiple central embeddings: see my 'From central embedding
        to corpus linguistics'.
   131. Bickerton, hierarchy in vocabulary: p. 43.
 131–2. Bickerton, 'we never make mistakes': p. 67.
   132. X-bar theory: Chomsky's suggestion, 'Remarks on nominalization',
        pp. 210–11; Jackendoff book, $\bar{X}$ *Syntax: A Study of Phrase Structure*, MIT
        Press, 1977.
   133. Kornai and Pullum assess X-bar theory: 'The X-bar theory of phrase
        structure', *Language*, **66**: 24–50, 1990.
   133. Pinker, arguments closer to verb than adjuncts: p. 109.
   134. English defers heavy elements to ends of clauses: my 'Depth in English
        grammar'.
   134. Bickerton, head noun obligatory, X-bar explains Quine's puzzle: pp. 63–4.
   135. Jackendoff, Universal Grammar 'stipulates that a language contains':
        p. 81.
   135. Measure words as a Pacific Rim phenomenon: Johanna Nichols and D.A.
        Peterson, 'The Amerind personal pronouns', *Language*, **72**: 336–71, 1996,
        p. 366.
   135. Borges, nounless languages: 'Tlön, Uqbar, Orbis Tertius', in *Labyrinths*,
        Penguin, 1970.

## Chapter 5   The Creative Mind

 137ff. Parts of this chapter were first presented as a talk at the First Convocation
        of *The Open Society and Its Friends*, New York, 1982.
 138–9. Interactionism: see also Popper's *Knowledge and the Body-Mind Problem*,
        based on a 1969 lecture series.
   139. Ayer, statements about morality not literally meaningful: *Language, Truth
        and Logic*, Victor Gollancz, 1936; p. 136 of Penguin edition, 1971.
   139. Smart, mental phenomena identical to physical: e.g. 'Sensations and brain
        processes', *Philosophical Review*, **68**: 141–56, 1959; reprinted in V.G. Chappell
        (ed.), *The Philosophy of Mind*, Prentice-Hall (Englewood Cliffs, N J), 1962,
        and in C.V. Borst (ed.), *The Mind-Brain Identity Theory*, Macmillan, 1970.
   139. 'Materialism' or 'monism': note that 'monism' refers to the belief that
        body and mind are one substance rather than two, but this need not mean
        reducing the mental to the physical — Bishop Berkeley's philosophy
        reduced the physical to the mental. People who hold monist doctrines
        nowadays, though, are normally materialists.
   139. Ayers, Locke shares dualism with Descartes: 'The ideas of power and
        substance in Locke's philosophy', *The Philosophical Quarterly*, **25**: 1–27,
        1975, p. 15. (I am not sure myself what is 'hesitant' about the dualism of
        Book II, Chapter 23 of Locke's *Essay*.)
   139. Chalmers restating dualism: *The Conscious Mind: In Search of a Fundamental
        Theory*, Oxford University Press, 1996.
   140. Chomsky, unusual sense of 'creative': see my *Liberty and Language*, p. 101ff.

Page 140. McDermott, expert system: 'R1: A rule-based configurer of computer systems', *Artificial Intelligence*, **19**: 39–88, 1982.

141. Warnock, Chomsky's use of 'creative' misleading: 'Free speech?' *The Listener*, 3 May 1979, p. 629.

142. Bartley, something can come from nothing: 'The philosophy of Karl Popper, Part II', *Philosophia*, **7**: 675–716, 1978, pp. 675–6; I have omitted references to footnotes.

143. Lees, 'close to gibberish': 'Trying to make sense', *British Journal for the Philosophy of Science*, **33**: 194–208, 1982.

143. Hurford, 'a serious philosopher of mind': review of my *Making Sense*, *Language*, **57**: 912–18, 1981.

143. Storr, 'I am one of those people': review of my *Making Sense*, *The Spectator*, 17 May 1980, p. 18.

143. Watkins, haunted-universe doctrine: 'Confirmable and influential metaphysics', *Mind*, **67**: 344–65, 1958.

144. Popper, 'promissory materialism ... a peculiar theory': *The Self and Its Brain*, p. 97.

144. Beloff, Popper and Eccles underestimate case for materialism: 'Is mind autonomous?', *British Journal for the Philosophy of Science*, **29**: 265–73, p. 271.

144. Putnam, linguists treat ideas they disagree with as logically impossible: 'What is innate and why: comments on the debate', in M. Piattelli-Palmarini (ed.), *Language and Learning: The Debate between Jean Piaget and Noam Chomsky*, Routledge & Kegan Paul, 1980.

144. Jaki, materialist arguments beg question: *Brain, Mind and Computers*, Gateway Editions (South Bend, Indiana), 1969.

144–5. Hurford, my most explicit critic: quotations from his review of my *Making Sense*, *Language*, **57**: 912–18, 1981.

145. Popper, 'All acquired knowledge': *Objective Knowledge*, p. 71.

145. I paraphrase Popper on new and innate ideas: *Making Sense*, p. 11.

145. Popper, 'If it were not absurd': *Objective Knowledge*, p. 71.

145. New ideas produced in response to problems arising with old ideas: it should be said, incidentally, that Popper may have changed his views on this issue, too; cf. the passage quoted from the first book he wrote, *Die beiden Grundprobleme der Erkenntnistheorie*, by Elie Zahar in 'Logic of discovery or psychology of invention?', *British Journal for the Philosophy of Science*, **34**: 243–61, 1983, p. 244.

146. Popper, 'As children we learn': *Objective Knowledge*, p. 63. 'The *tabula rasa* theory': *Objective Knowledge*, p.66. 'a "trial" or a newly formed "dogma" ': *Autobiography*, p. 37.

147. Chomsky, 'As a precondition for language learning': *Aspects*, p. 25. 'A child who is capable': *Aspects*, p. 30. 'it might very well be true': *Aspects*, p. 202 n. 19.

147. Popper, 'critical thinking may consist': *Autobiography*, p. 36.

149. Popper, 'One of the oldest': *The Self and Its Brain*, §7. 'From the amoeba to Einstein': *Objective Knowledge*, p. 261. 'It ... destroys ... the idea': *Objective Knowledge*, p. 222.

150. Popper, 'The idea of "creative" or "emergent" evolution', 'If something new seems', 'We can admit that the world': *The Self and Its Brain*, §8.

Page 151. Emergence in the early twentieth century: the first person to introduce the concept of emergence in the philosophical sense was G.H. Lewes (George Eliot's partner), in *Problems of Life and Mind*, Trübner, vol. I, 1874, pp. 97–8. Leading works by the authors named are: H. Bergson, *L'évolution créatrice*, Félix Alcan (Paris), 1907, published in English as *Creative Evolution*, Macmillan, 1911; S. Alexander, *Space, Time and Deity*, 2 vols, Macmillan, 1920; C. Lloyd Morgan, *Emergent Evolution*, Williams & Norgate, 1923; J.C. Smuts, *Holism and Evolution*, Macmillan, 1926.

151. Bergson, innate expectation of feeding at nipple: *Creative Evolution*, p. 155.

151. Lakatos, Popper's demarcation criterion developed from Bergsonian ideas: 'Popper on demarcation and induction', in P.A. Schilpp (ed.), *The Philosophy of Karl Popper (The Library of Living Philosophers, vol. XIV)*, Book 1, Open Court (La Salle, Illinois), 1974, p. 259.

151–2. Bergson, 'Le possible et le réel': in *La Pensée et le mouvant: essais et conférences*, 1934; 63rd edn, Presses Universitaires de France (Paris), 1966, quotations from pp. 102, 110, 112. An English translation is available as *The Creative Mind*, Greenwood Press (New York), 1968.

152. Popper, 'if there is such a thing as growing': *Poverty of Historicism*, p. vi.

153. Popper, 'the first emergence of a novelty': *The Self and Its Brain*, p. 30. 'There can be invariant laws': *The Self and Its Brain*, p. 25. 'my view of the matter': *Logic of Scientific Discovery*, p. 32. 'due to a fundamentally different approach': *Open Society*, vol. I, p. 202. 'a somewhat hysterical': *Open Society*, vol. I, pp. 314–15. The 'evolutionists' still interested in Hegel: *Open Society*, vol. II, p. 29, and note on pp. 304–5. 'evolutionary mysticism': *Open Society*, vol. I, p. 314.

154. Popper, Bergson 'utterly wrong in [his] theories': *Autobiography*, p. 143.

154. Bergson, 'in the animal ... routine': *Creative Evolution*, p. 278.

155. Popper, 'Western philosophy consists very largely': *Objective Knowledge*, p. 153. 'like Descartes, I propose': *Objective Knowledge*, p. 252. More extreme than Alexander: *Objective Knowledge*, p. 223 n. 35. Dualism 'compatible with the most radical': *Objective Knowledge*, p. 273.

156. Popper, 'I am unaware of the fact': letter to the author, 7 April 1980. 'It is my opinion that most': *Autobiography*, p. 37. Distinguished how ideas are assessed from how produced: e.g. *Logic of Scientific Discovery*, pp. 30–1. 'I do not think that the question': letter to the author, 28 April 1980.

## Chapter 6    Conclusion

159. Nativist style of linguistics attractive to language teachers: this has been pointed out, for instance, by C. Hagège, *La Grammaire générative: réflexions critiques*, Presses Universitaires de France (Paris), 1976, p. 17, n. 1, and by R.A. Harris, *The Linguistics Wars*, Oxford University Press, 1993, p. 75.

160. Publication of *The Logical Structure of Linguistic Theory* failed to redeem IOUs of *Syntactic Structures*: I analyse this in my review article 'What was transformational grammar?'

160. Air of irreverence and fun: to get an impression of the very un-Mandarin atmosphere of the first wave of nativist linguistics, see, for instance, Chapter 8 of Harris, *The Linguistics Wars* (as above), or the interview with J.R. Ross in G.J. Huck and J.A. Goldsmith, *Ideology and Linguistic Theory: Noam Chomsky and the Deep Structure Debates*, Routledge, 1995, pp. 120–5.

Page 161. 'Eclipsing stance': C.F. and Florence M. Voegelin, 'On the history of structuralizing in 20th century America', *Anthropological Linguistics*, **5:** 12–37, 1963.

    161. Pullum, nativist falsifications: 'Nostalgic views from Building 20', *Journal of Linguistics*, **32:** 137–47, 1996.

    161. Itkonen, Americans afraid to disagree publicly with linguistic nativism: 'Concerning the generative paradigm', *Journal of Pragmatics*, **25:** 471–501, 1996.

    161. Mary Lefkowitz vilified as racist for denying Aristotle stole his ideas from Africans: M. Gove, 'The woman who defied political correctness', *The Times*, 2 September 1996, p. 15.


## Works by Noam Chomsky referred to in this book

*Syntactic Structures (Janua Linguarum, 4)*, Mouton ('s-Gravenhage), 1957.

Review of B.F. Skinner, *Verbal Behavior*, *Language*, **35:** 26–58, 1959; reprinted in J.A. Fodor and J.J. Katz (eds), *The Structure of Language: Readings in the Philosophy of Language*, Prentice-Hall, 1964.

'Explanatory models in linguistics', in E. Nagel *et al.* (eds), *Logic Methodology and Philosophy of Science*, Stanford University Press, 1962.

'Formal properties of grammars', in R.D. Luce *et al.* (eds), *Handbook of Mathematical Psychology*, vol. II, Wiley, 1963.

*Aspects of the Theory of Syntax*, MIT Press, 1965.

*Topics in the Theory of Generative Grammar (Janua Linguarum, series minor, 56)*, Mouton (The Hague), 1966.

*Cartesian Linguistics: A Chapter in the History of Rationalist Thought*, Harper & Row, 1966.

*Language and Mind*, Harcourt, Brace & World (New York), 1968; my page references are to the Enlarged Edition, Harcourt Brace Jovanovich (New York), 1972.

'Remarks on nominalization', in R.A. Jacobs and P.S. Rosenbaum (eds), *Readings in English Transformational Grammar*, Ginn, 1970.

*Problems of Knowledge and Freedom: The Russell Lectures*, Fontana/Collins, 1972.

*The Logical Structure of Linguistic Theory*, Plenum, 1975.

*Reflections on Language*, Temple Smith, 1976.

*Language and Responsibility*, Harvester (Hassocks, Sussex), 1979.

Royaumont Symposium: various contributions by Chomsky to M. Piattelli-Palmarini (ed.), *Language and Learning: The Debate between Jean Piaget and Noam Chomsky*, Routledge & Kegan Paul, 1980 (proceedings of a symposium at the Abbaye de Royaumont, October 1975).

*Rules and Representations*, Blackwell (Oxford), 1980.

'Principles and parameters in syntactic theory', in N. Hornstein and D. Lightfoot (eds), *Explanation in Linguistics*, Longman, 1981.

*Lectures on Government and Binding*, Foris (Dordrecht), 1981.

*Language and Problems of Knowledge: The Managua Lectures*, MIT Press, 1988.

'Linguistics and cognitive science: problems and mysteries', in A. Kasher (ed.), *The Chomskyan Turn*, Blackwell (Oxford), 1991.


## Works by Karl Popper referred to in this book

*Die beiden Grundprobleme der Erkenntnistheorie*, written in 1930–3 (ed. T.E. Hansen), Mohr (Tübingen), 1979.

*Logik der Forschung: zur Erkenntnistheorie der Modernen Naturwissenschaft*, J. Springer (Vienna), 1935; English version published as *The Logic of Scientific Discovery*, Hutchinson, 1959.

*The Open Society and Its Enemies*, 2 vols, Routledge & Kegan Paul, 1945.

*The Poverty of Historicism*, Routledge & Kegan Paul, 1957.

*Conjectures and Refutations: The Growth of Scientific Knowledge*, Routledge & Kegan Paul, 1963.

*Objective Knowledge: An Evolutionary Approach*, Clarendon Press (Oxford), 1972.

'Intellectual Autobiography', in P.A. Schilpp (ed.), *The Philosophy of Karl Popper (The Library of Living Philosophers, vol. XIV)*, Book 1, Open Court (La Salle, Illinois), 1974; reprinted as *Unended Quest: An Intellectual Autobiography*, Fontana/Collins, 1976. My page references are to the Schilpp volume.

*The Self and Its Brain* (K.R. Popper and J.C. Eccles), Springer, 1977.

*Realism and the Aim of Science* (ed. W.W. Bartley III), Hutchinson, 1983.

*Knowledge and the Body-Mind Problem: In Defence of Interaction* (ed. M.A. Notturno), Routledge, 1994.


## Other works by the present author referred to in this book

*The Form of Language*, Weidenfeld & Nicolson, 1975.

*Liberty and Language*, Oxford University Press, 1979.

'What was transformational grammar?', *Lingua*, **48**: 355–78, 1979.

*Making Sense*, Oxford University Press, 1980.

'Popperian language-acquisition undefeated', *British Journal for the Philosophy of Science*, **31**: 63–7, 1980.

*Schools of Linguistics: Competition and Evolution*, Hutchinson, 1980.

'From central embedding to corpus linguistics', in Jenny Thomas and M.H. Short (eds), *Using Corpora for Language Research*, Longman, 1996.

'Depth in English grammar', *Journal of Linguistics*, **33**: 131–51, 1997.

# Index